Justification
by
Works

New Westminster Pulpit Series

Once Saved, Always Saved

All's Well that Ends Well

Justification by Works
Sermons on James 1–3

The Way of Wisdom
Sermons on James 4–5

Justification by Works

How Works Vindicate True Faith
Sermons on James 1–3

R.T. Kendall

Authentic
MEDIA

Authentic Media
We welcome your comments and questions.
129 Mobilization Drive, Waynesboro, GA 30830 USA authenticusa@stl.org
and 9 Holdom Avenue, Bletchley, Milton Keynes, Bucks, MK1 1QR, UK
www.authenticbooks.com

If you would like a copy of our current catalog, contact us at:
1-8MORE-BOOKS
ordersusa@stl.org

Justification by Works
ISBN: 1-932805-26-5

Cover design: Paul Lewis
Interior design: WestKey Ltd, Falmouth, Cornwall

Printed in United States of America

To
Lee and Sally, Linda and Neal, Lois and Bruce

Contents

Foreword

The Epistle of James is one of my favourite books. Not surprisingly, because of the hand of the Holy Spirit lying behind it, it is one of the greatest letters ever written. And yet Martin Luther called it 'an epistle of straw'.

So how dare I disagree with Luther? While he reportedly once threw an ink pot at the devil, I have to confess that there are times when reading James that I am tempted to want to return the favour!

What has provoked my fascination with the Epistle of James is the way that he consistently jabs at three of those areas in my life where I have felt weakest:

- my failure always to practise what I preach.
- my stubborn, unruly tongue which insists on getting me into trouble.
- my reluctance to show compassion to the poor.

Is there any wonder that most of us who are evangelical Christians struggle with the Epistle of James?

Now along comes Dr R.T. Kendall with a brand new two-volume commentary, and he asks me to write the foreword. There couldn't be a better subject, or a nicer author. R.T. is one of my heroes, and has been a very special gift to the church of Christ in Britain.

R.T.'s friendship is something that I have deeply appreciated, and his candor and ready wit make him a wonderful fireside companion. Yet it is his teaching of the Word of God that has made him a household name among British Christians, vast numbers of whom will readily acknowledge that he has opened their eyes to deeper truths in the Word of God.

But here's the rub. James has a 'dodgy' verse. And James 2:14 has created consternation for so many of us. You may not agree with R.T.'s careful exegesis, but for me, when I first heard him explain that verse many years ago, suddenly everything made sense.

May you sense a touch of the Spirit of God as you read these pages, and may the Lord Jesus himself continue to use his special servant to illuminate our hearts and minds. He may not preach for much longer in Britain – but the books will live on.

Clive Calver

Preface

I will never forget the summer of 1979 when walking with my family in Disney World near Kissimmee, Florida. I had been contemplating preaching on James a few weeks later, and was fully aware of James 1:2: 'Consider it pure joy, my brothers, whenever you face trials of many kinds'. I wanted to understand that verse more than anything in the world, and knew that I had little time to be ready for it – as I had announced I would start preaching from James when I returned.

It was the day before that I had an unforgettable incident when ordering a pizza in Kissimmee. I had become impatient with how long they took to make it, and then dropped the whole thing in a puddle of water when I got back to the motel! I was so upset and then I had to head back to the same pizza parlour to order another! But I can tell you, it was driving back to that pizza parlour that I thought of James 2. The whole thing looks ludicrous now, but it was vital to me then – when I said to myself, 'I must dignify this trial'. The phrase 'dignifying the trial' was born in that moment, and I asked God to forgive me for my impatience and had determined to let all that happened be for his glory. It literally changed my life!

I would never have remotely dreamed in those days that my preaching on James would be a book. It has of course been edited by professional copy editors with a view of making it read more like a book than a sermon. I want to thank those who have done this job – Tara Smith, David Page, Paul Compton, Helen Murphy and the staff at Paternoster.

I pray that this book will be a great blessing to you. An even greater breakthrough than grasping James 1:2 was understanding James 2:14 ff. You will see what I mean, and I thank God for this precious insight. The insight came to me the week before I preached it, but it happens that it was also the last time I ever had the privilege of letting Dr Lloyd-Jones hear what I was going to preach on. We used to meet on Thursdays, and he became seriously ill shortly after the Thursday that I was able to share my insights on James 2:14 with him. It is amazing that God kept him alive long enough that he could hear what I wanted to say, because his words to me were – having carefully listened: 'You've convinced me'. This of course was a great encouragement, although to be honest, I knew that the insight had to be right. It shows that Martin Luther was hasty in calling James 'a strawy epistle'. James and Paul do not contradict each other!

I warmly thank my old friend Clive Calver for writing the Foreword. Clive has been a dear friend and has opened more doors to me probably than anybody in Britain. He has made it possible for me to have a wider ministry and I thank God for Clive and for his Foreword.

I have dedicated this book to my wife Louise's brother and sisters and their spouses: Mr and Mrs Lee Wallace of Bradenton, Florida; Mr and Mrs Neal Otten of Rockfalls, Illinois; and Mr and Mrs Bruce Malpass of Boise, Idaho.

My thanks as always is to my wife Louise – my best friend and critic.

RT Kendall
Westminster Chapel, London
September 2001

1

Introducing James

James 1:1

James is one of the most controversial epistles in the New Testament. It is also one of the most underestimated epistles in terms of potential strength and growth that is to be found.

Addressed to 'the twelve tribes ... scattered abroad' (1:1), not any one person or church, this epistle provides a rare glimpse of a vintage, undeveloped, yet essential Christianity. It was written in all probability before James himself came into contact with the apostle Paul's more advanced theological views. It really is quite wonderful that we have this view of pre-Pauline Christianity, rudimentary in its innocence and seriousness but cohering perfectly with the teaching of the apostle Paul.

The practicality, even ruggedness and conduciveness to real growth in the Christian life is a striking feature of this epistle. As you read through these sermons I hope you will be challenged to put your Christian faith into practical action.

The Value of James

James has a very controversial history. While the modern father of existentialism, the Danish Lutheran Kierkegaard, regarded James as his favourite book, that was not quite the case with Luther. Obviously alluding to 1 Corinthians 3:12, where Paul said 'If any man build upon this foundation gold, silver, precious stones, wood, hay, stubble', Luther looked at James as 'a right strawy epistle'. As late as 1542 he said in Wittenberg in his Table Talk, 'We should throw the epistle of James out of this school [i.e. the University of Wittenberg] for it doesn't amount to much.'

Decisive for the acceptance of James in the western Church was
Jerome's full acceptance of the book, and in the Eastern church it needed
Athanasius' approval before it was given canonical status. Why was this?
For one thing they weren't quite sure which James wrote this letter, but
the real problem was its Jewishness. In a growing Gentile community the
epistle seemed outdated.

It will be our task from this first chapter to get into James' skin.
Reading this letter may require some shifting of gears. Paul, in Galatians,
admits that James was troubled, along with Peter and John, over his
teaching. There was this famous controversy in the early church. The
issue then involved the question of evangelism to the Gentiles and the
free offer of the gospel. People were asking whether the Gentiles could
be accepted into the Christian church without circumcision, what was
further required of the Gentiles if they were accepted, what kind of status
they should have and how they should be treated. There was the question
whether you should even sit with a Gentile if you were a Jew. So Paul had
this quarrel with these three men and upbraided them for their hypocrisy
and inconsistency.

You may want to say 'James' views were obviously wrong' because
Paul was vindicated and obviously James had eventually to abandon
certain views, biases and prejudices. But what made him willing to
change? We are dealing with a man who had a warm heart, who could
change and we see a godly mind at work. Many of us have been so much
like James, who had strong ideas and yet loved the Lord. Many have had
wrong views of this or that but have still been used of God.

We marvel that God would use us when we hold to certain things, but
he does. Why did God use Jesus? Because he saw an honest and true heart,
one which went after godliness. God, in his providence has let us see that
James had a heart of flesh and not stone, and he wants us to see how this
man was used. So I'm glad that God let James write this letter before he
had opportunity to digest Paul's discovery in Arabia. Had James written
this epistle ten or fifteen years later after he knew all about Paul's views, he
may have thought he should say things differently.

But does this epistle oppose Paul? Absolutely not. That is its genius.
The extra baggage that we know about James from Paul's inference
doesn't come out in this epistle, although it does have certain Jewish
biases, as we shall see. But what we have here is exactly right. Here
was a man who willingly received and responded to the truth as it was
given him.

I say there is a Jewish bias, but it is not obtrusive. God wanted James'
word preserved at this stage so that we might see a truly godly, if

embryonic, mind at work. James' obedience is glorifying to God; it is as useful and powerful as is the obedience that issues from the most developed and theologically sophisticated Christianity. This epistle demonstrates these words of our Lord: 'He that is faithful in that which is least is faithful also in much' (Lk. 16:10). James' epistle is as inspired, as spiritual, as theologically sound as any of Paul's. James' understanding of certain truths which many of us take for granted only went so far, but given that it was exactly right.

In the post-Reformation era, on this side of Luther, Calvin and Edwards, we have come largely to understand Paul first. We are sometimes tempted to look patronizingly at James, and I think some of us, if we are honest, see it as almost sub-Christian. I predict that we will change our minds when we see what a profoundly spiritual epistle it is. God's hand was no less on James than on Paul. Christianity is not essentially an intellectual enterprise; it is God's life in human personality. There are things that James does not say which Paul does say and vice versa. We can grow from James to Paul and we can grow just as strongly from Paul to James and conclude that the two mutually excel each other.

Listen to these lines in James:

> If any man among you seem to be religious, and bridleth not his tongue, but deceiveth his own heart, this man's religion is vain. Pure religion and undefiled before God and the Father is this, To visit the fatherless and widows in their affliction, and to keep himself unspotted from the world. (1:26–27).

> Who is a wise man and endued with knowledge among you? let him show out of a good conversation his works with meekness of wisdom (3:13).

> Resist the devil, and he will flee from you (4:7).

I'm so glad James said that. No one else did.

> The effectual fervent prayer of a righteous man availeth much (5:16).

Thank God for this epistle. If we find James' theology distasteful we show that we are not worthy of Paul. More than that, we show that rather than having understood Paul, we've misunderstood him.

A Different Approach to Church History

James also offers us a different insight on the general church history by opening us up to particular communities that may have developed their Christianity from this epistle alone, or maybe one other epistle. We forget that we are dealing with an era three hundred years before there was a canon of Scripture as we know it. Now we have a whole Bible, back then they didn't. With no printing presses and limited transportation it could be a hundred years before a Pauline epistle might even come into a community, and then it might not be understood or received that well. In the meantime a certain tradition gets established.

This explains what some think of as a defective Christianity in certain parts of the world. The kind of Christianity found in places like communist Russia. It would put many of you off, I am sure. Their theological grasp was, by our standard, shallow. But they loved the Lord, hated the devil and loathed worldliness.

We take mass communication for granted. I don't know whether you realize this, but an innovative idea nowadays peaks within a year of its emergence. What would have taken a hundred years in the Middle Ages now takes a year or two. When a new idea is put forward in our instant society, whether it's on the level of medicine, psychology, science or theology, ten of the world's greatest minds discuss and deal with it and perhaps lay it to rest.

The earliest Christian communities would have had one, two or maybe three books of the New Testament. Their tradition was established on the basis of these and was largely unchanged for centuries. We must never be unsympathetic towards these Christians – even with mass communication, even though we have the whole New Testament available to us and are without excuse for having a parochial or provincial Christianity, our own particular traditions have a way of perpetuating themselves and remaining largely undisturbed.

We must respect those that are not so erudite in terms of sound doctrine. James would have accepted them if they love the Lord, fight the devil and hate the world. If we accept James then we are accepting a pre-Pauline Christianity. If we see this Christianity in history and in our day, then we dignify this epistle by accepting these people.

I should point out that some scholars, usually liberals, think James represents a post- and not pre-Pauline Christianity. They argue that the epistle was written as late as AD 140 by an unknown author who used James' name and wrote these things long after the Pauline controversy had subsided. We will come back to the issue of dating this epistle later.

The Writer of James

There were four men in the New Testament who had the name James. Judas (one of the twelve but not Judas Iscariot) was the son or possibly the brother of someone called James (Lk. 6:16). There was 'James the less', as the Authorised Version calls him. A better translation is 'James the younger'; he was one of the twelve apostles (see Mk. 15:40) and the son of Mary and Alphaeus. Nothing more is said about these two Jameses and few people have ever seriously reckoned that either of them wrote this epistle.

Then there's James, brother of John, son of Zebedee and one of the twelve. Some have thought that this James was the author, but according to Acts 12:1–2, James, son of Zebedee was martyred by Herod Agrippa in AD 44. This gave him time to write an epistle which no doubt would have had a Jewish slant, but scholars do not think he wrote this epistle.

All signs point to another James, the brother of our Lord (Gal. 2). He was a most powerful man in the early church. We are not told why. If it weren't for Paul's reference that he was the brother of our Lord we would be in even greater doubt as to how this James could have such stature. James was probably the most powerful figure in the Jerusalem church, or at least one of three, along with Peter and John (cf. Gal. 2:9 where Paul refers to them as 'pillars').

In 1 Corinthians 15:5–7 Paul refers to the resurrection of Jesus and says that Jesus 'was seen of Cephas, then of the twelve: After that, he was seen of above five hundred brethren at once'. Then Paul says, 'After that, he was seen of James'. James had not always believed in Jesus – it is probable that it was the resurrected Christ appearing to him that sealed James' own conversion. James had such stature that Paul had to give notice of his special experience of the resurrected Jesus. When Peter was miraculously delivered from prison he said, 'Go shew these things unto James, and to the brethren' (Acts 12:17).

In the famous Jerusalem council of Acts 15 it was James who dominated the scene. Peter, Paul and Barnabas recount to James what happened to them. James listened and pronounced the word, and his word stuck. When James wrote this epistle some wondered why he didn't include more autobiographical material. He didn't need any. All he had to say was 'James, a servant of God and of the Lord Jesus Christ, to the twelve tribes which are scattered abroad' (1:1).

Bear in mind we're dealing with an epistle that was written by a man who probably not long before had counselled the Gentile Christian to 'abstain from meats offered to idols, and from blood, and from things strangled' (Acts 15:29). We don't know whether James still held to that when he wrote this epistle. Would it bother you if he did? If James still held to a peculiar idea would you be willing to learn from him?

The language used in this epistle is further proof that we are talking about the same James. The letter opens with an initial salutation or 'greeting' (Gk. *chairein*). It's the same word that the leader and elders of the council of Jerusalem used in the letter that they gave to Paul and his companions (Acts 15:23). As we have already noted, James was a prominent figure at this meeting and the word isn't used by any other apostolic writer.

The unique phraseology doesn't end there. There are plenty of examples, but I shall name just two. First there is the expression 'men and brethren', which is used throughout the epistle and is also found in Acts 15:13. Second there is 'upon whom my name is called', which we find in Acts 15:17 and James 2:7.

I have already mentioned the Jewishness of this epistle. It is accepted that James was the most Jewish and most conservative of the apostles. He wanted to maintain continuity with Moses and with the Jews. So it is not surprising that he would address his letter 'to the twelve tribes which are scattered abroad'.

In James 2:2 he says, 'If there come unto your assembly…' The Greek word here is 'synagogue', undoubtedly a Jewish term. When James refers to 'Abraham our father' (2:21) that's all he has to say. Paul would have said, 'Abraham our father according to the flesh'. This hints at how Jewish this epistle is. The early Jewish Christians looked to James and they trusted him. He was their link. They could do what he said it was all right for them to do. Yet he was also controversial in his acceptance of Gentile Christians.

We know that when Paul came back to Jerusalem in about AD 59 it was James who asked him to have his head shaved so as not to offend the Jews (Acts 21:23–24). What we have here is a composite picture. He's on the conservative side yet also has a conciliatory nature. He wanted to please the Jews, Paul and the Gentiles.

Dating the Epistle

It is important to date this epistle – that way we'll know whether it came before or after Galatians and Romans. According to Josephus, James the righteous, or James the just as he was nicknamed, was martyred in AD 61. This is generally taken to be reliable information, but Galatians and

Romans were probably written in AD 55 and AD 57 respectively. There were roughly four years, then, in which James could have written his epistle after Paul's major epistles.

I have, however, become convinced that James wrote his epistle in the forties, probably between AD 40 and 48. I wouldn't be at all surprised if it is the first New Testament writing we have. Surely no man had more authority than James. The opening words suggest that it was written before Gentile Christianity was on the rise. With his conciliatory nature James would not have wished to alienate Gentile Christians by ignoring them. The expression 'twelve tribes' can be taken to mean spiritual Israel, but it is not likely that Jews would have absorbed this heavy concept, and less likely that the Gentiles would have understood it.

Then there's the controversial verse: 'Ye see then how that by works a man is justified, and not by faith only' (2:24), which was a red flag to Martin Luther. Had James known about Paul's letters to the Galatians and Romans, he would have known how easily that line could have been misunderstood. I grant that you can compare and contrast Galatians and James, and there's no contradiction. But this verse was open to misunderstanding. In the light of James' conciliatory personality I conclude that he was not aware of Paul's letters or of Paul's advanced theological understanding.

James wrote to these Christian Jews who were in isolated pockets around the Mediterranean, probably before any of them anticipated the ascendancy, much less the eventual dominance, of Gentile Christianity. There was, however, enough time for them to have their quarrels and their questions. The wonder of wonders is that this book can be read with such profit by us Gentiles. No Christian Jew or Gentile has ever outgrown the epistle of James.

The Martyrdom of James

There's one final interesting point. Josephus tells us that the high priest Ananias arrested James on a charge of violating the law and he was stoned to death in AD 61. What an irony. This man James, who tried to be so conciliatory – especially to his Jewish countrymen by upholding the law and maintaining continuity with Moses – was in the end slaughtered not by Gentiles, nor by Caesar, but by the high priest for violating the law.

It shows that once you take your stand for Christ, however much you try to please your enemies, that offence is always sufficient to make you the object of hostility. So came the brutal end for this man who in his general epistle to the twelve tribes scattered abroad had one thing he wanted to say: 'Count it all joy when ye fall into divers temptations'.

The surprise of surprises that awaits us is, apart from its practicality, how profound and rich, how staggering the truth that will confront us. When we, like James, are faithful to that which is least then we come upon nuggets of truth with vast implications which we don't always perceive at first. Only later do we see the full marvel of it. If we are faithful in that which is least then we are faithful in much. Be encouraged to want to understand this godly man who can make a contribution to the lives of all today, knowing that he was slaughtered by the ones he was trying to please most. But he anticipated as much when he said, 'Blessed is the man that endureth temptation: for when he is tried, he shall receive the crown of life, which the Lord hath promised to them that love him' (Js. 1:12).

2

Reacting the Right Way

James 1:2

A Lesson in Patience

The epistle of James is a manual for godliness. Its central thesis is in 1:4: 'But let patience have her perfect work, that ye may be perfect and entire, wanting nothing.'

The theme *patience* underlies all that the writer says. He wants to produce patience in us, which in turn will provide us with the kind of Christian life that reflects the special grace of God.

James returns to this theme in chapter 5. He says that we must remember that it is God working in us that helps us to see our responsibility to the grace that is offered us.

> Be patient therefore, brethren, unto the coming of the Lord. Behold, the husbandman waiteth for the precious fruit of the earth, and hath long patience for it, until he receive the early and latter rain. Be ye also patient; stablish your hearts: for the coming of the Lord draweth nigh ... Take, my brethren, the prophets, who have spoken in the name of the Lord, for an example of suffering affliction, and of patience. Behold, we count them happy which endure. Ye have heard of the patience of Job, and have seen the end of the Lord: that the Lord is very pitiful, and of tender mercy (5:7–8, 10–11).

His final illustration is Elijah who prayed that it might not rain and then prayed that it would. And so we have these words: 'The effectual fervent prayer of a righteous man availeth much' (5:16).

But the whole thing centres on this point: patience. It is a most practical thing. In the AV the Greek word *hypomoneé* (1:4) is translated 'patience'. It means 'to bear up under', 'to endure'. The NIV translates it as 'perseverance', but the main thing we must see is that James is wanting all of us to establish patience as a habit.

The epistle of Jude maintains the subjective and objective sides of faith in balance. That is not quite true with James, although the objective side does come through, out of the blue at times. We know from this that James believed all that every other writer in the New Testament did. Yet his emphasis is, without doubt, on the subjective side.

James sees Jesus as the one to whom he is a servant. He sees Jesus not as his brother but calls him 'our Lord', We know from John 7:5 that, like Jude, James at one time didn't believe in Jesus, but we don't know when he was converted. We do know that as our Lord appeared to different ones he appeared also to James. That may have been his conversion, but it is likely that James believed before then. There is continuity between James, the brother of our Lord, and James, the servant of our Lord Jesus Christ.

There is no doubt that James heard many of Jesus' sermons personally. He frequently refers to Jesus' teaching. For example in 5:12 James says, 'But above all things, my brethren, swear not, neither by heaven, neither by the earth, neither by any other oath: but let your yea be yea; and your nay, nay; lest ye fall into condemnation.' It's taken almost word for word from the Sermon on the Mount. You might compare James 1:9 where he says, 'Let the brother of low degree rejoice in that he is exalted', with Matthew 5:3, 'Blessed are the poor in spirit', and so forth. Compare James 2:13 with Matthew 18:32–35 and James 4:9 with Luke 6:25. And so on.

This epistle reflects an interpretation of the teachings of Jesus applied directly to the Christian life. If Acts shows the continuation of what Jesus began to do and teach, James shows how the teachings of Jesus are to be interpreted and applied to the Christian life.

We are dealing with a man who heard Jesus preach at a time when he didn't even believe. But at some point along the way he was converted. James did not have a monopoly on the truth; much less did he have an intellect like that of Paul. But he had what all of us desperately need: namely, a practical way by which we may live out our Christianity. For such practical guidelines, there's no better book than this.

Establishing Patience as a Habit

In light of this emphasis on establishing patience as a habit, I'm interested in James' first word once he gets beyond the greeting. He doesn't simply say, 'Be patient'. He doesn't say, 'Avoid worldliness', or 'Pray more'. He's going to end saying those things but there's a proper way and a proper time to do it. James is not just wanting to moralize, to say how we are to be. He wants us to establish the habit. You can tell a person to be a certain way, but if the habit isn't there they are just imitating it intermittently. What kind of habit? That of doing good until it is an unconscious way of life. We don't let our right hand know what our left hand is doing. So that we will be like those in Matthew 25:37. We'll say, 'Lord, when saw we thee an hungred, and fed thee?' We weren't even aware we were doing it. That's the Christianity James wants us to have.

He is not talking about a superficial kind of Christianity, but a kind that is virtually unknown today. He's not talking about a happy-go-lucky kind of Christian who says, 'I'm going to give Christianity my best shot.' He's not talking about the kind of person to whom Christianity is one happy trip or a barrel of laughs or fun. We're dealing now with a kind of Christianity that you read about in the lives of the great saints, that we've all heard exists. Yet we must understand that this is something that is often not written about because for every Christian that becomes famous as a saint, like Francis of Assisi or Brother Lawrence, there are a thousand, hundreds of thousands, who never get recognition. I'm talking about a Christianity that dazzles. Whether it is an exception to the rule at the present time is beside the point. We can do it. And James gives us the clue.

What, then, is his first word? 'Count it all joy when ye fall into divers temptations' (or trials). Would it have entered your mind to give that kind of advice? If dazzling Christianity is what you are wanting to produce, would that have been the first thing you would have thought of? But it's trustworthy counsel from a godly mind. James says it.

Temptation and Trial: The Best Means of Grace

Why does he begin here? Because not only are trials the best *test* of grace, they are the best *means* of grace. This Greek word is *peirasmos* and it is translated 'temptation' or 'trial'. It comes from the root word which means 'to try' or 'to tempt'. Most of the time Greek is more expressive than English. But in this case the Greek is not helpful. James uses this one word which sometimes means 'temptation' and at other times it means 'trial'. So in your Authorised Version, every time you see 'temptation' or 'trial' it is the same word. Only the context can tell us the difference.

Five Differences Between Temptation and Trial

Before we go any further it will be helpful to see some differences and similarities between temptation and trial. They often overlap. We must not drive the distinction too far, but there are differences.

The first of is all in their immediate origin. Temptation usually comes from within. Trials usually come from without. The fact that James could say, 'Blessed is the man that endureth temptation: for when he is tried ...' (1:12), makes it obvious there that he's referring to trial. But the very next verse says, 'Let no man say when he is tempted, I am tempted of God ... but every man is tempted, when he is drawn away of his own lust, and enticed' (1:13,14). Obviously James means temptation there. The difference is in this point: temptations generally come from within, trials come from without.

The second distinction is their moral relevance. Temptation generally has great moral relevance. Right and wrong, good and bad are at stake. But when it comes to a trial it is usually presented as though morally neutral, if not morally irrelevant.

The third distinction refers to what is tested. A temptation is an attack upon a weak spot that we have. A trial tests a strength.

The fourth difference has to do with providence and environment. Temptation involves ourselves and our watchfulness and it therefore can often be avoided. Trials refer more to circumstances and our reactions to events over which we have no control.

Finally there's the difference with reference to time. Temptation is usually constant, continuous. It is almost always present. But a trial is intermittent. It can be sudden and often suggests discontinuity in our lives.

Five Similarities Between Temptation and Trial

What are the similarities between a temptation and a trial? Both are immediately the devil's activity but ultimately are by God's sovereign permission and pleasure. Secondly, there is a similarity in their timing. Temptation or trial usually comes at the worst possible time and yet at the best possible time. At its worst you can see the devil's hand, how evil he is, how unfair and how clever. Yet with every attack and every trial you can always see a mercy. And you are constrained to say, 'Well, if it had to happen, at least it happened in such a way.' You can see the devil but you can also see God.

The third similarity is that they are never beyond our ability to cope. I now think the most important verse a new Christian should master and memorize is 1 Corinthians 10:13: 'There hath no temptation [trial] taken you but such as is common to man: but God is faithful, who will not suffer you to be tempted above that ye are able; but will with the temptation also make a way to escape, that ye may be able to bear it.' I challenge you to memorize that verse because it is something we must believe. All trials come within our ability to cope. All trials have been filtered through the throne of grace and have come by God's permission. It shows that God imputes to us sufficient strength to bear it or he wouldn't allow it.

The fourth similarity is that, whether trial or temptation, they are invariably accompanied by the suggestion that the only thing to do is to give in. If it's temptation it always looks providential and therefore you are to yield to it. If it's a trial it always looks as though it's beyond your ability to cope and so the suggestion is to cave in.

The fifth similarity is that both are given as wonderful opportunities for spiritual growth. If you cave in, yield, or throw in the towel and say, 'It's no use', and let the devil have the victory, you will forfeit a unique opportunity for blessing that will never again be presented. Every temptation, every trial must be looked upon in that way. This is why James said, 'Count it all joy'.

I was talking to somebody who had just come back from Romania where he had been with Josef Tson. He told this story of how Josef Tson was brought in before the secret police. They had been harassing him for months and finally said to him, 'Why don't you give up and co-operate with us? You must be miserable. He said, 'No. You've done me the greatest favour. For since you've started I've really known the presence of God and blessing.'

Having a Spiritual Reaction to Trials

James knew this. He didn't want his readers to misinterpret adversity, much less miss the opportunity which a trial affords. In Hebrews we read, 'Despise not thou the chastening of the Lord' (12:5); when the trial comes it's the devil, but God lets it happen. We are not to despise it. James wants to instill in us a spiritual reaction, not a natural one to the phenomenon of a trial.

What then is the spiritual reaction? It is to count the trial a basis for rejoicing. I want to be careful here. I'm not talking now of a glib, superficial, shouting, 'Glory! Hallelujah!' every time something goes wrong – when you can't find your keys, if the hammer misses the nail and lands it squarely on your thumb, when you are laid up with illness or you have been severely maltreated at work, by a friend or by an enemy. That's a lot of nonsense.

But I do mean this. Counting it all joy is to dignify God's providence because it shows that you see God's hand in every area of your life. It shows that you pay tribute to a loving God who would give you such personal attention and who would impute to you sufficient strength to bear it. So you don't shake your fist in God's face. You do not murmur.

What you do is you think, 'Ah, here is my chance to get a blessing.' Begin to look for the blessing, anticipate it. After all, you know that when the trial comes it's not going to last forever. When it's over you can look back with shame because you panicked or caved in, or you can look back with a real sense of justifiable pride.

This is what Galatians 6:5 means: 'For every man shall bear his own burden.' James gives this practical advice for your own good. Esteem this trial as a thing of joy rather than despise it.

Avoid Temptations and Trials

There is, however, this condition: the trial is a thing of joy only if you fall into it. The Greek word here is *peripipto*, 'to fall upon and fall in with' or 'fall into'. It is used by our Lord in Luke 10:30, the parable of the good Samaritan: 'A certain man went down from Jerusalem to Jericho, and fell among thieves.' And by Jews in Acts 27:41 when Paul's ship ran aground: 'And falling into a place …' It is a word that denotes a passive falling into trouble or difficulty, not something that you plot to happen. Jesus told us that when we pray the Lord's Prayer we should say, 'Lead us not into temptation'. You are to pray that way. You avoid temptation and trial at all costs. Paul said, 'Make not provision for the flesh, to fulfil the lusts thereof' (Rom. 13:14). Billy Sunday once said that the reason most Christians fall into sin is that they treat temptation like a strawberry short-cake rather than a rattlesnake. The best way to avoid falling into sin is to avoid the temptation.

So a trial is not something you ask for or bring about, but something you fall into, something appointed by God. Dignify the trial by enduring it gracefully and refusing to sin, determine to find the blessing that God has for you; don't despise it.

One thing more. James says to rejoice because you fall into diverse trials. The Greek word here means 'of various shades', 'variegated', 'diverse'. In other words, not the same trial all the time but different trials.

This suggests that Satan needs a slightly different method each time he goes for you, that you have overome his previous attacks so he has to get after you differently now. The fact that you are falling into diverse trials is an implicit compliment. It shows the devil is on the run. He can't just bring you into the same trial every time. It's always different, coming from behind, in an unexpected way. It's a compliment from God who knows that you can handle it.

What, then, makes the trial different? It's different because of the initial impression that always comes with the trial that here at long last is the trial that is beyond your ability to cope with. This one is different. All other trials have had commensurate grace but not this one. The devil will give that suggestion every time. In temptation Satan always goes for the Achilles heel, but in the unexpected way, so that a trial always seems to be the one beyond my strength. Satan gives us the horror of inevitability, i.e. he suggests that you must give in, if you haven't already, because you will do so eventually. 'You don't have the strength to resist this one. Give in. God understands. It's all here. It's providential. You probably won't even get caught. Give in.'

Then, if you have already given in, you start justifying it by saying, 'Well, I had no choice. It was one of those things.' My fellow Christian, there is no temptation, no trial taken 'but such as is common to man'. God will, with the temptation, always, always 'make a way to escape, that ye may be able to bear it'.

The One Success in Life that Matters

Why does James say, 'Count it all joy when ye fall into divers temptations'? All joy? The answer is, because it points to the one success in life that really matters. All other joys are derived joys, secondary joys. But there is no greater joy than discernible growth in grace.

Finally, I'm giving the kind of advice that when you are older you wish you had taken when you were young. Let me give you two illustrations. One is that of the elderly lady who was in my mother's church in Springfield, Illinois. She was one of those ladies the young people just loved. And she loved young people. One evening with lot of young people there, she blurted out this comment – she said, 'You know, I've been a Christian so long that I can hardly tell the difference between a blessing and a trial.' Do you know what she meant by that? I think I do.

The second illustration is that of an elderly man in my home church in Ashland, Kentucky. One day I was sitting in the front row of the church after the service had finished. Tears were rolling down his cheeks and he said: 'The world looks for something that will make it laugh. I'm looking for something that will make me cry.' I've thought a lot about that statement and it's puzzled me. But after twenty-five years I think I know why he made it, especially knowing a little more about that man – he wasn't always the saint he appeared to be then. Aged about eighty, he was reflecting across the years of missed opportunity, of not meeting trials with the dignity that would have paid great dividends. So that if something would make him cry now, at the age of eighty, it would be one more opportunity to increase his heavenly treasure.

Did you ever hear an older person say, 'If only I had bought that property years ago it would be worth a lot of money now'? Older people are always looking back upon, 'if only I had done this'. Here's my word to you today. Regard diverse trials in terms of property – a good buy while you are young. Jesus called it 'treasure in heaven' (Mt. 6:20). It is like saving for retirement. The dividends will pay you with increasing interest as you get older. Do you see now why James said it? 'Count it all joy when you fall into divers temptations; knowing this, that the trying of your faith worketh patience.'

3

The Path to Maturity

James 1:3–4

We have seen that trials not only afford the best *test* of grace; they are the best *means* of grace. Peter said, 'That the trial of your faith, being much more precious than of gold that perisheth, though it be tried with fire' (1 Pet. 1:7). James 1:3–4 is saying precisely this. Verse 3 is best translated: 'Knowing this, that the trying of your faith brings out as a result a patient frame of mind.'

Trials Beget Growth

James uses the strong word *ginoskontes*, the participle of *ginosko*, showing that we know by revelation and by experience that trials help us. As Paul said, we enter the kingdom of God 'through much tribulation' or 'through many hardships' (Acts 14:22). Here is a fact that every new Christian must learn: a trial begets growth and is the quickest way to see the glory of God. If you as a young Christian can endure trial with dignity, there will be such a sense of the presence of God that you will never be the same again and would not take anything for that very trial.

We may ask, how is faith tried? Mostly by sudden disappointment. It is not that you don't get your way, for non-Christians know what it is not to get their way – but the trial refines faith by bringing the unexpected, which appears to be just beyond our ability to cope. This is what makes a trial a trial. It is no great compliment to our spiritual state if we are being tried the same way over and over again: be thankful that we are not having the same old trials. A spiritual reaction to a new trial will result in what James calls 'the patient frame of mind'.

Patience

Patience is *the ability to endure hardness without murmuring*. It's a wonderful virtue and you do not get it by prayer alone. It comes by your reaction to sudden disappointment that at first seems beyond your ability to cope with. Patience is what I would term a crossroads virtue. It simply shows that you have come so far and you have met the test that determines which way you are going from here. Simon Peter shows that if you are now being pestered to see whether you are going to have patience, you have already come far. It means that you had much faith, virtue, knowledge, temperance, and now patience is the next step.

The goal of the Christian life is to bring us to perfect love, for there are virtues that follow patience. Add to your 'patience godliness; And to godliness brotherly kindness; and to brotherly kindness charity' (2 Pet. 1:6). That's the goal. But there are no short cuts. We cannot come to perfect charity, or love, until we know what brotherly kindness is. And we cannot come to brotherly kindness until we know what godliness is. But the crossroads virtue is patience. And this comes if we pass the examination of examinations: the trial of our faith. Peter and James agree that how you react to trial will determine the result, whether there follows that patient frame of mind.

What is this patience? The NIV calls it 'perseverance'. I'm sticking with the word 'patience'. I think most of us have a view of this that makes it closer to where we live. It is what Isaiah meant about having perfect peace (Is. 26:3), and the peace that passes understanding which Paul talked about (Phil. 4:7).

Nicholas Hermain, affectionately known as Brother Lawrence, called it 'the practice of the presence of God'. He said he wouldn't turn his hand for the difference between picking up a piece of straw or preaching to thousands. It's the mind that knows no panic, no hurry.

> Like a river glorious
> Is God's perfect peace,
> Over all victorious
> In its bright increase;
> Perfect yet it floweth
> Fuller every day;
> Perfect, yet it groweth
> Deeper all the way.

A patient frame of mind knows no need for vengeance, panic,

hostility or resentment. It is a mind at rest, undisturbed. Do you have this?

> Hidden in the hollow
> Of his blessed hand,
> Never foe can follow,
> Never traitor stand;
> Not a surge of worry,
> Not a shade of care,
> Not a blast of hurry,
> Touch the spirit there.

How to Have Patience

Is this foreign to you? Is this beyond anything you've known? Wouldn't this be wonderful to have? You may say, 'Perhaps I need a greater vision of the sovereignty of God.' Or, 'I need more theological refinement.' Or, 'I should pray more, read my Bible more.' We could go on and on and all these things help. But there is one way to come to this, and that is by the trial of your faith and your reaction to it.

James is not finished. He says, 'But let patience have her perfect work'. What on earth does that mean? It means first of all that you don't panic by hastening the end of the trial prematurely. After all, we are talking about a trial that has come about by God's appointment. You didn't plot it.. You didn't plan it. You fell into it. 'Every joy or trial *falleth* from above.' It is something that God has done, it happened to you. Its origin was outside yourself. Therefore it is not your job to solve it or to end it but rather to react to it with honour. The same God who appointed the trial and timed it will end it. I promise you – and my authority is God's infallible word – your trial will not last one moment longer than you can bear. That's the first thing that this means: 'Let patience have its perfect work'.

Secondly, it means that the trial did not come without purpose. After all, we are not existentialists who believe there is no meaning or purpose in what they call existence. Rather, we believe that every trial has purpose, design and lesson. James is urging us not to sweep the trial aside and miss the lesson that God has for us. For example, if somebody has said something about us that is not true, our reaction is to rush to defend ourselves. There's something more important than your personal pride, and that is your Christian growth. Let God vindicate you in his way and in his time. Then you'll have both vindication and growth, the establishment of a new habit. And you are never the same again. Indeed, God is more concerned about your influence and reputation than you are. There is no way to calculate the Christian growth that awaits you if you yield to his sovereignty.

The third thing this verse means is that patience itself is a living virtue which works wonders in and by itself. While we wait we can worship, and our perspectives are broadened. The things which were once fuzzy to us become clear. We begin to have objectivity about things around us and even about ourselves, which so few of us have. We begin to enjoy the simple things of life that once bored us. Do you remember that story of Corrie ten Boom when she was in prison? She made friends with a little ant that crawled into her cell. God can make everything precious. We see things we hadn't seen before. And the simplicity of life becomes glorious. In our busy lives we rush from A to B, but you will be amazed how much there is to see between A and B if you let God do things his way.

The Trial's End

During a time of trial, one of the best things you can do is start praying for other people, not wasting so much precious prayer time being preoccupied with your own personal and sometimes selfish concerns. While patience is bringing forth its perfect work we can learn so much. We begin to apply truths that we had never before soaked in and see the wonder of God's providence. The worst thing we can do to a trial is to abort it before God ends it his way. 'Let patience have her perfect work'.

You will want to ask, 'What is the perfect work of patience?' Ultimately it is God's redemption. 'He that endureth to the end shall be saved' (Mt. 10:22). One of these days, everything will be finished and Jesus shall come back. We should live every day as though this were the day Jesus is coming so that we will 'not be ashamed before him at his coming' (1 Jn. 2:28).

So it is with the phenomenon of trial. There is coming a time when it will be over, when God will step in. And often the trial will end as suddenly as it began. How are we going to feel when it's over? Are we going to say, 'Well, I'm glad that's over'? Or are we going to say, 'It's over but I endured it with dignity'? This is the meaning of the words, 'count it all joy when ye fall into divers trials'.

God will end the trial. When it ends and we are caught manipulating things, defending ourselves, seeking others' approval, and all the time God was working behind the scenes to do it himself, we will be embarrassed and we will blush. We will think, 'I missed the blessing that I might have had.' The trial is over and we are no better off.

But oh, the joy that comes when we endure a trial without murmuring and then God ends it! We can say with the prophet, 'Lo ... we have waited for him' (Is. 25:9). The test is this: how do you get your joy? Do you get your joy simply because the trial is over and done with and you think, 'I feel good again'? Do you get your joy because you got your vindication or your financial need was supplied after all?

Two Kinds of Superficial Joy

Stop for a moment. There are two kinds of superficial joy. And often one or both of these are mistaken for the kind of joy that James is talking about. The first superficial joy is what I call a secondary joy – the sheer relief that the trial is over. If you have that kind of joy and you think it's primary joy you have misunderstood James.

The second kind of superficial joy is what I would call artificial joy. This is when you make the effort to defuse the trial by your own manipulation. An example of this is the joy Abraham knew by following Sarah's advice and accepting Hagar as the mother of the child of promise. The trial was that God gave a promise but the child wasn't coming along. So what did Abraham and Sarah do? They manipulated things and Ishmael came along. They didn't believe God was big enough to keep his own word his own way.

Artificial joy comes when we try to sidestep trials by manipulation, making out that things aren't as bad as we'd thought. Take the promise of Romans 8:28: 'We know that all things work together for good to them that love God, to them who are the called according to his purpose.' Many of us lean on that verse. I do at least once a day. But if you think that things work together for good because you manipulate and make them work together for good you have missed the point. For that verse is in the context of a chapter that shows that everything is by grace. We don't have to keep ourselves saved. We didn't even initiate salvation. Things work together for good because of God.

Real Joy

So the real joy that James is talking about is knowing that you've got a God
in heaven who cares. I want you to see the honour that comes from him
only and wait on him.

My fellow Christian, come to see that even our hurt is God's divine
plan. My trying to end the trial by manipulation will make the whole
ordeal not only imperfect but botched and ugly. When God ends the trial
without my help it's beautiful. It has symmetry, design and his glory is
there. As Ecclesiastes 3:11 puts it: 'He hath made every thing beautiful in
his time'. On top of this is the establishment of a new habit of grace and
incalculable growth.

There's another thing I want us to see from this fourth verse. When
James says, 'Let patience have her perfect work, that ye may be perfect and
entire, wanting nothing', there is contained a hint of a larger and greater
principle that characterizes all of God's dealings. What do we learn about
God from Genesis to Revelation? That he never does anything idly or
without purpose. When people attempt to interrupt or hasten or embel-
lish his straightforward purpose and way, the result is always a diminished
reflection of how lovely things would have been. We can see it throughout Scripture, from the fall of man to our present situation, whether it's in
the realm of evangelism, church growth, or guidance, it is always the case.

Take, for example, a new convert who is brought prematurely to a
decision for Christ. That Christian life suffers from arrested development
for a long time. Or take the contemporary emphasis upon church growth
– trying so hard to build up a congregation, trying not to offend, trying to
please. What happens is that our haste deprives people of seeing how God
might have added to the church had things been done his way. Abraham
and Sarah had Ishmael, but how much grief might have been avoided...?
Do you know that every tragedy in the Bible is an illustration of how
people would not let patience have its perfect work? How true it is: 'He
hath made every thing beautiful in his time'.

When patience reaches a full term, completing its purpose, there is
nothing wanting. There is no way that things might have been better. So
Paul, referring to the incarnation could say, 'But when the fulness of the
time was come, God sent forth his Son, made of a woman, made under
the law, To redeem them that were under the law, that we might receive
the adoption of sons' (Gal. 4:4–5). Here is a perfect illustration of how
lovely things are when God works unhindered, for no mistakes are made
then. James wants each of us to participate in this divine principle, to
watch God work and wait on him.

Three Illustrations of Worldliness

Finally, James does not limit this truth to a matter of one particular trial. After all, he has as his goal for us this unconscious habit of godliness. He's not simply saying, 'This particular trial will bring about great fruits', he's talking about what patience will do for the whole person. When James says, 'perfect and entire, wanting nothing', he is obviously not talking about a sinless perfection or a sinless maturity. As John said, 'If we say that we have no sin, we deceive ourselves, and the truth is not in us' (1 Jn. 1:8). Yet there is to be enjoyed a far more advanced maturity than some of us care to admit.

What, then, does James mean by 'perfect and entire, wanting nothing'? This perfection is first of all in terms of a godly contentment. The man of God does not crave the things of this world. John said, 'Love not the world, neither the things that are in the world. If any man love the world, the love of the Father is not in him' (1 Jn. 2:15). And then he gives us three illustrations of worldliness that we are to avoid.

The first is '*the lust of the flesh*': we are not to sin outwardly. Then '*the lust of the eyes*': we are to avoid temptation. The best way to avoid sin is to avoid temptation. When you begin to avoid temptation you are beginning to grow in the way the New Testament writers envisage for the people of God. But there's still a third, highest level of worldliness: '*the pride of life*'. Our egos are to be subservient to the honour of God. We live for that, not for what people think, for honour comes from God only (Jn. 5:44). That's the first thing that James means here in terms of being 'perfect and entire'.

The second thing that is intended is the possibility of us having a forgiving spirit. Do you remember that Jesus said, 'Be ye therefore perfect, even as your Father which is in heaven is perfect' (Mt. 5:48)? We pray, 'Forgive us our trespasses as we forgive those who trespass against us.' I wonder how many are made out to be liars by praying the Lord's Prayer. But our Lord Jesus envisaged a spirit of forgiveness like God's. Do we only love those who love us and forgive those who don't hurt us? But James speaks of a maturity beyond such simple worldliness.

Finally it means protection and maturity with reference to God's will for our lives. When we pray, 'Thy will be done on earth as it is in heaven', we do not simply mean that we are willing to do God's will – of course that is necessary and we must be willing to do God's will, but many of us never move beyond that. It is one thing to say, 'I am willing to do his will', it's quite another to be so in the hand of God that we are actually what he wants us to be. Do you know the story about D.L. Moody sitting on the platform, hearing a minister say: 'The world has yet to see what God could do with one man who was totally yielded to him'? Moody said to himself, 'I propose to be that person.'

We should be so utterly subservient to Christ that we are not merely willing to do what God wants us to do, but actually doing it. This is what Paul meant in Colossians 4:12: 'That ye may stand perfect and complete in all the will of God.' As long as we have the same old trials we will never grow. In ten years from now we will be no more spiritual than we are today.

Patience leads to real maturity because we are exactly what God wants us to be. Do you know where this kind of Christianity is being exemplified at the moment? There may be one person here and one person there. But what would happen if all of us were exactly what God wants us to be? We learn from church history that this kind of godliness is the next best thing to revival.

Many people are put off by Evan Roberts because he seems not to have had a clue about the doctrine of imputation. He didn't, as far as we know. He went around talking about living for each other, loving Jesus and hating the world. Many of us sophisticated theologians say we're beyond that. Are we? This simplicity of holy living is what we must attain to before we can expect God to bless us. Is God preparing us for something? I certainly hope so. But what matters is our reaction to trial.

4

Growing in Wisdom

James 1:5

Prayer, to James, is not the end but the means to the end. There's no particular virtue in how much time we actually spend in prayer. Some people get more accomplished in one hour of praying than others can with two. What matters is what prayer can do for us. If there is a need, we pray. Particularly if we lack wisdom, we ask God.

Why does James turn to wisdom here? It is obviously what is lacking. In the previous verse he said: 'Let patience have her perfect work, that ye may be perfect and entire, wanting' – or lacking – 'nothing.' Now he addresses what we so often lack: wisdom.

Ask God

I think of Romans 8:28 almost every day. I also think of James 1:5 almost every day. James has the hope that even what we lack – wisdom – we may receive. Having dealt with trials, and the great perplexity they may bring, he knows that they require not only patience but also wisdom of Christians.

James addressed those 'scattered abroad'. It may be that, having been transplanted to different soil, met new people and been confronted with different surroundings, they were asking 'Why?' We may be sure that these Jewish Christians once had a traditional view of the Messiah. That they had overthrown, but they still didn't understand what was taking place. They needed theological wisdom to know God's whole purpose. But I think we may safely say that the main reason James brings up this question of wisdom is because he is telling us how to live the Christian life. We all face questions: What shall I do? Can I do this and be a Christian? Is this all right? If you don't know, perhaps you lack wisdom. Here's the beauty of it. James wants you to see that it is God you ask. Don't expect a book of rules. James does not say, 'Look to the Lord God', or 'Read the Bible', he says, 'Ask God'.

James primarily wants to establish the conviction that God can and will lead the Christian, and do so by an immediate, personal and direct relationship with himself. This relationship is to be known by the instrument of prayer. No Christian, no church leader was more Jewish than James, and if anybody could be expected to give the counsel: 'Look to the Lord God', it would be James. This whole book is one continuous exhortation to live the Christian life without law.

The first reference to the law is in 1:25, the 'perfect law of liberty'. The next time James mentions the law he refers to the 'royal law according to the scripture, Thou shalt love thy neighbour as thyself' (2:8), cohering with Paul who said that love is the fulfilling of the law (Rom. 13:8). James is saying here that by respecting persons one violates the perfect law of liberty. How can he do that? Because it becomes a moral standard that even unregenerate humanity can live by and will be judged by. Like Paul, James is convinced that there is a way, a glorious way, to live the Christian life without the law: a living that exceeds the righteousness of the law but always fulfils it. James believes that if we live by the law of liberty purposefully, we will fulfil the moral law accidentally. If you lack wisdom, ask of God.

What Kind of Wisdom?

At the beginning James quietens the weakest Christian before God. That is what he wants to do. He says, 'Count it all joy if ye fall into diverse temptations ... Let patience have her perfect work, that ye may be perfect and entire, wanting nothing.' Then he suggests you are going to be wanting in one thing – subjective wisdom – but even that will be supplied.

I might point out that, from an objective point of view, we don't lack wisdom. Have you forgotten: 'Of him are ye in Christ Jesus, who of God is made unto us wisdom, and righteousness, and sanctification, and redemption' (1 Cor. 1:30)? What Adam lost, Christ got back. Objectively we have Christ 'in whom are hid all the treasures of wisdom and knowledge' (Col. 2:3). But James is talking about a subjective lack of wisdom.

The Greek word in question here is *sophia*. It is a word that differs from other Greek words with similar meanings. *Sophia* was originally derived from an adjective that denotes a quality, never an activity, and it always implied an unusual knowledge and ability. Originally, in Hellenistic literature, *sophia* was the possession of the gods alone. But then along came Socrates who gave it new meaning by comparing *sophia* to *philosophia*. Socrates said that *philosophia* referred more to rhetoric and the ability to dispute, whereas *sophia* was critical knowledge about oneself. It is the wisdom of knowing that you don't have wisdom and this, he said, is the highest kind of knowledge. In the Septuagint (the Greek translation of the Hebrew Old Testament) *sophia* is the word used in the wisdom literature (e.g. in the famous statement in Proverbs 9:10 that 'The fear of the Lord is the beginning of wisdom'). In Hellenistic Judaism knowledge mediated by *sophia* had the character of direct revelation. As far as the Stoics were concerned, *sophia* was actualized knowledge whereas *philosophia* had a practical application.

The New Testament writers used words that had meanings understood by the people who read them. James did not use the word *techna* which referred to an art, craft or skill (used by Paul in Acts 17). Nor did he use the word *phren*, meaning cleverness or intellect (used in Matthew 25 of the five wise virgins).

James used *sophia*. What we have here is what Socrates long before regarded as the highest form of self-knowledge, with which we can be critical about ourselves. It is the kind of understanding that matters most and that eludes the greatest minds. They can be efficient in rhetoric. They can be ingenious in skill. They may have brilliance in intellectual aptitude but not have *sophia*. And James says the Christian can have it.

Sophia is the same word used to refer to our Lord Jesus when he was a child. We are told that he 'waxed strong in spirit, filled with wisdom' (Lk. 2:40), and that he 'increased in wisdom and stature, and in favour with God and man' (Lk. 2:52). *Sophia* is also used in Mark 6:2 when they asked of Jesus: 'From whence hath this man these things? and what wisdom is this which is given unto him, that even such mighty works are wrought by his hands?' This is very interesting because the Greek here is referring to power, energy which flowed or was derived from wisdom. The very fact that Jesus was able to perform miracles was regarded as the result of his wisdom.

When in the early church the apostles felt a need for deacons, what did they say? 'Look ye out among you seven men ... full of the Holy Ghost and wisdom' (Acts 6:3). And later on it is said that when Stephen, one of the seven, preached 'they were not able to resist the wisdom and the spirit by which he spake' (Acts 6:10).

Do you lack wisdom? Well, ask of God. You may want to ask, for example, when you are aware of your lack of wisdom or when a trial makes no sense to you. You may be aware of your lack of wisdom because of a sudden or approaching need for decision. Or you may ask for wisdom when the law of liberty doesn't give you the answer. Can I do this or is it wrong? That's the law of Christian liberty.

The Philippians said, 'If only we had Paul here we could just say, what about this?' Paul replied, 'I'm not with you. I'm not worried that I'm not with you because it is God that works in you.' He was not afraid to leave them. He said, 'The only thing I would say is do all things without murmurings or disputings.' That's what matters. James' way of saying it is: 'Count it all joy when you fall into divers temptations'. 'As long as you do that,' James says, 'I'm not too worried about you.' When the law of liberty doesn't give you the answer, you ask for wisdom.

Is there anybody who doesn't lack in wisdom? In 1 Corinthians 12:8 one of the gifts of the Spirit, we are told, is the 'word of wisdom'. What is that? I'm not exactly sure, but I would have thought it is given to somebody who has a good deal of the Greek word *phren* already. I would have thought that the gift of wisdom is a combination of *phren* and *sophia* – intellect and wisdom – and yet nobody has it all the time. It is given as it is needed. Those who have it know more than anybody else that they could lose it, and they're aware of their dependence upon God.

Our Lack of Wisdom

There was never a wiser man than Solomon, but a greater fool never lived. We are wiser if we admit to our lack of wisdom rather than to our possession of it. Paul said, 'If any man among you seemeth to be wise in this world, let him become a fool' (1 Cor. 3:18). James says 'Ask God' because when you ask God you are thereby admitting a deficiency and James is later going to say, 'God resisteth the proud, but giveth grace unto the humble' (4:6).

But why ask God? Because he knows everything and is able to keep you. You don't need a code of ethics to go by, like a tourist with a map in a strange city. You ask God because he's a God of power. And he communicates. He's not dead. He's not deaf. He's there and he knows everything. There is no searching of his understanding (Isa. 40:28). He knows the right answer.

O what peace we often forfeit,
O what needless pain we bear,
All because we do not carry
Everything to God in prayer!

How much have you been praying recently? Jesus taught that 'men ought always to pray, and not to faint' (Lk. 18:1). Why did he say that? Because we lack wisdom. Why does God withhold wisdom? That we might see what we are in ourselves and have no choice but to acknowledge that we need him.

The Christian is not one who goes by cleverness and skill. We are all equal here. You may have a high IQ or you may have an ingenious ability. You may be a dentist or a surgeon, a professor or a barrister. You have skill and aptitude and knowledge, but when it comes to this you're in the same situation as the rest of us. It's wisdom that we all need and it's that which our leaders should recognize they need.

There's a feeling in politics that if somebody has been to Eton or Oxford then they're automatically qualified for government service. But wisdom eludes the brightest of people. May God hasten the day when those over us see that wisdom is not cleverness. What we need is a break-through from God. When that comes righteousness will exalt the nation (Prov. 14:34). And revival will come when our congregations are governed by a spirit of wisdom. Will we be governed because chastening is the only language we understand? Or will we wait before God, crying to him for a spirit of prayer? I long to see that because revival will begin with the emergence of divine wisdom.

They said of Jesus, 'From whence came this wisdom that there is such power about his ministry?' Stephen also had it. People were not able to resist the wisdom and spirit by which he spoke. This is what Jesus meant when he said, 'But when they deliver you up, take no thought how or what ye shall speak: for it shall be given you in that same hour what ye shall speak. For it is not ye that speak, but the Spirit of your Father which speaketh in you' (Mt. 10:19–20). Wisdom is given by God. And when wisdom is present all see that it is not a natural endowment.

God Gives Wisdom

James says three very important and encouraging things about this God to whom we pray when we have the need of wisdom. The first is that God gives wisdom to all. You don't pay or bargain for it. It's like salvation.

The gift of wisdom is a peculiar gift of the Spirit which Paul said is given to some, not all. Not all may have the gift of wisdom, but all of us may have wisdom as a gift in the moment we need it.

Secondly, James says that God gives wisdom 'liberally' (AV), 'generously' (NIV), though neither translation really gets at what James means. The Greek is *aplos*. It comes from the word used throughout the Bible to mean 'simply' or 'given with simplicity'. It's from the word Paul used when he said, 'I fear, lest by any means, as the serpent beguiled Eve through his subtlety, so your minds should be corrupted from the simplicity that is in Christ' (2 Cor. 11:3). James is saying that wisdom is given simply. James goes on to say that 'the wisdom that is from above is first pure, then peaceable, gentle, and easy to be entreated' (3:17). The marvel of this wisdom is its simplicity, its gentleness, its unpretentiousness.

When a breakthrough comes it's always so simple. When we see it we say, 'That's it. Why didn't I think of that?' But that's the wisdom that comes from above. It eludes us until God gives it. When he gives it, we know it's right. It is 20/20 hindsight vision before the fact. It's the same with understanding Scripture and with theological wisdom. A passage of Scripture that had seemed dark and obscure becomes so simple because the Spirit gives us light. This is what James wants us to see in living the Christian life. The most learned among us and the most illiterate may both have this simplicity of wisdom.

The third thing James says about God is not only that he gives wisdom to all and he gives it simply, but he 'upbraideth not'. That means he doesn't insult you. When God is approached because you need wisdom he doesn't say, 'Don't bother me with that,' or 'Surely you're not saying you don't understand that?' or 'You should already know the answer to that.' God accepts. His wisdom is gentle, easy to be entreated.

Many Christians don't go to another Christian for any kind of counsel because they feel stupid and fear that the reply will be 'You've got that problem? Well, you should know the answer to that.' James says, 'God won't make you feel that way.' The truth is that what you feel stupid about everybody else has problems with too. They've got problems worse than you, but they wear masks so you will be intimidated. The wonder is that God will forgive any sin, listen to any problem. 'In all thy ways acknowledge him, and he shall direct thy paths' (Prov. 3:6). Later James says 'Ye ... have seen the end of the Lord; that the Lord is very pitiful, and of tender mercy' (5:11).

James concludes that such wisdom as you ask for will be given. The key word is *given*. This, incidentally, is the most offensive thing about the Christian faith, it's what everybody stumbles over, the fact that it is given.

This is what people hate about God, that God gives freely, not according to our works. The Christian faith is a religion of given knowledge. People, by nature, don't like that. They want a gathered knowledge, a speculative knowledge, the kind of knowledge that they have to use deductive reasoning with whereby everybody will see how clever they are. For example, one Dutch theologian once said that if he had his life to live over he would rather have the quest for truth than truth itself. Now think about that. That shows he was no evangelical, and that he was a proud man. As long as we have the quest for truth we can use our knowledge and everybody will clap and say, 'Oh, you're brilliant, marvellous.' But if it's just given to us we can't boast about it. This is the whole thing about Christianity. It is given knowledge.

This is why people hate the infallibility of Scripture. It's given. We don't have to think it up. We don't have to use philosophy. We don't have to argue. Christians who have put their trust in Jesus Christ are to do all things without murmuring, to count it all joy when they fall into diverse trials. 'You've passed that test', James says. 'You're on your way. You that lack wisdom are going to get it. Ask of God.'

How Wisdom is Given

How is wisdom given? In one of three ways. First, it may be given by an immediate apprehension. I do not say how often this happens, but it does happen. It just comes. There is a quiet assurance of the right thing to do that you know is from God.

Secondly, wisdom may come through the use of practical reason: 'sanctified common sense'. The Christian is one who lives in the real world. You consider the realities and the alternatives. Often the wisdom you are seeking is your best judgment unless there is a check. What do I mean by a check? Two things. One, when there is a negative witness of the Spirit, when God smites you and you know something is wrong. Or two, God's overruling providence; he blocks you off. Otherwise, your best judgment may be the wisdom that you are praying for.

Thirdly, wisdom comes when God works providentially behind the scenes in events and circumstances. In other words, he makes the decision for you. There is nothing to think about: it's done. If you are not given an immediate apprehension or if your practical judgment fails, it is a sign that God is going to solve your problem by his overruling providence. And you just wait and watch him do it. I have many problems solved like that. I pray about it and nothing happens and I am still confused. I just wait a bit and God settles it. God does it and he's never too late, never too early, always just on time. As Jesus put it in Matthew 10, don't even think about what you are going to say. In the moment you need it, it will be given. The Spirit will do it. It's not your wisdom. It's what the Father gives you.

James does, however, attach this condition: 'But let him ask in faith, nothing wavering.' Your first reaction to that verse will be, 'Well that spoils everything.' But that is not the case. The opposite is true. For this is a promise for you that you are going to have wisdom. The same God who will not put upon you a trial beyond your ability to cope will not let a need for wisdom emerge for which there is not commensurate faith. As surely as you have a need for wisdom, you will have the faith to pray for that wisdom and it will be given you.

You may want to say to me, 'But if that is true why did James make a point of saying, "Let him ask in faith, nothing wavering"?' We'll deal with that in some detail in the next sermon, but I will say right now that James had to say that because this is what protects the kingdom of God from bizarre claims of direct revelation. For this attached condition is a key that unlocks but also locks the windows of heaven. And it disqualifies the godless man who wants useful knowledge but despises God's chastening. He who wavers is bound to know that he is asking for something which is not his real need and therefore which he should not expect to receive.

But you will want to ask, 'Is there never a valid need to which a wavering faith will result in the forfeiture of that need being supplied?' The answer is yes. But a valid need met by a wavering faith stems from double mindedness. Double mindedness stems from murmuring.

And so we are back to whether we count it all joy when we fall into diverse trials, whether we can do all things without murmurings and disputings. James wants us to dignify the phenomenon of trial. When your faith is tried by fire and it brings you to maturity so that you want nothing, you will probably lack wisdom. It may be that you need to repent because you would not let patience give its full-term birth to God's perfect work. But if you follow James up to there and your real need is wisdom, you will get it. I will stake my reputation, my whole ministry on this. It may come none too soon, but it will come soon enough.

5

Single-Minded Faith

James 1:6–8

Wisdom Through Faith

There has been a tendency to look at the book of James as though it emphasizes works and not faith. As a matter of fact, most superficial interpretations of James always zero in on the latter part of chapter 2. Consequently, it is often thought that James has no doctrine of faith. In fact, the reverse is true, though James actually prizes faith, he recognizes only one kind of faith – a faith without doubting.

To the promise of wisdom there was an attached condition. 'It shall be given him. But let him ask in faith, nothing wavering.' As we have seen this condition is grounds for great encouragement to us. For this is something that safeguards the kingdom of God generally and our own state particularly. We are talking about guidance, self-knowledge, and grace that comes from God. What more do you need? If we have this wisdom we are set. If we don't have it we are 'Like a wave of the sea driven with the wind and tossed.' This wisdom is promised to all, but received only by faith.

But that should not surprise us, for this is the pattern of the whole gospel. For the gospel is promised to all but received only by faith. Not to receive the gospel means that there is 'a certain fearful looking for of judgment and fiery indignation' (Heb. 10:27). So is the Lord's Table offered to all but only the one who discerns the Lord's body is blessed. Not to discern the Lord's body is to eat and drink damnation to oneself (1 Cor. 11:29). You can see the pattern here. The Lord's Supper, the gospel, and also with wisdom: promised to all 'but let him ask in faith, nothing wavering'.

The absence of wisdom, then, means confusion and every evil work. James would do us no favour to omit this condition, for it is what safeguards the throne of grace from abuse. It is protection against antinomianism and bizarre claims of direct revelation. And the consequence for us is this: doubt is a sign that you are seeking that to which you are not entitled. God never promotes us to the level of our incompetence and never requires us to pray beyond the level of our confidence. For if wisdom is your immediate need, wisdom you will get.

The Entitlement to Wisdom

At this stage we have got to make something quite clear: many are guilty of asking for wisdom when they are not entitled to it. For if we have not first dignified the phenomenon of trial, wisdom isn't our need. When James said, 'If any man lack wisdom', the assumption is that wisdom is the only thing you do lack. The kind of person who despises God's chastening is the person that wisdom always eludes. Why? Because until we let patience bring forth a full-term birth to God's perfect work, we cannot ask for wisdom.

Peter shows that we must have certain virtues in a certain order. For example, we add to our faith virtue; to virtue knowledge; to knowledge patience and so forth (2 Pet. 1:5–8). Now, Peter concluded, 'If these things be in you, and abound, they make you that ye shall neither be barren not unfruitful in the knowledge of our Lord Jesus Christ.' In other words, there are certain disciplines, certain graces, that are already assumed when we are in a position to ask for wisdom. And the final test is whether we can pray without doubting.

This attached condition is for the sake of the kingdom of God. It is for our own sakes, because if we start praying beyond the level of our confidence we know at once something is wrong and we are not praying in the will of God. We must back up and bring ourselves in line with what our faith really is. God does not promise wisdom when there is a particular area of prior need – patience should have its perfect work.

You may say, 'Why does James bring up wisdom so early on in the epistle? Surely he should wait till the very end?' But the fact is, if we let patience have its perfect work we are ready to ask for wisdom. We don't have to be old and grey-headed to qualify for that. Often young Christians manage to prevail in great wisdom and knowledge because they are obedient straight away, whereas other Christians never find this wisdom.

If we let patience have its perfect work, we are ready then and there to move on and grow in grace.

Faith as a Mirror

Faith is both a negative and a positive thing. The windows of heaven are locked by wavering faith. But to the degree that faith is without wavering, 'Eye hath not seen, nor ear heard, neither have entered into the heart of man, the things which God hath prepared for them' – that wait for him – 'that love him' (1 Cor. 2:9). You may be able to move all mountains or you may have nothing more than apprehension of what you are to do for the next five minutes. The point is, we are not required to pray beyond our own faith. Faith then becomes a clear mirror by which we can see and know ourselves with objectivity.

Now what is a mirror? We have all looked into a mirror at least once today. And when we do, the mirror does not lie to us. We may not like what we see, but there it is. Faith is like that because we apprehend in it what God is doing in us. This is why Paul said that all should think of themselves with objectivity, soberly, not more highly than they ought, but recognize their own measure of faith (Rom. 12:3). Within that measure of faith there is this wisdom that becomes a gift.

In prayer there may be an immediate release of wisdom which allows you to pray beyond what you thought yourself capable of. This is what Jude means by 'praying in the Holy Ghost' (Jude 20). But sometimes prayer is nothing more than sanctified common sense; we pray in line with the overruling providence of God. The point is, as we pray we do not think of ourselves more highly than we ought to, but recognize what faith is there. And so we do not impute to ourselves the gift or strength that is not there. We don't have to play games with ourselves; Christianity lets us find ourselves. By seeing what we can pray for and what we cannot pray for we begin to eliminate certain possibilities that we may have desired. This is a humbling process which many of us don't like, and we want to quarrel with God.

Finding our niche in the kingdom of God is so satisfying. It is so gratifying. Not everybody can be an Athanasius or an Augustine or a Calvin or a Saint Francis of Assisi. But there is a place you can fill that nobody else can fill. And your reward in heaven will be as great as that given on earth to the most eminent of saints. God requires that we are faithful in that which is least. Finding our niche is such a wonderful thing.

Our Meaning of Faith

Is there such a thing as a doubting faith? Strictly speaking there is no other kind of faith but a faith that does not doubt. We may doubt, but our faith does not. Our task is to bring ourselves in line with the faith that we have. We may say, 'Lord, increase my faith'. 'Lord, I believe; help thou mine unbelief' (Mk. 9:24). It could be that the degree to which we doubt reflects the fact we have not let patience bring forth its perfect work.

We often refer to weak faith, yet it is not that really. For to the extent that it will accomplish its intended purpose it is as strong as the faith that removes mountains. We sometimes call it weak because our faith is good for passing out a tract rather than writing one. But God gives us faith commensurate with our calling and does not require that we play games with ourselves, praying for what we have no faith to pray for.

I once heard a talk by a very prominent man associated with giving out Bibles. I told him I had a chance to go to Russia and asked how many Bibles I should take. His answer was, 'As many as your faith will let you.' He said some can take hundreds. I took two. I couldn't have taken three but I felt I could take two and I did. The first night we were in Russia, we went on this trip in a bus, terrified that the KGB were watching and trying to trap us. Then we stopped to eat. There must have been hundreds of people there, queueing for food. A man came rushing across to us and said, 'You're Christians, aren't you?' And he asked 'How many Bibles do you have?' I said, 'Well, how many do you have?' 'Two hundred.' I said, 'You've got two hundred?' He showed me his bus and it was the same kind of bus we had: the same make, the same year. I said, 'You don't have two hundred Bibles in that bus.' He said, 'Yes, we do. How many do you have?' I said, 'I've got two.' But he had the faith. I didn't.

We may earnestly covet the best gifts but we don't have to pretend to have the gifts simply because we've coveted them. But when we pray in faith and see our prayers answered, when we operate with contentment within the measure of our faith, however strong it is, we ourselves can sense that God is using us. And it's a great confirmation that we are in his will.

The Double Minded

At this stage we see the emergence of a new, parallel theme in James. What we have here is the first word about what we will see over and over again in this epistle as the alternative to true godliness, the folly of the 'double minded man'. He's not actually called this until we get to verse 8, but he's described in verse 6 as 'he that wavereth', as being 'like a wave of the sea driven … and tossed'. And then his faith expectancy is described in verse 7: 'For let not that man think that he shall receive any thing of the Lord.' He is also described as 'unstable in all his ways' (v. 8). Who is the double minded man? He is the man who prays for wisdom when he's not a candidate for wisdom. He has a prior spiritual need which he will not let be supplied. Here's a man in fundamental rebellion. He asks for wisdom but takes his own intellect to be the answer. He's described as being unstable and imagines himself to be in the will of God when he is deceived. Here's the man who always promotes himself to the level of his spiritual incompetence.

James said that we must ask in faith, nothing doubting. This expression 'nothing doubting' comes from the Greek word *diakrinomenos*. It means those who are at odds with themselves; who believe and yet don't believe; who has no certainty about judgment or actions; who do with bad conscience what they cannot refrain from doing; who do not know the fruition of patience, for patience has not been allowed her perfect work; who took Ishmael to be God's ultimate purpose: 'the double minded man', those who let personal ambition dictate God's will, who make pride their barometer and others' praise their confirmation. Instead of waiting on God the double minded keep on walking. Instead of dignifying the trial, responding positively to chastening, or resisting temptation, they listen to people. They say, 'I cannot be all that bad.' They never stop long enough to know God's will. Wisdom always eludes them. They survive by their natural endowments.

We have differentiated between *sophia*, *techna* and *phren*. But the double minded always call their ability wisdom. They know nothing but whims. Today they think one thing, tomorrow another. So James says, they are 'like a wave of the sea driven with the wind and tossed'.

What makes a wave in the sea? Wind. And the shape of waves is also determined by the wind, by the wind's direction and velocity.

Here are those who are driven by the wind. Whatever the direction of the wind, that is the way they go. If a new doctrine comes along they take it. They are those who always do what is in vogue, regardless. They have no real character of their own. They're afraid to be themselves; they're always imitating others. They have never found themselves.

But the wind also has velocity. On a day with no wind the double minded do quite all right. They're in a good mood, at peace with themselves. They think everything is all right spiritually. But let the wind come and they soon fall to pieces. Why? They're double minded, informed by the direction and speed of the wind. Velocity, if there's any strength to it at all, causes them to collapse.

I'm putting my finger on what is wrong with so many who profess the name of Christ and with the modern church that makes no impact on the world. We are driven not by inner peace, not by wisdom, not by conviction, but by wind.

James adds a bit of advice to the double minded, in case one is listening: 'Let not that man think that he shall receive any thing of the Lord.' James did not say that this man would not receive anything of the Lord. For, after all, he's going to say in verse 17, 'Every good gift and every perfect gift is from above'. Obviously the double minded do receive something. But James says that as far as wisdom is concerned they should not expect any. The Greek word is *oiomai*, to presume, or imagine. James says, 'Don't even expect wisdom.' It will elude the disobedient and the double minded.

So when you fall into confusion, into every evil work, 'Let not that man think he shall receive any thing of the Lord.' Of course those like this won't listen, because they think they are receiving. They ask for wisdom but take their skill or intellect to be that wisdom. My fellow Christians, there is no greater folly than thinking common grace is the wisdom and virtue that comes from the Holy Spirit.

James' nickname for this miserable state is being double minded. It comes from the Greek word *dipsuchos*, and means two minds. It is those who believe and yet don't believe; who want to follow God but also the world's attractions, justifying themselves by saying, 'I'm just weak and, after all, there is the warfare between the flesh and the spirit.'

Are the Double Minded Saved?

The question we must deal with sooner or later is are the double minded Christians? The answer is yes. James obviously thinks so. He addresses them again in 4:8: 'Purify your hearts, ye double minded.' James' concern is for Christians who, though they've made a profession, want to hold onto the world. He says, 'Know ye not that the friendship of the world is enmity with God?' (4:4). This whole epistle is a devastating attack upon the worldly Christian. May God grant that it will help us to shake loose anything that would grieve the Spirit of God and cause any of us to forfeit wisdom. If God will give us this wisdom then we'll have a power, a purpose that will cause the unconverted to be unable to know us and remain unchanged.

James is after the double minded who think their lusts are beyond subduing, that their temptations are supposed to be lived with, nurtured, fulfilled and gratified. They do not war against the flesh. The single-minded Christians are the ones who are in control, who walk in the Spirit and do not fulfil the lust of the flesh (Gal. 5:16), who set their affections on things above.

Finally what is the result for the double minded? They are unstable in all their ways. They know nothing of this Holy Ghost wisdom. They have no objectivity about themselves while the rest of the church and even the world can see there's something wrong. They may carry a Bible under their arm. They may refuse to do this or that, but there's something odd about them, something unattractive. Why? They're unstable in all their ways. The unspiritual Christian is the poorest possible witness for the Christian faith.

This is why I long to produce under God a congregation of people that love God, who flee temptation, who put Christ first. What an opportunity we have in this wicked world to be the kind of Christians that once caused the world to take notice, to say, 'Behold, how they love one another.'

We can see how relevant this epistle is for all of us. How wise this man James was. Count it all joy when you fall into divers trials. Verse 2 and the following verses are the key to James. They determine whether we qualify for this great wisdom: how we respond to trial, how we respond to temptation, whether we will know this faith that knows no doubting. Yet all of us have been double minded. Who do not see themselves described? But James is telling us there is a better way to live. When we begin to take James seriously then we will live lives that dazzle the world because they'll see not a schizophrenic Christianity but a living of the Christian life that is single minded and pure.

6

Religion for the Poor

James 1:9–11

This is the beginning of a commentary on the first part of the epistle of James, for the rest of James is really an enlargement of the original thesis put forward in verses 2 through 8. Some people have looked at the book of James much like a string of beads that's broken. Beads fall all over the floor and are put back on the string with no definite order. They see the book of James as a series of sermon notes, some nice but random sayings. This is quite wrong. James has a definite order. Its original thesis may be understood in terms of three ordered arguments or propositions. First, said James, 'Be sure to dignify or sanctify the phenomenon of trial or temptation.' Second, 'Be sure to let patience give a full-term birth to God's ultimate purpose in this trial, so that the only thing lacking is wisdom.' And third, 'The presence of an undoubting faith is the assurance that you have found yourself.'

Now James has put forward the thesis we come to the commentary, or the enlargement. He said at the beginning, 'Count it all joy when you fall into divers temptations,' 'rejoice'. So now he's beginning to go back. In verse 9 he says, 'Let the brother of low degree rejoice in that he is exalted.' This is the first hint that the trial James has in mind is how financial temptation or trial can bring Christians to despair if they don't react in the right way. The Greek, *tapeinos*, really means 'a man of humble circumstances' (as the NIV translates it). It means that person who is insignificant, who has been economically and sociologically deprived. The one at the bottom.

It has been suggested that there are five classes in England. There's the aristocracy, the upper middle class, the middle middle class, the lower middle class and class five – the working class, the poor. *Tapeinos* describes the person who just barely makes it into class five, the one of most humble circumstances. James says, 'Let that person rejoice.'

The Poor

That's not exactly the kind of philosophy that people embrace today. But why would James say to the poor, 'Rejoice'? Because the poor are precisely the kind of people Jesus came to save. In other words, if a man is poor, if he is economically and socially deprived, he's halfway into the kingdom. This is why Jesus said, 'The Spirit of the Lord is upon me, because he hath anointed me to preach the gospel to the poor' (Lk. 4:18). When John the Baptist wanted to know what was going on Jesus said, 'Go and shew John again those things which ye do hear and see: The blind receive their sight, and the lame walk, the lepers are cleansed, and the deaf hear, the dead are raised up, and the poor have the gospel preached to them' (Mt. 11:4–5).

One of the strangest and most ominous developments of modern Christianity, especially in the West, is its gradual identification with the bourgeoisie, with middle-class society. We must feel this is wrong. Do you know how to test someone's character? Look at how they treat another person who cannot possibly do them any good. Where did Jesus go? To the poor. Who followed Jesus? The poor. He was constantly doing things for people who couldn't possibly have done him any good. James, the brother of Jesus, heard him preach and knew about his followers. James wanted to keep Christianity from becoming a religious bourgeoisie, a sociologically elitest movement. Yet Christianity can quite easily become middle class.

However, this can be explained. It almost always happens like this: because Christianity gives a woman real dignity for the first time in her life, she wants to better herself. She now has reason for living. She becomes ambitious, a real worker. Think about this for a moment. Marxism talks about the worker, but Marxism makes people lazy. Christianity emancipates people from laziness. One can see how a Christian becomes better and her standard of living quite naturally rises.

There's nothing necessarily wrong if poor Christians becomes middle class as long as they never forget the pit from which they were dug. As long as they remember that Christianity is by design a religion for the poor. The trouble is, when the poor better themselves and become middle class, they often only want to witness to the middle classes. From then on they want the church to be middle class.

Nobody enjoys being patronized. It's humiliating. It's disgusting. Often, new Christians feel as if they are somebody for the first time. But others might continue to treat them in a condescending fashion. And it hurts. They come to realize that even though they're Christians, heirs of

the kingdom and children of the King of kings, they're back in the real
world where people are going to spit on them.

James said, 'Wait a minute. Be glad of your humble circumstances
which put you at the head of the queue to receive patience, which paves
the way for the wisdom that eludes other people.' Because the gospel is,
by design, for the poor, no others need apply. 'So,' James says, 'let the
humble rejoice straight away in that they have been exalted.' The Greek
word is *hupsei*, honour. They are straight away honoured by virtue of the
way they were born. They may not know it, but the humble have been
born with silver spoons in their mouths because it is they who have
been made heirs of the kingdom.

A Missed Opportunity

The poor people of England have been almost completely untouched by
the gospel in the twentieth century. It has become a middle-class religion.
Yet what an opportunity we have to follow in the steps of those who have
not been ashamed to go to the poor. We can say to the poor people, 'You
can ratify your birthright. You're halfway there. The gospel is for you.'
But not only does birthright, being born into poverty, put the poor right
there next to the kingdom, they also have an opportunity to grow into
patience, godliness, wisdom and joy such as most people will never know.
This is an important point. Financial trial can be the greatest means of
spiritual growth. What you can do if you are sociologically and economically deprived is 'count it all joy'. You're at the head of the queue to
receive the glory and James recognizes this. Many Christians want to
better themselves so they won't have to trust God so much.

I knew a lady back in Ashland, Kentucky. She was really poor and
everybody knew it. Her husband wasn't a Christian. When he got a little
money he would just use it for drink. She lived a hard life, but she came to
church regularly and there was a glow on her face: a glory rested upon her.
If you ever had a request for prayer you went to her. You knew that she
would pray for you and that you would rather have her praying than
anybody. She was godly and felt God with her. Then one day her husband
was killed in an automobile accident and the insurance company made her
independently wealthy. She came to church less frequently and when she
did come she had classy-looking clothes. The glow was gone. Nobody
went to her any more for prayer. Something happened. It need not have
happened, but it did. And this is what often happens to us. We think we
want to get beyond where we are but God withholds things from us.

James is saying, 'Let the brother of low degree rejoice in that he is exalted'. It's a wonderful thing if we can make poverty into something that counts.

Attitude Makes the Difference

Let's be clear about this. What will make the difference as to whether your poverty will be a blessing? Your attitude to it; whether you are poor in spirit. This is why Jesus said, 'Blessed are the poor in spirit' (Mt. 5:3). In other words, you are poor not only in the eyes of others but you also see yourself as poor in the eyes of God. Poverty alone will not save you, poverty of spirit will.

If poverty is all you know, you can shake your fist at God. You can take the attitude, 'From now on I'm going to have the kind of lifestyle that just takes from those who have.' That's the Marxist solution. Or you can know that 'godliness with contentment is great gain' (1 Tim. 6:6). Jesus said the gospel is for the poor but also for 'the broken hearted'. It is possible to be poor and proud and go on to hell just like the rich who die in their sins.

Your reward in heaven will be in proportion to your faithfulness to your calling on earth. Glory enjoyed on earth is not in proportion to the rewards that will be given in heaven. In the church, as in the world, it's the one who has natural gifts that goes places. Even in the church we recognize that for now the head may have more glory than the foot, eye or hand. That is why Paul said, 'The eye cannot say unto the hand, I have no need of thee: nor again the head to the feet, I have no need of you. Nay, much more those members of the body, which seem to be more feeble, are necessary: And those members of the body, which we think to be less honourable, upon these we bestow more abundant honour; and our uncomely parts have more abundant comeliness' (1 Cor. 12:21–23). But heaven will be a place where the trophy given to the little finger or the little toe will be greater and more glittering than the one given to the head. You may think that Athanasius, Augustine, Calvin, a Christian king or queen or the philanthropist who gave millions of pounds will have the greater reward in heaven. Don't believe that.

Do you want to know what the judgment seat of Christ is? It is where King Jesus honours that slave who was mistreated year after year, day after day, but endured it. King Jesus will honour that one who had it so hard but didn't murmur. King Jesus will honour that unvindicated man or woman who kept turning the other cheek, that man or woman that didn't have the chance to go to Oxford or Cambridge but found their niche in the kingdom of God. King Jesus will honour that one who never had an invitation to Buckingham Palace but still prayed for the nation. James says, 'See this now. Rejoice. After all, you've been exalted. What is more, your day is coming.'

A Word to the Rich

James now turns to the rich because there are some rich and mighty people in the kingdom of God. Not many. As Paul put it: 'For ye see your calling, brethren, how that not many wise men after the flesh, not many mighty, not many noble, are called' (1 Cor. 1:26). The Greek word here is *plousios*, 'the rich'. The word comes from the root word *plero*, 'fullness'. It means simply those who have everything.

What does James say to the rich? If you had a chance to say something to the rich, what would you say? Would it be, 'If you are really a Christian you'll sell all that you have and give it to the church'? Would you say, 'Give to the have-nots. Sell up. Become a pauper yourself and repent of your riches'? James didn't say that. If you had said it you would be following Marxism, motivated by nothing but a spirit of jealousy – and that will never do.

In fact James has an even harsher, more offensive word for the rich, one which the church has failed to say. Firstly, James tells the rich that they should rejoice. Rich and poor, all should rejoice. You might want to say, 'Well, of course. Why shouldn't a rich man rejoice? I would too if I had his money.' But that's not exactly what James means. He doesn't mean the rich should rejoice in money or noble birth, social standing or class. 'The rich man', says James, 'is to rejoice in his humiliation', 'in that he is made low' (AV). This takes us right back to the Greek *tapeinos* – just as the humble rejoice in their exaltation, the rich are to rejoice in their humiliation.

We're talking about rich Christians, so James is saying that the rich are not even at the back of the queue to receive the gospel. The rich have to be told that the gospel, by ordination, is for the poor, for the deprived. The rich, the mighty, the noble were deliberately omitted from the list of those receiving the most coveted invitations in the universe. Not an invitation to dine at Windsor Castle or to own a Jaguar. Not a chance to run for public office or have a public-school education. The rich person's humiliation is that, by design, they were left off the invitation list to receive the gospel.

If a rich man should find himself in the kingdom of God, he should be reminded that he's got no right to be there. 'You're out of place. You don't really belong here. How did you get in?' The gospel was for the poor and, yet here he is, a mighty man in the kingdom of God. James is saying to him, 'Mind your manners. Watch how you stand or sit at the table.' This is his humiliation, his stigma. It is by special dispensation that the rich are converted and offered seats at the banqueting table. 'They don't actually belong. That is their humiliation.' If the rich don't accept that, then they forfeit patience and wisdom. If you are a rich or mighty person and you are a Christian, count yourself doubly thankful, for the gospel wasn't designed for you. And if you can't rejoice in this humiliation then you'll never know patience or wisdom.

Furthermore, James says, 'Your humiliation consists also in this: remember that when you come into church and are with the people of God, don't expect to enjoy the prestige that this world gives you. In church the rich are no different. This may be a trial for you but count it all joy. When you come among the people of God you are just like anybody else and you leave your earthly status behind. That may be humiliating, but rejoice in it. If you can't, then you're double minded. You will always be at sea, unstable in all your ways.'

Earthly prestige doesn't impress God. As Jesus said to the Pharisees, 'Ye are they which justify yourselves before men; but God knoweth your hearts: for that which is highly esteemed among men is abomination in the sight of God' (Lk. 16:15). Jesus also said, 'A rich man shall hardly enter into the kingdom of heaven ... It is easier for a camel to go through the eye of a needle, than for a rich man to enter into the kingdom of God' (Mt. 19:23, 24).

But James still isn't through. He's giving an awful lot of attention to the rich man. 'As the flower of the grass he shall pass away. For the sun is no sooner risen with a burning heat, but it withereth the grass, and the flower thereof falleth, and the grace of the fashion of it perisheth: so also shall the rich man fade away in his ways.'

Not only should the rich be doubly thankful that they got on the list of invitations, they must also be ever aware that they're exceptions and should be self-conscious. They must live by the humiliation that whatever the world sees in them, when they come into the presence of God they're just people (and the church should look at them the same way). Then James says that the earthly status of the rich is destroyed by the course of dying nature. The grass, the flower, the plant shall pass away. So Mr Mighty Man, Mrs Rich Woman, God sees you as grass, here today gone tomorrow.

What makes nature nature? That it is transitory, that it dies. The rich are called upon to rejoice in the fact of their transitory status. 'What you have is temporary. You are to rejoice in this. You may think that you are somebody important and that you are going to live on and maybe future generations will talk about you. But don't count on it too much.' In Westminster Abbey you can see all these people who were so well known in their own day. Nobody knows who they are now. Americans come over here to do brass rubbings of this or that figure. They don't know who they are. Is that the way you want to be thought of a hundred years from now? No, your glory will fade. Recognize this and rejoice in it.

'A rich man shall hardly enter into the kingdom of God.' Do you know why? He can't bear to think like this. The mighty are called upon to rejoice that all that matters is that they're invited to the marriage supper of the Lamb.

In verse 11 James says four things about the rich. The first is the comparison between the sun in its size and stature and a little plant or blade of grass. How do you compare the sun to a blade of grass? That's how much greater God is than the rich and the mighty. If you are a person of some means or earthly glory you may think you are somebody. But look at yourself as a blade of grass compared to the sun. God does not need you. Second, the grass owes its life and its sustenance to the sun. So, rich person, know that everything you have you owe to the sun, to God. Third, the same sun that gives light to the plant, the grass, the flower, will be what kills it. As the sun will bring the loveliest flower to withering, so will the rich man 'fade away in his ways'. God will see to that. The fourth thing you need to know is the suddenness by which all this will happen. It can happen two ways. It can happen by death. Suddenly you will be called to give an account of how you've lived your life before God. 'Thou fool, this night thy soul shall be required of thee' (Lk. 12:20). God can take your life at any time. But the other way is not physical death. God can take your glory away from you even while you are alive. For as the sun can bring the loveliest flower to withering just like that, God who controls all destinies and events can withhold common mercies from you so that overnight you lose your money, your health, your friends, even while you are yet alive. It's not a question of whether this is going to happen to you. It's a question of when. If you are a Christian and God has blessed you financially, recognize that you owe all this to him. He can take it away from you. Rejoice even in that.

Why all this talk to the rich? You may say, 'I've not been listening to you because I'm not rich.' 'Are there many people like that in the church? Isn't this irrelevant? Isn't James wasting his time?' No, because he's been talking to you all the time he's been saying this. He knows the temptation for all of us.

Don't be Jealous

Jealousy has been a temptation for the people of God throughout the ages. Even the Psalmist said, 'Fret not thyself because of evil-doers, neither be thou envious against the workers of iniquity. For they shall soon be cut down like the grass, and wither as the green herb' (Ps. 37:1–2). You may feel greatly deprived and think, 'If I could only be like that person.' But James is saying, 'You wouldn't want to change places with that person for anything in the world.' Save yourself from the sorrow of jealousy and anxiety. When you are tempted to feel sorry for yourself, understand that Christianity is a poor man's religion.

Isaiah said it long ago: 'Every valley shall be exalted, and every mountain and hill shall be made low: and the crooked shall be made straight, and the rough places plain: And the glory of the LORD shall be revealed, and all flesh shall see it together ... All flesh is grass ... The grass withereth, the flower fadeth: but the word of our God shall stand for ever' (Isa. 40:4–6, 8).

There's a word for us today. To see things in this perspective: that when it comes to the glory of God we all stand naked and this world is passing. What matters is the state of our immortal souls when we stand before God. And on the way the test of our religion is how we treat those who cannot possibly do us any good.

7

The Crown of Life

James 1:12

As a commentary on verses 3, 4 and 5, James 1:12 shows us what the purpose of trial or temptation is, namely that we might 'receive the crown of life'. The crown of life is life's highest goal. It is that which eludes the most brilliant and the most successful of people. Only Christianity offers the crown of life, and yet only the Christian who has learned obedience through suffering receives it.

Paul said, 'If any man's work shall be burned, he shall suffer loss: but he himself shall be saved; yet so as by fire' (1 Cor. 3:15). We are dealing now with something that only Christians can know about but that not *all* Christians know about. What a pity if we go right through this book and are able to understand some of the contents but never experience what James puts before us, for it is a wonderful way to live.

Who will receive the crown of life? James tells us, 'Blessed is the man that endureth temptation, for when he is tried, he shall receive the crown of life.' The word temptation comes from the Greek word *peirasmos*, which has two English meanings: trials of enduring hardness and temptations of our natural lusts. This verse shows us both of these meanings simultaneously. Had there been two Greek words – one for trial, one for temptation – James probably would have used both. But we shouldn't draw too clear a distinction, for we must react in the proper manner to temptation or trial; they both come down to the same thing ultimately.

It is our reaction to temptation and trial that determines whether we are going to receive the crown of life. If we are in trial, we dignify and accept it graciously. If we are in temptation, we resist it and do not give in. But there is a sense in which all trial is temptation because temptations may go beyond what we normally think of as lust.

Temptation may be that which arouses bitterness. The temptation to murmur, to cheat or to lie.

The Significance of our Reaction to Trial and Temptation

As I said, it is our reaction to trial or to temptation that determines whether we receive the crown of life. And this reaction is put in terms of endurance. Blessed is the man who endures temptation. This word endure comes from the Greek *hypomeni*, meaning to remain and stay behind when others have departed. In other words, the one who remains as everybody else leaves is the exception. *Hypomeni* is not in itself intrinsically connected with temptation. It is simply a normal word that shows what people normally do. How do people normally react? Well, if we have a sudden inconvenience we are tempted to complain. When traffic is held up we start honking our horns, looking out of our windows and wanting to know why. So, when it comes to temptation, people normally give in. If people are tempted they just do what they're tempted to do, especially if they won't get hurt or caught. But here is a word that shows that you *don't* do what everybody else is doing. It is staying behind when everybody else leaves.

James is showing that the Christian is different from the non-Christian. Whereas most people normally do what they do, the Christian is the exception. The normal thing when trial comes is to be bitter. The Christian dignifies trial. Non-Christians, when temptation comes, give in to it, thinking that they can get away with it. The Christian endures, resisting temptation.

The whole of Christianity is one great demonstration that we are the exception to the rule. We have many illustrations of this in the New Testament. For instance, when the disciples realised the crowd could not feed where it was and said to Jesus, 'This is a desert place, and the time is now past; send the multitude away, that they may go into the villages, and buy themselves victuals.' Do you know what Jesus said? Here's the seeming impossibility, the exception: 'They need not depart.' Or take the example of the disciples when they were enduring Jesus' intermittent resurrection appearances. They didn't know what these appearances meant. Jesus would be there and then he would not be there. And there was one time when Simon Peter said, 'I'm going fishing', and the others said, 'We're going with you', and this of course would have meant to Galilee. But the final word to the disciples was that they should not depart from Jerusalem. The whole of Christianity is one demonstration to show that we need not depart. We don't have to do what everybody else is doing.

There is great blessing for doing what God says. Jesus said, 'They need not depart; give ye them to eat' (Mt. 14:16). And, we are told, 'They did all eat, and were filled: and they took up of the fragments that remained twelve baskets full' (v. 20). We're talking about five thousand men besides women and children. Whenever God says, 'Stay', you need not depart. God's reason is always worth waiting around for. Blessed are those who endure temptation.

You may ask, 'What if I fail?' If you fail, the question is, what is your response to that failure? First of all, consider Jesus who endured. We are told that he endured the suffering for the joy that was set before him (Heb. 12:2). God does not ask us to do anything that Jesus did not do. But he does ask us to do what he did. Peter said 'Because Christ also suffered for us, leaving us an example, that ye should follow his steps: Who did no sin, neither was guile found in his mouth: Who, when he was reviled, reviled not again; when he suffered, he threatened not; but committed himself to him that judgeth righteously' (1 Pet. 2:21–23).

So if there is a trial what are you to do? Sanctify it. Esteem it as something God has handed to you on a silver platter. If there is temptation resist it, knowing that God will enable you to do so. We have this glorious promise: 'There hath no temptation taken you but such as is common to man: but God is faithful, who will not suffer you to be tempted above that ye are able; but will with the temptation' – or trial – 'also make a way to escape, that ye may be able to bear it' (1 Cor. 10:13). No trial or temptation is given beyond your ability to bear. What did Cain say about his punishment? 'My punishment is more than I can bear' (Gen. 4:13). But when it comes to trial, to temptation, you are a child of God. You may know it is not beyond your ability to cope, but say, when this particular temptation comes, 'I can't go through with it.' God says, 'You can.' You can go on, for it is his word.

Become Mature

Your response to trial, to temptation, will indicate whether you are different from a non-Christian, whether you really love Jesus. James says the crown of life is promised to those who love him. Incidentally, whether you endure temptation will show whether you are a 'man'. What is a man? One who is physically strong? The he-man, endowed with great muscles? One who has mannerisms that are unfeminine or who is attracted to the opposite sex? The Greek word in James 1:12 is *aner*. 'Blessed is the *aner* that endureth temptation.' It is a word that refers to an adult as opposed to a child. It's not referring to a man as opposed to a woman. It's not a reference to sex or to masculinity. This is why Paul could say, 'When I was a child, I spake as a child, I understood as a child, I thought as a child: but when I became *aner* I put away childish things' (1 Cor. 13:11). The trial which God has in mind for you is what separates the adults from the children. We are not to remain in childhood forever. The New Testament acknowledges that there's such a thing as a 'babe in Christ'. Yet nearly every time we have the expression we find the writer upbraiding them because they are still on milk and not meat.

We have a tendency to want to stay at a certain level. Maturing is never a pleasant process. From the moment of birth, as we grow up, we want to stay as we are. But what makes a mature adult? It is that we move on and grow. We are not meant to be babes in Christ forever. The New Testament recognizes and emphasizes this. The writers are always unhappy about those with retarded growth. Most of the Old Testament kings, priests and prophets were wicked. Not all the priests were like Aaron, all the prophets like Elijah, or all the kings like David. Yet must we be like the majority? Do we take our comfort by saying, 'Look at so and so. Look at that group'?

You may have heard the story about Methodists and Baptists running revival campaigns in southern Alabama. They were constantly quarrelling with each other, the Methodists saying you can lose your salvation, the Baptists arguing until they were blue in the face that you can't. They were having revival campaigns at the same time and both were complete flops. After it was over the Baptists were overheard to say, 'Well, we didn't have much of a revival but, thank God, the Methodists didn't either.' That shows the tendency in us to get comfort from what others are.

Look at Christianity today. What are most Christians like? They're worldly. They vacillate. Must we be like them? The challenge is for us to be mature, to take James seriously. I promise you, revival will come to no other kind. Blessed are those who endure temptation.

So what if you have failed? I simply ask, how do you respond to your failure? Do you justify it? Are you defensive about it? If you haven't been the kind of Christian that you ought to be, do you identify with Peter who went out and wept bitterly? There is hope for every Christian who is ashamed when they're not what they ought to be. If you can be ashamed it shows that you have a broken and contrite heart.

It shows that you are a Christian. My counsel to you is, prove your sorrow by your repentance, by hating the garments spotted by the flesh (Jude 23). 1 John 1:9 says, 'If we confess our sins, he is faithful and just to forgive us our sins, and to cleanse us from all unrighteousness.' So I say to you, if you have failed, accept your forgiveness and then don't look back. Go on and know that God still wants to use you. And you may turn out to be as radiant a Christian as there ever was and as useful in the kingdom of God as anyone. My counsel is to become mature and put away childish things.

The Trial Will End

The next thing James wants us to see is not only that all this is promised by God in his word to those who prove their love for the Lord by their endurance, but it's a fundamental rule that trials and temptations will end: a rule, incidentally, that Satan does not want you to believe. The Greek shows something which no translation can possibly make clear, that we're dealing with something that always comes to an end. 'When he is tried' is the translation, or 'When he has stood the test' (NIV). But that doesn't quite say it. The word is *genomenos*. It comes from the Greek verb *ginomai* which means to be born, to be created, to be brought into existence. James uses this word in an inverted kind of way. Instead of the trial being born, the trial gives birth to the end of itself.

James uses the same word later on: 'Sin, when it is finished' (v. 15). It's the same point: the trial will end. When the trial gave birth to its end and was left unhindered, it ran its full course, then something wonderful happened. It's the same thing we have seen back in verses 3, 4 and 5: 'Let patience have her perfect work'. When enduring trial we are in the heat of a battle which looks as though it will never end. As a matter of fact, that which makes a trial a trial is the uncertainty of its ending.

But remember 1 Corinthians 10:13. 'There hath no temptation taken you but such as is common to man'. God will make a way to escape. This promise refers not only to the quality of the trial, the nature of the temptation, but to the quantity of it, the time limit. God shows, in that trials always have an end and are never beyond our ability to cope, that the trial is controlled temporally, at both ends. How it all began and that it happened at a particular time will help you to see something of the glory of God in that the trial didn't come sooner. Had it come sooner, you know you couldn't have made it. It is quite remarkable to think that God controls the trial's timing, both its beginning and its duration.

I don't know about you but I look at the way I have been led across the years and I'm convinced that I've had many trials which six months earlier I couldn't have managed. Consider what you are being put through. There was a time when you could not have endured it, but God spared you. He knows how much you can bear. It shows the sovereignty of God. And it shows that these things are out of our hands. It's the wonder of it all.

Trials as Mirror

There's another thing to see in this. Every trial mirrors your present development. Each trial will tell you a lot about yourself and how well you are doing spiritually. For the greater the trial, the greater the compliment God has given you. God will not test you on grounds you have not covered, for every trial presupposes adequate preparation. Every trial should make you realize that you are ready for it. It is not a good sign when you are having the same old trial time after time. Yet it's a sign of mercy in this way: that God is giving you a second or third chance to pass the test. You will never move beyond the level of your present trial until you pass it.

Some people, after years and years, only know one kind of trial. They have arrested spiritual development. They are still babes in Christ, despite the years since they were saved. Why? They've never dealt with a particular trial and it comes back again. It throws them. They murmur. They complain. Finally it's over. They breathe a sigh of relief and go on. Same trial, no growth, no development. We ought to see that if we dignify the trial, accept it graciously, we'll be tested. We'll pass and be able to move on and grow, becoming mature.

You may well wish that your trial would be easier. I will acknowledge that God often tries us to the limit, for there is your opportunity to grow. The devil always says, 'You can't make it.' But you can. James and Paul both say, 'You can do it.' And there are a host of saints throughout the ages that testify, 'You can do it.' May God help us to see it. The trial will end, often abruptly. God permits it to come, but not one moment sooner than we can handle it, and allows it to last one moment longer than we can cope with.

At the End of the Trial?

Now we turn to the ultimate question in this verse: what happens at the end of the trial which has been endured with honour and dignity? James says, 'We shall receive the crown of life.' If we are not careful we could miss the glorious truth here. James is talking about a crown that we can wear both in the present and in the future. There is a crown to be given in heaven. Jesus said so: 'Be thou faithful unto death, and I will give thee a crown of life' (Rev. 2:10). Peter talked about 'a crown of glory that fadeth not away' (1 Pet. 5:4). Paul could say, 'There is laid up for me a crown of righteousness' (2 Tim. 4:8). James means this too, of course, but is equally speaking of a present possession. It is not something physical or visible that will be on our heads but something that is spiritual. It is internal but equally real and it comes to every Christian at the end of the trial endured with honour.

Now what is a crown? The word is used in the Bible in various ways. For example, it is described as a wreath of victory in the game. 'Every man that striveth for the mastery' – in Greek means 'in the game' – 'is temperate in all things. Now they do it to obtain a corruptible crown; but we an incorruptible.' Paul goes on to say, 'I keep under my body, and bring it into subjection: lest that by any means, when I have preached to others, I myself should be a castaway' (1 Cor. 9:25,27). Paul didn't want to lose that crown. He could say to Timothy that we are crowned if we strive lawfully (2 Tim. 2:5). The crown is described in the Song of Solomon as a festival ornament: 'Go forth, O ye daughters of Zion, and behold king Solomon with the crown wherewith his mother crowned him in the day of his espousals, and in the day of the gladness of his heart' (Song of Songs 3:11). In Hellenistic literature a crown was always a symbol of public honour granted for distinguished service.

James calls it 'the crown of life' and it is something both for the here and now, and for the life to come. There's a moment after the trial when the one who has endured with dignity gets a little bit of attention from heaven. God comes down. It is that wisdom James has been talking about. It is a wonderful thing that, in that interval between the end of the bitter and the beginning of the sweet, God notifies us of our deposit in the heavenly treasury. Jesus said, 'How can ye believe, which receive honour one of another, and seek not the honour that cometh from God only?' (Jn. 5:44). God delights in giving us that honour that comes from himself. This is prefigured by our Lord's own temptation. We are told that Jesus was tempted by the devil but he kept resisting and finally the devil departed. Then angels ministered to Jesus (Mt. 4:11). The trial was over and God was pleased. This is what I mean by the crown of life. It is that strong assurance that we passed the test.

There's no greater joy than the end of a successfully fought trial. We can say, 'Lo, this is our God, we have waited for him' (Isa. 25:9). When the trial ends there are two possible kinds of joy. One is simply the relief that it's over. For some that's the only kind of joy they know, because they murmured throughout the trial. That's all they get – the fact that it's ended. They have trials like that across the years. They end, but not one degree of growth comes from them.

But there's another kind of joy and that's the crowning, when God comes down and puts the wreath on our heads. This internal crowning can be enjoyed in three ways. First, it's the happy reflection that you endured gracefully. The second thing is the immediate witness of God's Spirit. Often the sealing of the Spirit comes right after the trial. 'The God of all grace ... after that ye have suffered a while ... strengthen, settle you' (1 Pet. 5:10). But the most important thing is the bestowal of fresh grace for all remaining trials. For by passing this trial, you have grown. In the past, every trial threw you. You murmured and there was no crown. But the glory is that when you pass the test a new godly habit is formed and you are equipped for a higher level of service.

Do you know something else? You are, to use an American expression, in the big league – you know what the saints have known. You are not like the wicked or everybody else. You've become mature and you recognize what John was going through. 'I John, who also am your brother, and companion in tribulation' (Rev. 1:9). This is why Paul could talk about being a partaker 'of the inheritance of the saints in light' (Col. 1:12). You suddenly realize you are in great company with those men of the Bible. Proverbs puts it like this: 'He that ruleth his spirit [is better] than he that taketh a city' (Prov. 16:32).

Blessings for Endurance

One last thing. James describes the state of mind of the one who endures temptation. 'Blessed', *makarios*, the word used in the Beatitudes, simply means 'happy'. In Greek literature it was a transcendent happiness of life beyond care: inner happiness. This happiness is there because one is anointed with wisdom, which is another synonym for the crown. It goes back to verses 3, 4 and 5. The trial gives birth to the crown of life. Patience gives birth to wisdom. In Proverbs we read: 'Wisdom is the principal thing; therefore get wisdom: and with all thy getting get understanding ... She shall give to thine head an ornament' – or a wreath – 'of grace: a crown of glory shall she deliver to thee' (Prov. 4:7, 9). When we get to heaven we will be crowned with the wisdom of God. We will know things we cannot know now. We will understand the mystery of evil and why each trial happened, and there will be no need for faith.

The crown of life, then, is prefigured by these intervals when God endows us with special wisdom and we see things other people don't see. We have a grasp of life that other people don't have. That is what James wants us to enjoy. Yet if this crown of life is bestowed on us here and now and if the angels surround, and God lets us know that he's pleased with us, what will heaven be like?

After all, Jesus had these intervals. The voice came from heaven: 'This is my beloved Son, in whom I am well pleased.' The angels ministered to him. And he cried out on the cross, 'It is finished.' He did everything exactly right. He ascended to heaven, went behind the clouds to receive the glory of his Father. And some day he shall come with many crowns. We shall participate in his exaltation and he shall participate in ours, for we are made 'joint-heirs with Christ' (Rom. 8:17). A day is coming in which we will have our last trial, our last temptation, in which the devil will depart for the last time and the angels will minister to us for the last time. A day is coming when the angels will bear us up to the bosom of Abraham and we shall be welcomed home. There will be no more sorrow, nor crying, nor pain, nor death, nor sin. For the day will come when we will receive that crown of life, the ultimate. 'Blessed is the man that endureth temptation: for when he is tried' and has stood the test, when it's all over 'he shall receive the crown of life.' And we shall see his face and sing. It will be worth it all when we see Jesus.

8

Resist Temptation

James 1:13–14

The main thing that we have seen up to now is James' stress on our reaction to trial or temptation, the importance of counting each one a joy as they result in that wisdom called 'the crown of life'. Up to this point James has used the Greek word *peirasmon* largely with reference to trial rather than temptation, but in verse 13 he changes the subject, and speaks of temptation (the context – what verse 14 goes on to say – proves this).

James introduces the subject of temptation by anticipating an objection you are likely to make, or a natural conclusion you are likely to draw, if you have understood him up to this point. You are likely to say, 'Since God, in his providence, permits trials, the same must be true with temptation.' James knew that you would be thinking this. We have seen the sovereignty of God in trial. The trial comes at a time when we can cope, yet it lasts not one moment longer than we could have borne. If this is true with trials, why not with temptations? It is precisely at this point where our natural minds are always offended. The natural mind wants to think logically, mathematically. Two and two are four, therefore four and four are eight. Well, two and two are four: trials are by God's permission. But it does not follow, in his sovereign will, that four and four are eight. This is the thing we don't like, that makes us angry. Yet it should make us humble, realizing that we just cannot understand everything. We like to think that we can put God in a little package and open it up any time we wish. But God isn't like that. Trials are something that you are to esteem and to count all joy, but not so with temptation.

We are moving into a realm of mystery. We must not rush in, or jump to conclusions. We must be willing to take off our shoes, stand back and know that there is more here than our natural minds can grasp. This in itself – the very fact that our logic fails – is a trial for us, and we can dignify it by rejecting natural reason and simply following Scripture. We don't like having to bow to God's word, but that is what determines whether we really are obedient Christians. Great wisdom will come to us if we let James speak. He says, 'Let no man say when he is tempted, I am tempted of God.'

No One is Tempted by God

The first thing James does in this connection is to remove any exception to the rule: 'Let *no man* say when he is tempted, I am tempted of God.' If there had been one exception, every single one of us would be at the front of the queue saying, 'That's me. I am that exception.' The same is true of when our Lord said, 'My sheep hear my voice, and I know them, and they follow me ... and no man is able to pluck them out of my Father's hand' (Jn. 10:27, 29). If there had been one exception then not a single one of us could enjoy our salvation: we would constantly be thinking, 'I'm the exception.'

James makes it clear here that none of us can ever say we're being tempted by God. But suggesting otherwise is the devil's favourite trick. The devil turned God's word right around when he went to Eve and said, 'Ye shall not surely die' (Gen. 3:4). And he does the same thing with this. He says that you are the exception. He knows your personality. He knows the circumstances. The devil will do this every time you are being tempted to make you think, 'God understands. I couldn't talk about this to anybody else. They wouldn't understand but God knows. It's quite all right.' The devil will point to circumstances in the light of your own weaknesses. He will point to the sovereignty of God, how God controls events. He will point you to the fact that God knows you and understands your ways. He'll say: 'Surely God would not allow this circumstance if he did not expect you to react as he knows you will.' Have you ever heard that before? You didn't read that in Wordsworth or Shakespeare, but you heard it. That's the devil. He weakens you with this very thought. The devil is very clever. He will use your most refined theological thinking to make temptation a thing that you can give in to.

There's another thing working here. Don't underestimate Satan's dominion, wherein he has limited control over certain events and providence. He's called 'the god of this world' (2 Cor. 4:4) and 'the prince of the power of the air' (Eph. 2:2). The devil has a very subtle but real way of making things happen. You are inclined to say, 'Surely God made this happen.' But the devil is also allowed to make things happen. For example, Paul wanted to go to the Thessalonians. The great apostle Paul – whose theological grasp I don't think we would question – could actually say, 'We would have come unto you, even I Paul, once and again; but Satan hindered us' (1 Thess. 2:18). 'Satan hindered us.' God wants us to see that the devil can shape certain events. The devil's subtle way of making things happen is calculated to make you think that God does the tempting, to say that yours is a special case. All of us think we are special anyway. The devil doesn't have to work overtime on that point.

The Temptation to Blame God

Not only is James ruling out any exceptions, but he says that if you think you are one, you are thinking something that is not true. For God does not tempt any one. God *does* try us; he does *not* tempt us. Trials do not originate in us, but temptation does. We dignify trial, but flee temptation. But there is more to James' point. We are most tempted to charge or blame God when we are actually being tempted. This is something the Authorised Version doesn't quite make clear. The Greek word is *peirazomenos*, a present passive participle. '*When being tempted* let no man say' – in other words, when the heat is on. Temptation, by its very nature, is weakening. Our minds get fuzzy and we are not able to think clearly. That is when it becomes easy to believe that God is doing the tempting. But remember that the weakness is already there.

We all have weaknesses. What may be your weakness may not be mine. What may stimulate me may not stimulate you. When the right circumstance, the right conditions, the right person, the right words all coalesce into one obvious suggestion which plays into an internal volcano waiting to erupt, it is called temptation. The Christian (and this is dealing with Christians primarily) who is being tempted needs just one more piece of information to overload their system. What is that? 'I am being tempted of God.' As I said, temptation reveals an existing weakness, and yielding is the easiest thing in the world. All I need to do is to convince myself that God is behind it and I can yield and feel good about it. Eve convinced herself she was in God's will, that God knew she was going to yield. She saw all of the fruit would 'make one wise', it was 'pleasant to the eyes' and she ate.

When we are being tempted we need but the slightest shove. 'I'm being tempted. This is God's will.' But that is the devil's talk. He's appealing to that natural conclusion that must be rejected. I could give you many examples of how this works out in everyday life. Take, for example, when you are tempted to be bitter over mistreatment. Say somebody has said something about you that isn't very nice. It may be true, it may not. But you are hurt. Or perhaps something tragic has happened, something accidental that seems so unfair. You want to shout to the highest heavens, 'Why?' Mistreatment and circumstances may be God's trial but temptation comes to be bitter against God. We must fight against being bitter.

Do you know what else will happen? After all of that, Satan can still arrange for something worse, because if you are beginning to get bitter then the devil in his limited domain can bring other things. And you say, 'That does it!' You are tempted to murmur and to scream and to give up. You say, 'God is making me do this and I'll just do it. It is certainly God's will.' But that bitterness, if you give in to it, will get you out of God's will. Your spirituality will be impoverished to the degree that you give in to bitterness.

What if you are tempted to steal? You say, 'Well, nobody is going to know and I have a particular need at this time. God knows I could use that. It will never be missed. It's so convenient. Thank you, Lord.' This is the way our minds work. It's the same when it comes to tithing. Tithing is always inconvenient. I don't know of very many people that really feel led to tithe. Yet we receive joy when we give joyfully in gratitude to God, as Abraham did. The easiest thing in the world is to look around and say, 'God knows I've got this bill. There's inflation. He can use others to support the work. Nobody will ever know if I don't give.' God does know. But that's the devil talking, not God.

I could go on. Sexual temptation. Do you know that sex is the most natural appetite in the world? Sex is a physical need. It is not good for man to live alone (Gen. 2:18). There's a good excuse to begin from. 'It's a physical need. God knows I've got this need.' We are living in a day of promiscuity. Never has sex outside of marriage been more available than at the present time. That which makes temptation temptation is the convenient nature of it. But don't confuse availability with God's will, that's the devil using your natural mind.

James wants us to establish new godly habits by narrowing down the number of weaknesses we have. We can learn not to be bitter or murmur. Stealing need not be a temptation at all. Tithing can be the most natural thing you do. And you can overcome sexual lust. But as long as you play around with it, live on the edge of Sodom and are constantly making provision for the lust of the flesh, you will not overcome it. You will convince yourself it's something that has to be done. But it does not. It can be overcome. One sure way to overcome temptation is to do away with the suggestions that God winks at sin and that he tempts us. You will never develop a new habit until you begin consistently overcoming temptation and put aside any notion that God causes it.

Now we come to what I think is one of the most eloquent and sublime statements about God in all holy writ. James described God using a which explains why all this is true. It's a word not found anywhere in Hellenistic literature before the New Testament. James uses a word which means God is *untried in evil.* The Authorised Version says, 'Let no man say when he is tempted, I am tempted of God: for God cannot be tempted with evil.' That's as good a translation as any because it's a word that means *incapable of being tempted by.* God is without any experience in evil. He's incapable of being tried in evil because he's untemptable where evil is concerned. So, God does not tempt because God doesn't know how to tempt you to evil.

The reason we know how to tempt another person is because we have lust within by which we measure what will tempt another. I know how to make people jealous. So do you. You start talking about what you are going to do, mention your great holiday, your pay rise, drop a few names, and so on. We know how to make others angry by threatening their pride or calling attention to their insecurity. We know how to tempt people to lust by flattery.

But God is absolutely pure and is beyond being tempted. He has no weak spots by which he can gauge what will tempt others or which he can project to cause temptation. You cannot find any weak spot in God or any shady dealings in his actions. You can't blackmail or threaten God. 'God is light, and in him is no darkness at all' (1 Jn. 1:5). You cannot entice God to do anything contrary to his will. You cannot flatter him. You cannot name-drop with him. You cannot bluff him. You cannot provoke him to do anything, to show you mercy.

If you are not a Christian, let me tell you something. Don't think you are impressing God if you say, 'I'm not going to become a Christian until he explains this to me.' God takes no notice of that. As James says later, 'The wrath of man worketh not the righteousness of God' (Js. 1:20), for God is no respecter of persons.

Similarly, do you wonder why God doesn't deal with the evil blaspheming in the world? Some years ago a man came to the high school of my home town in Kentucky. He made a speech to prove that there is no God. His final illustration was: 'Everybody, get out your watch. If there's a God we are going to give him fifteen minutes in which to strike me dead. I'm going to blaspheme him and if there is a God, let him strike me dead.' And he blasphemed. Then he took out his watch and gave God fifteen minutes. The minutes rolled by. Fifteen minutes were up. 'See, there is no God.' One man at the back stood up and said, 'Sir, do you think you can exhaust the patience of God in fifteen minutes?' God cannot be influenced by evil.

When God shows mercy it is because he loves to show mercy. 'I will have mercy on whom I will have mercy.' And he hardens whom he will. If he's unwilling, nothing can change him. Who can coerce God by finding fault. This is James' point. He concludes, 'God cannot be tempted with evil, neither tempteth he any man'. It is the reflexive pronoun, as if: 'He himself tempts no man.' My fellow Christian, this is a promise that you can lean on.

Resist Temptation

Another difference between temptation and trial is that we cannot end trials, God does that. But how long temptation lasts is up to us. Some people are tempted all the time. They like it and live right on the edge of Sodom so that they have temptation. You cannot end trials, but you can end temptations. The responsibility, scarily, is put right on our shoulders. James is telling us that when it comes to temptation, it's a question of whether we make a 180-degree turn and walk the other way.

The responsibility is ours, but we don't like it. We love to shift responsibility. God said to Adam, 'What is this that you've done?' 'Oh, Eve made me do it.' 'Eve, what is this you have done?' 'Oh, the devil made me do it.' James says, 'Every man is tempted, when he is drawn away of his own lust.' We are all weak and full of infirmities. It is the carnal mind that says, 'God has a lot to answer for.' But the Christian says, 'God is inexperienced in evil. He cannot be tempted by evil.'

Here, my fellow Christians, is an opportunity for us – if we'll take James seriously and just believe him – to grow in grace, to establish a godly habit that the world knows nothing of and to have the wisdom that bypasses the greatest brains: divine wisdom. God will give it to us.

Another way of putting this is that God is not influenced by evil. The prophet Isaiah said that 'our righteousnesses are as filthy rags' (Isa. 64:6). We can't bargain with God: 'I'll do this if you'll do that.' That is sin.

> In my hand no price I bring,
> Simply to thy cross I cling.

So much of our service is nothing but carnal ambition. So much of our praying is selfish. God is not influenced by evil. Is God influenced by anything at all? Yes. God is influenced by good, true good. But what is that? 'This is my beloved Son, in whom I am well pleased' (Jn. 3:17). Our Lord Jesus Christ at the right hand of the Father has the ear of the Most High God. This is why we come to God, pleading nothing but the merit, the name, the shed blood of Christ. Jesus has influence with God.

Yet there's one more thing. And this is even more staggering. We can please God by dignifying trial and resisting temptation. It is actually true, though a great mystery. God blesses our obedience, faith and works by love. James will end the epistle by saying, 'Ye ... have seen the end of the Lord; that the Lord is very pitiful, and of tender mercy', but 'the effectual fervent prayer of a righteous man availeth much' (Js. 5:11, 16).

God delights to bless us. He honours those who honour him. The love that flows from his will is met with great blessing. This is a great mystery, but it is true. We must take off our shoes, not try to understand it. We must let God be God and worship him through 'the King of kings, and Lord of lords; Who only hath immortality, dwelling in the light which no man can approach unto' (1 Tim. 6:15–16).

9

Temptation and Sin

James 1:14–15

We are seeing more and more just how practical – painfully practical –James is. It tests whether or not we really want to be the kind of people that bring honour to God's name.

The Classic Objection to God

We have seen that none of us can say, when being tempted, that we are tempted of God. That's the classic, if not eternal, objection to God: that he must be the author of evil. The Bible refutes this, leaving us with one of life's unsolvable questions. But those are what makes faith a possibility; answer those questions and there's no need for faith. We only know that evil has been dealt with through the death of Christ and that we are to resist temptation.

Rule number one is that Christians are not given the luxury of saying that their temptation is different from that which non- Christians experience, or that their peculiar temptation has God's special sanction.

Rule number two is that I cannot blame God for temptation, neither can I blame him if I yield to temptation. I cannot blame the devil if I yield to temptation. James – it seems so cruel and may make us very Hhostile – is putting the burden of temptation on our shoulders. He says, 'every man' – no exception – 'every man is tempted'. We are responsible not only for our response to temptation but for the very temptation itself.

Temptation's Perfect Work

We have seen that patience has a perfect work, but now James shows us that temptation also has a perfect work. We see this progression which, if not aborted, will give birth to four stages of heinous things. Stage one: suggestion. Stage two: temptation. Stage three: sin. Stage four: death. With patience we don't want there to be an abortion. We want to see what God will do if we wait and watch him work, dignifying the trial so that patience may 'have her perfect work'. For patience leads to godliness, godliness to brotherly kindness, brotherly kindness to love (1 Peter 1:6–7). We want to experience this.

But what James gives us here is a description of the origin of temptation. It is not from God. It is not even from the devil. 'But every man is tempted, when he is drawn away of his own lust' or desire.

Some Distinctions

At this point we need to see several distinctions. We need to see the distinction between the temptation that our Lord endured and the temptation which we endure. Because our Lord took upon himself unfallen nature, there was no inherent weakness in him already. Much less was there any corrupted desire in him already, for our Lord was born without sin. We are told that he was made 'in the *likeness* of sinful flesh' (Rom. 8:3), not sinful flesh. Our Lord, though really tempted, was 'without sin' (Heb. 4:15). Our temptations are essentially different because we are already weak in our fallen nature.

Temptation is anything that tries to get us to disobey God. James says uses the same Greek word *peirasmon*, but now in the present passive as a verb form *peirazetai*, meaning 'every man is tempted when'. In other words, something must happen before you can call it temptation. A trial is not like this. A trial comes from without and is out of our hands. We don't start or stop it. Temptation is different. A trial, when wholly dignified, may be endured without temptation. Look what Job's wife said to him, 'Curse God, and die.' He said, 'You talk like a foolish woman' (Job 2:9–10). That wasn't even a temptation for Job. It was a suggestion.

We need to distinguish not only between temptation and trial, not only between our Lord's temptation and our temptation, but also between suggestion and temptation. For suggestion is not always temptation. All of us know what it is to encounter evil suggestions that don't have any effect upon us. I, for example, could be standing next to

£100,000 that wasn't mine. The suggestion might be, 'Take it.' But it wouldn't be a temptation for me. Stealing in that way has never been in recent years!

James' concern is that we develop godly habits so that we narrow down the number of our weaknesses and the devil has a much harder time getting at us. One of the aims of the Christian life is to reduce temptation to the level of suggestion. Suggestion remains suggestion if we have grown immune to it, if there is no corresponding internal volcano waiting to erupt. Temptation emerges when suggestion corresponds to an evil desire in me. What may be a temptation for me may be but a suggestion for you – we all have our weaknesses. This goes back to the very reason James in urged us to count it all joy when we fall into diverse trials (1:2). If you do that, you have an opportunity to kill two birds with one stone. Dignify the trial and you simultaneously resist the temptation that comes alongside. And the more we strengthen our resistance to temptation, the more likely temptation will be reduced to the level of suggestion.

Two questions follow. The first is, where does the suggestion originate? The other is, what makes a desire evil?

Where Does Suggestion Originate?

Suggestion originates either from the world, the flesh or the devil. As long as we are in this present evil world we will have evil suggestions coming to us. We cannot avoid them. If you don't have evil suggestions you're either dead or have one foot in the grave! So until God destroys the world itself, there will be evil suggestions. And we will face them without any restraint, without any qualification. Such suggestions may or may not be temptations for us but we will always have them. Television, newspapers, magazines, people, circumstances: the world will put certain suggestions before our eyes and into our minds.

Suggestion can also originate from the flesh, from our own sinful nature, without any contribution from the world. This is especially true with a weaker Christian. I do not say *younger* Christian, for many old Christians are weak. For Christians who make no attempt to mortify their flesh there will be a constant and an acute sense of temptation, which is not a sign of spirituality. You may be persuading yourself that this is the way it is supposed to be. I can tell you, you are in the most horrible kind of bondage if so. You will have no measure of growth until you begin to mortify the flesh and find that it is not the way you have to live.

Those of us who know constant and acute temptation from the flesh ought to search our hearts to see whether we are encouraging it. Sometimes a faulty theology, antinomianism, can keep it going. Yet even a very strong Christian can know great struggle and endless suggestions from the flesh. We must keep on. It is warfare. Victory is to be sought and daily discipline.

The devil can also put an evil suggestion into your mind that plays upon your natural desires. Keep in mind that the devil is the father of lies (Jn. 8:44) and he will suggest things that correspond to your weaknesses. He knows just the things to say to you. He will put it into your head that a person doesn't like you, has said something about you or is physically attracted to you, making you dwell on it, hoping to tear you up inside. By the way, don't forget William Perkins' great statement, 'Don't believe the devil even if he tells the truth.' It could be that the suggestion is right. But refuse to listen to it. Know that it's the devil trying to stir you up within.

What Makes a Desire Evil?

Temptation happens when an evil suggestion succeeds in exploiting a desire or weakness. It may be a natural desire that the evil suggestion exploits, or a corrupted or unnatural desire. The Greek word is *epithumias*. It simply means 'desire'. In the seventeenth century when the Authorised Version was translated, the word 'lust' didn't have its modern connotations. The Puritans would talk about 'lusting after God', but today we see lust in a slightly different way. We need realize, then, that the Greek is a neutral term meaning 'desire'. Ambition is a natural desire, but it becomes evil if it is not subservient to the will of God. Sex is a natural desire, but it becomes evil outside of marriage. Self-preservation is a natural desire, but it becomes evil if it succumbs to the love of money. An evil suggestion presented to a natural desire may be rejected. If not, the desire becomes corrupt. If the desire is corrupt already, the chances are that the evil suggestion will succeed and can be called temptation.

Now what about the unnatural desire? The fact is that an unnatural desire need not be corrupted. For example, the Bible says homosexuality is unnatural. A person may say, 'Well, it seems natural to me', but the biblical order of creation says it is unnatural. A Christian with homosexual tendencies may no more think of yielding to that desire than another godly person would to suggestions that are natural. So an unnatural desire need not be corrupted.

You can see that James is making us utterly responsible for our own temptation. The Greek is actually to be translated 'tempted by his own desire'. We cannot help having the suggestion, but we are responsible for the temptation. If the evil suggestion meets my desire successfully I cannot blame God. I can only blame myself. I cannot say God or you or the world or the devil or the flesh made me do it. I did it after all.

Christians are given a certain autonomy. They are in the flesh but are to rise above the flesh. They are in the body but are to rise above it. So Paul could say, 'Walk in the Spirit, and ye shall not fulfil the lust of the flesh' (Gal. 5:16). Paul could also say, 'I keep under my body, and bring it into subjection: lest that by any means, when I preached to others, I myself should be a castaway' (1 Cor. 9:27). I am responsible. It is my duty to defeat the success of the evil suggestion.

What about this success? How is it described? James tells us, 'Every man is tempted, when he is drawn away of his own lust, and enticed.' Two Greek words – 'drawn away' and 'enticed' – with synonymous meanings pointing to one thought: entrapment. This is what temptation does. As a matter of fact, the word translated 'enticed' is *deleazomenos*, which can even mean 'be deluded'. It's the same word used in 2 Peter 2:14: 'Having eyes full of adultery, and that cannot cease from sin; beguiling unstable souls'. Temptation has a beguiling quality. We become deluded once temptation sets in. A fire begins to burn and an enslavement of some sort is effected. The wish is there. Then comes contemplation. And then you begin to dwell upon it, which is in itself weakening. It tends to make our thinking processes cloudy. Delusion sets in and we begin to say, 'Well, this desire can't be all bad. After all, God knows I need this money.' Or, 'God knows I must get ahead. I must take care of myself and I must pull this string or that. I must look out for number one.' Or, 'After all, God knows that I am lonely and this person accepts me and understands me.' Temptation weakens our thinking. The result of temptation is almost always confusion, our thought processes lose clarity and lucidity. That's temptation.

Temptation and Sin

Perhaps the most helpful distinction is yet to be seen. Although temptation is the offspring of our own desire, it is not sin. At least not yet. Thank God for the distinction between temptation and sin. Obviously, the best way to avoid sin is to avoid the temptation. Temptation emerges because I am drawn away of my own desire. Yet temptation's emergence does not mean that sin has also emerged.

We ought never to feel safe in being tempted. We must be careful to 'make not provision for the flesh, to fulfil the lusts thereof' (Rom. 13:14). We must run from living at the edge of Sodom. There are certain things we must avoid if we know ourselves, some TV programmes we cannot watch. Maybe others can, but you can't, I can't. Certain magazines I cannot read. There are certain people I know it is best that I don't go out of my way to be around. It is no certain sign of strength that you can say, 'But I know how to resist temptation.' Strong Christians avoid temptation, rather than resist it. Jesus said, 'Watch and pray, that ye enter not into temptation' (Mt. 26:41). He didn't say, 'Pray and watch.' Because if we pray and watch we just say, 'Lord, I've prayed about it. Look what happens.' No, 'Watch and pray.' You are not entitled to pray until you've been watching. Keep watching as though there were no God to help you.

But temptation, when it comes, is not sin. Temptation gives way to sin. James says, the desire must *conceive*. The Greek word is *sullabousa*, used in Luke 1: 'Elizabeth conceived'. It also means 'to catch up', 'to seize', 'to apprehend'. Suggestion becomes temptation when the evil suggestion successfully exploits a desire. Temptation becomes sin when desire becomes consent. Temptation is anything that tries to get us to disobey God. Sin is when we become willing to disobey, even if in our own hearts. Sin need not be an outward act. Jealousy, hate, sexual fantasy are not merely temptations but sins (Mt. 5:21, 22, 27, 28). Sin is in the will. It is when we become willing to follow temptation whether or not it is carried through outwardly, whether or not it physically involves another person. Once sin has set in we need to confess and to ask forgiveness in repentance. So says 1 John 1:9: 'If we confess our sins', thank God, 'he is faithful and just to forgive us our sins, and to cleanse us from all unrighteousness.' We do not confess the suggestions or the temptation. We confess the sins.

In 1 John, sin is referred to in two ways. First, we are told 'If we say that we have no sin, we deceive ourselves, and the truth is not in us' (1 Jn. 1:8). This refers to our sinful nature. Our sinful nature will continue until we are glorified. Only Christ had a sinless nature. He had no earthly father. God was his Father. He was conceived by the Spirit. But our sinful nature needs the daily cleansing of the precious blood of Christ. 'If we walk in the light, as he is in the light, we have fellowship one with another, and the blood of Jesus Christ … cleanseth us from all sin' (1 Jn. 1:7). Our fellowship with the Father shows that our sin is being cleansed.

Second, 1 John also refers to sin that has been carried out by the will. 'Write I unto you, that ye sin not. And if any man sin, we have an advocate with the Father, Jesus Christ the righteous; And he is the propitiation for our sins: and not for ours only, but also for the sins of the whole world' (1 Jn. 2:1–2). We are told not to sin, yet also told that, if we do, 'we have an advocate with the Father'. We are to confess our sins. 'There is forgiveness with thee, that thou mayest be feared' (Ps. 130:4).

Could it be that you have not only experienced the power of temptation but you've sinned? You've sinned in your heart? There's jealousy, hate or lust there and you nurture it? I say to you, ask forgiveness. Plead the precious blood of Christ and repent. Turn from your sins. Could you have gone so far as to plot your sin? You've already thought out how you are going to get even or how you are going to take something that is not yours? You've already decided to have illicit sex with someone? I say to you, break it off right now. Stop it and pray not only for forgiveness but also that you may be spared the final stage: 'Sin, when it is finished, bringeth forth death.'

10

The Goal of Sin

James 1:15–16

We are in the middle of James' important statement about how sin emerges: how it emerged originally, how it continues to emerge. He says to us, 'Let no man say when he is tempted, I am tempted of God: for God cannot be tempted with evil, neither tempteth he any man: but every man is tempted, when he is drawn away of his own lust, and enticed. Then when lust hath conceived, it bringeth forth sin: and sin, when it is finished, bringeth forth death' (Js. 1:13–15). You can see here a downward progression.

Upward and Downward Progressions

In fact, it's the second progression in this chapter. For there is the upward progression of verses 2–4 where we see the advantage of doing everything God's way. Now James is making the converse point: those that do not do things God's way pay for it. Paul put it like this: 'Be not deceived; God is not mocked: for whatsoever a man soweth, that shall he also reap. For he that soweth to his flesh shall of the flesh reap corruption; but he that soweth to the Spirit shall of the Spirit reap life everlasting. And let us not be weary in well doing: for in due season we shall reap, if we faint not' (Gal. 6:7–9). Now the reaping is what Jesus described in the Sermon on the Mount as treasure that we are laying up in heaven (Mt. 6:20). In that same sermon Jesus talked about rejoicing when people attack you for your faith, 'for great is your reward in heaven' (Mt. 5:11–12). When persecution comes, when trial comes, it can be seen as God dealing with us. And there's no more wonderful thing than to be dealt with by God. 'No chastening for the present seemeth to be joyous, but grievous: nevertheless afterward it yieldeth the peaceable fruit of righteousness unto them which are exercised thereby' (Heb. 12:11). This is why Peter could say, 'The trial of your faith, being much more precious than of gold that perisheth' (1 Pet. 1:7). We reap of the Spirit life everlasting, the crown of life.

But it is true that the converse goes in a downward progression. Proverbs tells us that the way of the transgressor is hard, that 'He that covereth his sins shall not prosper' (Prov. 28:13). 'Be sure your sin will find you out' (Num. 32:23). Paul summed it up. If you choose to live in sin what do you get? 'The wages of sin is death' (Rom. 6:23). This is what happened to Adam and Eve. They experienced spiritual death. 'In the day that thou eatest [the fruit] thereof dying thou shalt die' (Gen. 2:17): spiritual death followed by physical death.

James' important statement is, then, a general description of how sin emerges and also of how sin ends. Sin begins with temptation which is seated in the flesh. Temptation arises when an evil suggestion to disobey God meets a desire within with success. But temptation is not sin. Sin, seated in the will, is when desire gives consent. James puts it: 'lust when it has conceived'. Lust is not sin but lust which conceives is sin. That's the difference. For example, we are told in the description of the original sin, 'When the woman saw that the tree was good for food, and that it was pleasant to the eyes, and a tree to be desired to make one wise, she took of the fruit thereof, and did eat' (Gen. 3:6). It was not sin that she saw the tree was good for food. That was temptation. It was not sin that it was pleasant to the eyes or to be desired to make one wise. Sin emerged when 'she took of the fruit thereof, and did eat'.

Our Responsibility

James gives us two irrefutable reasons why we know we are not tempted of God. The first is that God cannot be tempted with evil. God knows nothing of evil and so cannot tempt. Second is the fact that temptation and sin lead to death. Temptation leads to sin. Sin leads to death. And God did not bring death into the world. Paul said, 'Wherefore, as by one man sin entered into the world, and death by sin.' This is how it began. Death came by sin 'and so death passed upon all men, for that all have sinned' (Rom. 5:12). The same God who cannot be tempted with evil did not bring death into the world.

But we are to see something else. James' succinct description of the emergence and end of sin puts before us a general principle of the cause and effect of sin. Not only do we see the fall of humankind and what happened when sin came into the world described here, we see how that fall took place. Temptation followed suggestion. Sin and death followed temptation. But James also shows us how all have their own fall. As Jeremiah said: 'In those days they shall say no more, The fathers have eaten a sour grape, and the children's teeth are set on edge. But every one shall die for his own iniquity: every man that eateth the sour grape, his teeth shall be set on edge' (Jer. 31:29–30). And as Ezekiel put it, 'The soul that sinneth, it shall die. The son shall not bear the iniquity of the father, neither shall the father bear the iniquity of the son' (Ezek. 18:20).

All people are responsible for their own sin and their own temptation. It is in us to want to refuse God and blame somebody else – our background, our parents, the state or education – that's the way our evil nature works. But the word is: you are tempted because of your own lust and you shall die for your own sin.

Non-Christians know that your final journey will not be in the hearse on the way to the cemetery or the crematorium. Your final journey will be when you are escorted by God's angels into everlasting torment. And you will go there for your own sins. Nobody will be able to help you. Now is the time, now while you are in this world, with the love of Christians or parents available to help you. If God sends you to hell you will have to say, 'I played the fool.' You will not be able to blame God, the state, the devil, your parents. You will have to say, 'I am now being paid for my own sin.'

Unfinished Sin

However, James' statement is not a description of everyone who sins or is tempted. It is a description of every one who *yields* to temptation, in whom sin is finished, brought to a completion. The Greek word is *teleo*, from which we get teleology which seeks to explain the universe in terms of final purposes. It is showing here the final purpose of sin. 'Sin, when it is finished, bringeth forth death.' But the wonderful news of the gospel is that sin is not yet finished for all.

Why is sin not finished for every one? Because Christ tasted death for everyone (Heb. 2:9). It is therefore possible for each one of us to abort the ultimate consequence of sin. How? By looking to the sin bearer who cried out on the cross, '*Tetelestai*' (from the same word) 'It is finished'. There and then sin was brought to an end. Jesus Christ, by tasting death, finished sin. He didn't say, 'I've done my best,' or 'I've tried but I have failed.' If Jesus had said that day, 'I have failed', the angels in heaven would have dropped dead on the streets of gold. God would have retreated into ever-lasting silence. Hell would have triumphed and there would have been no resurrection on the third day. But Jesus shouted, 'It is finished!' And because of that, sin was brought to an end. The downward progression from temptation to sin to death was aborted by the Son of God who bore the sins of the world. All who look to him may know that sin has been finished in him, not in us. He tasted death and therefore I shall live. I can sing with Augustus Toplady:

> The terrors of law and of God
> With me can have nothing to do;
> My Saviour's obedience and blood
> Hide all my transgressions from view.

Deceptive Temptation

James' statement is nonetheless a firm warning to every Christian because he goes on to say, 'Do not err, my beloved brethren.' Why did James say that? First, remember that he is concluding a statement that began in verse 13: never think when you are tempted that you are tempted of God. James does not want you, at the end of this statement, to be deceived. He says, 'Do not err', but he means, 'Don't be deceived by this. Don't ever think that when you are tempted you can say that God did it.' And he says 'do not be deceived' because we have already seen the deluding character of temptation. Temptation is in its very nature weakening. He wants us to come to our senses and see what is going on.

But there is also a subsidiary warning contained in this description of the emergence and end of sin. For every Christian is warned not to sin. You have no right to tamper with sin. When you sin you are venturing into the realm of death from which you've been redeemed. You are therefore commanded to stay utterly out of it. There is nothing more incongruous than a Christian who sins deliberately. There's no way that you can sin and be happy about it. You cannot sin and receive the crown of life. The issue here is not whether you are a Christian but the kind of Christian you are going to be. James is putting forward an implicit analogy between the upward progression which begins with patience and has its perfect work and the downward progression of temptation and sin. Patience brings about the crown of life which is both future and present, when God steps in and blesses us.

Every Christian May Receive the Crown of Life

What is the crown of life? It is the reward for mastery. As Paul put it to Timothy, 'If a man also strive for masteries, yet is he not crowned, except he strive lawfully' (2 Tim. 2:5). Here is an opportunity to be ambitious in the kingdom of God, to have a Master's degree in godliness! Every field has its top performers, its Nobel or Pulitzer prizewinners. The crown of life is the top prize in the field of godliness, in the realm of the Spirit. But all of us may have it. It doesn't matter what your IQ, your educational background, your sociological status or position in the church. Anybody can receive the crown of life.

This is our opportunity as Christians, as followers of Jesus to participate in what Paul calls 'the inheritance of the saints in light' (Col. 1:12). We don't profess to be like most Christians. We don't have to be wicked like most of Israel's kings, prophets and priests were. We can be different. We can be like those described in the eleventh chapter of Hebrews. All of us can qualify for the crown given to men and women like that.

After all, when you are in eternity, which isn't far away, it will not matter whether you received the Nobel prize or were made prime minister or were written about in *The Times*. It will not matter whether you shopped at Harrods or dined at Claridges. Eternity will be the time that lasts forever, where our reward for how we were on earth is put into everlasting hold.

The reward is commensurate with your faithfulness to your holy calling, and all may qualify. It comes through how you rejoice in trial and how you resist temptation. Why is it called the crown of *life*? There's nothing you can do in eternity to make it glitter any more or make it any brighter. It depends on what happens in this space and time. John said, 'He that is unjust, let him be unjust still: and he which is filthy, let him be filthy still: and he that is righteous, let him be righteous still: and he that is holy, let him be holy still. And, behold, I come quickly; and my reward is with me, to give every man according as his work shall be' (Rev. 22:11–12).

Now to the heart of James' point. As the crown of life is given to those who overcome sin, so the forfeiture of that honour pertains to those who let sin run its course. What James is warning us about here is what happens to Christians who deliberately venture into that from which they have been saved. Here is what we are to see: to the degree that there is a trespassing into death's realm there follows what the New Testament calls 'dead works'. What is a dead work? It is when a Christian suffers loss but is yet saved. It is when Christians suffer loss because their works are to be burned (1 Cor. 3:15). With every trial, with every temptation, there comes a possibility of either a good work or a dead work. A good work is when the trial is dignified, when the temptation is resisted. And if sin does emerge and if that sin is confessed and broken off, repented of before it goes too far, there's still a vestige of a good work to be seen.

Three Stages of Sin

The downward progression has four major stages: suggestion, temptation, sin and death. This third stage, sin, sometimes has three stages of its own. The first stage is when the will consents to the desire or temptation. There may or may not be overt sin, but it is there in the heart and it is nurtured, furthering the grudge, the lust, the greed.

Then there is the second stage, when one is confronted with the possibility of repentance. One sees what one is doing, what one is participating in. Sometimes a person filled with a grudge, with hate and with lust suddenly thinks, 'What have I been doing?' and wakes up. It could be because the Holy Spirit is dealing with them, possibly through the rebuke of a friend (Prov. 27:6), or of a minister in the pulpit. They stop, turn around, ask God for forgiveness and go on. There's a vestige of a good work that is still profitable.

But then there is the third stage, when someone deliberately disobeys God, knowing repentance was offered. The awakening came but this person kept on going. Like Jonah they keep on running from God. They not only will to do it, consent to it, but go down to the docks to find a ship going to Tarshish. They could still turn around and go back but no, they pay the fare and leave. This is sin running its course, when there is continued, unrepentant disobedience to God.

What is the aim and purpose of sin? It is that we will continue in disobedience to God and will render any repentance too late to please God. This is like Esau, who would have inherited the blessing but finally found 'no place of repentance, though he sought it carefully with tears' (Heb. 12:17). What the devil wants you to do is to run your course and reach the place where repentance is too late. The aim of sin is to make complete fools of us, to depersonalize and defeat us before repentance sets in. You would have thought that Simon Peter, when he first denied his Lord, would have stopped. But he went on. He denied the Lord again and again. Did Peter repent then? No, not until he heard the crowing of a cock. Then he 'went out and wept bitterly' (Lk. 22:57–62). Peter himself was saved, but he had to live with that denial for the rest of his life. The aim of sin is to produce a dead work:

to ensure that you will never have victory over a particular temptation in a particular trial or situation.

Am I speaking to someone right now who is in the midst of sin? It may be too late. I don't know, but in the name of God stop it. Come to yourself before it's too late and turn around. The aim of sin is to produce a dead work so that you have no awakening until it's all over and you hear the crowing of the cock and cry, 'What have I done?' The damage will have been done and no amount of repentance will change what will have happened. You may be sorry, you may weep bitterly, but it will be too late.

I will put it another way. When suggestion turns into temptation there's still a chance for victory. Even when temptation turns into sin there's still space for repentance and therefore some chance of victory. But if repentance is procrastinated the victory will be lost. As every trial has its end, so every sin runs its course. And then you wake up one morning and realize you've been deceived, you've been had. So James is saying, 'Do not err, my beloved brothers and sisters. Do not be deceived.'

Claiming God's Mercy

Is there such a thing as repentance from dead works? Of course there is. Your works are to be burned, but you go on. It's like the prodigal son. We are told that he went 'into a far country, and there wasted his substance with riotous living' (Lk. 15:13). There was famine and he began to be in want. He knew he'd done everything wrong. He was an utter failure. So he said, 'I will ... go to my father, and will say unto him, Father, I have sinned against heaven ... and am no more worthy to be called thy son' (vv. 18–19). He didn't know what would happen. He just said, 'I'll go and lay myself upon the mercy of my father.' And this is the thing for you to do. If sin has run its course you may weep bitterly but come to your heavenly Father and claim his mercy. You know what he will do? He will say to his servants, 'Bring forth the best robe, and put it on him; and put a ring on his hand, and shoes on his feet: And bring hither the fatted calf, and kill it; and let us eat, and be merry: For this my son was dead, and is alive again; he was lost, and is found' (vv. 22–24). For God will seek you. Your works will be burned but you will come to the Father.

You may ask, 'Will there be no crown of life for me?' You lost that victory and can never get it back, but there will be other trials and more temptation. Vow, 'Never again', and put yourself in the hands of God. Start all over again. But you will say, 'Will God hold that sin against me?' The answer is: 'He hath not dealt with us after our sins; nor rewarded us according to our iniquities ... As far as the east is from the west, so far hath he removed our transgressions from us ... For he knoweth our frame; he remembereth that we are dust' (Ps. 103:10, 12, 14).

Not only that. Those dead works which are good for nothing will nonetheless be thrown into God's great melting pot. As Romans 8:28 says, 'we know that all things work together for good to them that love God, to them who are the called according to his purpose'. This is true because Christ finished sin. He bore our sins in his own body. Death has no hold on us. His grace is greater than our sin. God will restore the years which the locusts have eaten (Joel 2:25). He can turn you around, make you anew and you can start again. God does this in order to demonstrate that sin will never finally achieve its purpose with his people.

11

The Good and the Perfect

James 1:17

This is a most remarkable verse, one with far-reaching implications both practical and theological. But why is this remarkable verse inserted here? Does it fall out of the blue, put in without any kind of arrangement or purpose, or is there a reason that it comes at this particular place? The answer: this verse has been carefully positioned at a strategic place in the epistle.

The Origin of Evil

James has finished his second set of progressions. We saw the upward one that leads to perfection, and the downward one that leads to sin and death. This was sparked off by James' assertion in verse 13 that if any are tempted they should never think – much less say – that they are tempted of God, for that is impossible.

James knows that it is easy to blame God for temptation. So convinced are we of God's power and sovereignty that we assume that everything that happens is of God. James says, 'Be careful about that. It's an easy mistake to make.' But are we going to follow our reason or Scripture?

The translations are divided over whether verses 16 – 'Do not err, my beloved brethren' and 17 – 'Every good and every perfect gift' – mark a transition in James' thought. The answer is that James is not yet finished. There is no change of thought or new paragraph because he's still dealing with this question of the origin of evil and temptation. He began in verse 13, 'Let no man say when he is tempted, I am tempted of God', and is still going in verse 17, which is another proof that God cannot tempt us. James is not finished with this question.

What Comes From Above?

If temptation, sin, death come from below, the question follows, what comes from above? James tells us, 'Every good gift and every perfect gift is from above, and cometh down from the Father of lights, with whom is no variableness, neither shadow of turning.'

The easiest mistake for us to make as Christians is simply to attribute everything as being from God. We become sheer fatalists, accepting a doctrine like that of Islam: 'Allah wills it. Whatever it is, that's the will of God.' My fellow Christians, this is not so. 'Do not err, my beloved brethren.' There are things that do not come from God. We need to be clear about this or we will fall into the gravest error.

Having stated the negative and shown what is from below, James moves to the positive. Vast theological truths are at stake here: our doctrines of providence, of common grace, of predestination. As James says in verse 18, 'Of his own will begat he us with the word of truth, that we should be a kind of firstfruits of his creatures.' James wants to show that, being of God, we may know what comes from above.

Not everything is from below. Not everything is from above. We know that evil does not come from God. What comes from above? James, coming to the positive, becomes very emphatic, dogmatic and makes no exceptions. 'Every good gift and every perfect gift is from above.' He made no exception when it came to what is evil ('Let no man say when he is tempted, I am tempted of God') and now, when it comes to what is from above, he's just as emphatic. If it's God's, it's from above. If it's good and perfect it's obviously from above.

But how do we define 'good' without making it sentimental? We can safely say that the good is that which either transcends or replaces evil. If it is good it comes from God, and anything that replaces evil is good. For example, disease is evil. Anything that overcomes disease is good, whether it be the use of penicillin or direct healing. Both are from God, for only God can overcome evil.

The Distinction Between Common Grace and
Saving Grace

But James contrasts evil not only with the good, but also with the perfect. The perfect is contrasted with the stages of temptation, sin and death or a remarkable contrast. James is not saying, 'every good and perfect gift', he's saying, 'every good gift and every perfect gift'. It is a clear distinction, the distinction between common grace and saving grace. Common grace does not necessarily have a connection to salvation. As a matter of fact, all are showered with grace from God but not all are saved. Saving grace is that which is perfect and comes to just some. Common grace is whatever is good for humankind. The instrument of that good need not itself be regenerate.

Four Classifications of Common Grace

Now, so that we might understand more of common grace, we can say that there are four classifications of it.

- *The classic good.* Things which teach us how to think about and appreciate God's world. E.g. learning, music, culture, poetry, literature, the arts and sciences. They come from God.
- *The common good.* That is what we have in government with law and order, and in the police and fire services for our protection.
- *The created good.* That which comes from God: our natural endowments, gifts, intellectual aptitude, etc. Such gifts should not be a cause for pride, nor should Christians expect to be more gifted than others. Being regenerate isn't going to increase your IQ, enable you to compose like Tchaikovsky, be a poet or whatever. You need to see the distinction.
- *The changing good.* Under this come the improvements wrought to human life wrought by ever-improving technology, medicine and science. These things are good and come from God. They replace evil and so come from God irrespective of whether or not they are developed by Christians. Jesus put it like this: 'He maketh his sun to rise on the evil and on the good, and sendeth rain on the just and on the unjust' (Mt. 5:45). Do not be surprised if a non-Christian has a brilliant mind or is used in remarkable ways that surpass anything you do. Rather, appreciate what non-Christians do more than they themselves can. For we know we are in God's world. 'Thou art worthy, O Lord, to receive glory and honour and power: for thou hast created all things, and for thy pleasure they are and were created' (Rev. 4:10, 11). Have a true world view: this is God's world.

The Connection Between Common Grace and Saving Grace

Though there is a distinction between common and saving grace there is also an important connection. James inserts the Greek word *kai*, 'and'.

'Every good gift *and* every perfect gift.' I think that there are three principles that connect common grace and saving grace.

Principle 1. Common grace is most abundant where saving grace has also flourished and been abundant. As Jesus said, speaking to Christians, 'Ye are the salt of the earth' (Mt. 5:13). That the greatest advances in learning, technology and prosperity have been where there are traces of the Judaeo–Christian tradition is, I think, beyond any doubt. Western civilization and the history of the Christian church are inseparable. You cannot know one without the other. It is an undoubted fact that the Reformation gave birth to modern science. It is no coincidence that technology has flourished where true revival once flourished.

Principle 2. Common grace loses its momentum if it is not continually upheld by the flourishing of God's perfect gift, the gospel. Jesus said, 'Ye are the salt of the earth: but if the salt have lost his savour ... it is thenceforth good for nothing, but to be cast out, and to be trodden under foot of men.' If the church becomes good for nothing, then all the world will be affected and the next generation will suffer. There will be a diminishing development in the field of knowledge. Since all knowledge leads to knowledge, there must be successive breakthroughs or knowledge will come to a standstill and, eventually, will start going backwards. Scientists predict advances in light of what progress has already been made. The fact is, though, that if God doesn't give the light, things will stand still and start going backwards. There must be a continual flourishing of the gospel or there will be a diminishing of the evidence of common grace.

Several years ago *Time* magazine had a major article on Thomas Edison on the 100th anniversary of his invention of the light bulb. In the same *Time* magazine there was a supplementary article entitled 'The Sad State of Innovation'. Here's what it said: 'The centennial of Edison's great achievement comes at a time when American innovative genius, so well personified by Edison, has begun to fade ... Over the past decade America has been losing its traditional leadership in technological innovation.' This illustrates the point. If the church, the salt of the earth, ceases to flourish, the whole world is affected.

Principle 3. To the degree that common grace loses its momentum, good will be turned to evil. This is not unlike Jesus' words: 'If therefore the light that is in thee be darkness, how great is that darkness!' (Mt. 6:23). A person's genius is usually their downfall. So with science and the nations. The medical world that can discover penicillin can also produce a thalidomide baby. Science invents that which destroys as well as good things. Technological advancement is accompanied by its bastard offspring, air and water pollution. America, the country that for years has fed the world, is now the object of hostility. When a nation forgets God, everybody is affected by it. 'Righteousness exalteth a nation: but sin is a reproach to any people' (Prov. 14:34). There's nothing more lovely than great music and literature. But look at what we have today. Look at today's literature. Listen to today's music.

Despite these connections, James is keen to distinguish common from saving grace, what comes from below from what comes from above. What comes from below and what comes from within is imperfect to start with. What we have here are these things that are changeable. Temptation, for example, just cannot stay temptation. Either it must be aborted or it becomes sin. God's gift that comes from above is perfect, unchangeable. There's 'no variableness, neither shadow of turning' because this perfect gift is God himself.

The good gift is derived and therefore imperfect and improvable. But when it comes to the perfect gift, it is God himself. 'God so loved the world, that he gave his only begotten Son, that whosoever believeth in him should not perish, but have everlasting life' (Jn. 3:16). This is God's perfect gift. Rain and sun are good. The rain falls and the sun shines on the just and the unjust. Consequently, penicillin will heal the wicked as quickly as it will heal Christians. An aeroplane will not take Christians any faster to its destination because they're Christians. An atheist may be the inventor of electricity or may discover relativity. But when it comes to God's perfect gift God does for us what common grace cannot do. He gives us a forgiveness of sins and an assurance of everlasting life. The Christian may know that the downward succession from suggestion to temptation to sin to death may be aborted because Jesus Christ stopped it all by tasting death himself. The Christian is the one who has the perfect gift.

Confusing Common Grace with Saving Grace

The curse of the modern church is confusing common grace with saving grace. How many of us exist by common grace and think that it is saving grace simply because we are Christians? If the Holy Spirit were completely withdrawn from the church today, it would go right on as though nothing had happened.

How much of what characterizes you and of what you do is just the fruit of God's common grace? Are you existing by virtue of the good?

Many of us know the perfect only at a very superficial level. Many of us, because we are Christians, are taking our gifts and the good things that happen to us to be the evidence that we are in God's will. But if you were to talk to your non-Christian friends about the good things that may be happening to you, you might be embarrassed and begin to blush when you find out that they can say the same things. For non-Christians will know of a coincidence and a sudden occurrence that makes them happy. God may indeed be with you, but the evidence is not that you are experiencing this realm of the good, for everyone knows this.

James wants us to know something of this perfect gift. It is not for all, but for the believer only. Here is a dimension that so few of us know anything about. We settle for the good, we talk about how lovely things are and how nicely they are going. But I fear that so much that happens to us can be explained at a natural level. Your work is cut out for you if you are going to try to prove these things show that you are living on a higher plane.

I wonder how many of us are seeing the evidence of God's perfect gift in our lives. We ought to be those who live differently, who know what it is to resist sin. For this is what separates common grace from saving grace. Brilliant men that can understand physics, science, medicine, philosophy, still look around for the other man's wife. They still lust for the sensual appetites of the world. Are we different from them?

But there's one thing that cannot be explained or overcome at a natural level, and that is resisting temptation and sin: to know what it is to say 'No' to the world, to the flesh, to the devil. If we enter into this realm of the perfect, where the Christian alone has the right to be, we will demonstrate to the world that we are different. We will not convince the world because we are better equipped, because we have better facilities or better intellects. What will make us different is that we can resist the devil, sin and temptation.

My fellow Christian, I ask you, are you counting it all joy when you fall into diverse trials? After all, the non-Christians that you rub shoulders with have trials. What do they do? They complain. They gripe. They curse. Maybe you don't use the same language, but are you having the same thoughts? What makes you different? It's that you can look to God and know that he's there. And he has grace, grace to make you different from the natural man, the natural woman. Oh, this realm of the perfect, may God grant that we may enter into it and see it working. Best of all we know that we are looking to a God who cannot lie, who cannot change, but is always there. 'O Thou who changest not, abide with me.'

All I see around the world is decay and sin, succumbing to the lust of the flesh. But the Christian is different. We have a God who cannot lie. We live by his promise. Humanity is created variable or we would never have fallen into sin. The devil was created variable or he would never have rebelled against God. We see in this world fluctuation, change, everything moving, improving or going backwards. But in the realm of the perfect there is no change. God is always the same. A word, if he ever once says it, will always be true. Has God ever told you that you are his child? Well, you are his child. That doesn't change. Has God ever told you that he's with you? Well, he's with you. Whatever else happens, whatever others may do, God doesn't change and his word is the same. Any promise he gives us we may lean on and live by.

Worldly people cannot be like that. We know what it is to see fickle men and women, to have a person who is friendly one day and not the next. You wonder what you've done, but it's just the way people are.

Are we different from that? The wonderful thing is that we can experience not only the good, but the ultimate perfect gift from God. The world has yet to see in our generation what would happen if we lived entirely by that which is from above, not from within. When this happens we will become 'the salt of the earth' again and all the world will be affected by us. At the moment we are influencing nobody. The world takes no notice. The world is in decay and it is the church's fault.

May God hasten the hour when we begin to live in that ultimate realm that is our real inheritance. Then the church will flourish and the world will see that we are different. We may not be appreciated. They may reject or persecute us. We may die. But generations will rise up to call us blessed because we dared not to be content with just the good but wanted that which is the ultimate, which is ours, which proves who we really are.

12

The Father of Lights

James 1:17

All Good is by God's Active Will

James shows us that even the good, not simply the perfect but the good, comes from above. He's not only saying that it originates from above but that it *comes* down. He puts it in the present tense. He did not say that it came down. He's showing that the good that does happen is by the active will of God. In other words, there is no such thing as accidental good. It may appear to be accidental, as penicillin and anti-freeze were discovered accidentally, but they and all other goods are the gracious consequence of a sovereign God who steps in and affirms his creation by giving special benefits to humankind, thus showing that he is still active in the world.

We must not think that God has forgotten the world. We ought to remember, when we see the evil around, that God mixes mercy with wrath. We ought to look for the positive good. God is not an absentee watchman who simply turns the world over to natural forces. For if God did turn his back on creation then every living thing would instantly collapse. We are upheld by the very power of God. All life is that which God has granted and maintains. Why, then, does God tell us to recognize that he gives it? Why does James say that it comes down?

It's simply to show that the good already down here cannot continue without God's active will. In other words, God need not kill anything to make it die. All he has to do is to leave it alone and it will die of its own accord. This is why the apostle Paul said, 'In him we live, and move, and have our being' (Acts 17:28). We read that 'all things were made' by the Lord Jesus Christ. 'Without him was not any thing made that was made. In him was life; and the life was the light of men.' 'That was the true Light, which lighteth every man that cometh into the world' (Jn. 1:3–4, 9). We are to look at any living or good thing, whether an invention or special knowledge, as being something that God does by his active will. But we must distinguish between that which is from below and that which is from above. That which comes from below is always dying. To the extent that there is life in nature it is God's special grace within nature. That which comes from below is shifting and changing. The very character of that which comes from below cannot stay the same. There is not the remotest degree of stability or permanence in nature. This is why Jesus said, 'Heaven and earth shall pass away' (Mt. 24:35).

If you look around, you can see that this is obviously true. Why are things so unpredictable? Why is the world changing? Why is it that we are changeable people? Why do we have moods? Friends disappoint. People don't keep their word. Why is this? It is the character of sin. It is that which comes from below. It is always transitory.

But is there anything that is permanent and unchanging? Is there a quality of mercy that is not strained? Is there a friend who will not forsake? James says there is. It is the one who is above and he is called 'the Father of lights'. We are told that the good comes from him.

You will perhaps want to ask, then, if God gives good and he is unchangeable, why is the good changeable? Why does a flower wither? Why must a bird or a pet die? The answer is that there is a distinction between that which is good, which may change, and that which is perfect, which does not change.

The good that is in the world will change because it is attached to nature. We must be careful not to put our trust in the good that we see – the non-Christian's mistake. Non-Christians don't see the distinction between the good that is attached to nature and the God who sends the good. If there is peace in Israel or the Balkans it doesn't mean that there's going to be permanence or stability. It doesn't mean we should bow at the shrine of the brotherhood of man. For the good that is in the world is a derived good and capable of change.

What the good ought to do is make us worship God who gave the good, whether it is through a surgeon who performs a delicate operation or through a politician who by special grace can bring peace. Whatever it is, it is from the Father of lights. Again the error of humanism is seen in the failure to make this distinction. Remember that the good is changeable.

Is there anything that flows from above which is not changeable? There is. This is what James calls the 'perfect gift'. It is that which aborts that downward progression from temptation to sin to death. It is perfect because God does in salvation what he did not do in creation. Creation was pronounced good. But salvation is perfect. Adam was created without sin but he was able to sin. Then he fell, leaving all humankind unable not to sin. But the perfect gift is when God steps in and gives us the grace to resist temptation and to overcome sin. In the end, when redemption is complete, we will be unable to sin for ever and ever.

The Father of Lights

Both the good and the perfect flow from above. The good represents that which flows from God as Creator. The perfect represents that which flows from God as Redeemer. But James wants us to see that the origin of what flows from above is God, the Father of lights.

But this name of God raises some questions. Why, firstly, is the father of lights called 'Father'? Is this one of the verses that gives credibility to the cliché, 'fatherhood of God, brotherhood of man'? Does it mean that God is Father of all whether they are born again or not?

James is talking about what gives birth to what. What is a father? A father is a sire. Throughout James we've been seeing how one thing gives birth to another. We are told that patience brings forth her perfect work which brings forth wisdom. Then there is temptation which brings forth sin which brings forth death. So it is quite natural that James would talk about the Father of lights. What gives birth to what? James is showing us that God is the Father of the good as well as the perfect.

But why is he called Father of *lights*? Why is lights plural? I wondered when I first saw it whether it was a misprint or whether the Authorised Version accidentally said 'lights'. But this is exactly what James wrote. Just as there are the good and the perfect, so are there two kinds of light. There is the light of nature which the Bible calls conscience. This too flows from common grace. As Paul says: 'Because that which may be known of God is manifest in them; for God hath shewed it unto them' (Rom. 1:19). The light of nature is that which is in all humanity. All good, whether it comes by created light or in terms of advanced knowledge, is in nature, but it proceeds from God. It is sufficient to condemn but not to save.

Common grace ought to make us thankful, but it is insufficient to produce real gratitude. Paul goes on to say, 'when they knew God, they glorified him not as God, neither were thankful; but became vain in their imaginations, and their foolish heart was darkened' (Rom. 1:21). The only thing that will produce genuine gratitude and thankfulness to God is the light that flows from the gospel. Paul put it like this: 'For God, who commanded the light to shine out of darkness, hath shined in our hearts, to give the light of the knowledge of the glory of God in the face of Jesus Christ' (2 Cor. 4:6).

What is Light?

We might ask, what is light in the first place? I think the Bible says three things about light.

- Light is brightness. 'God said let there be light: and there was light' (Gen. 1:3). It was brightness as opposed to darkness.
- Light is heat. The psalmist said, 'The heavens declare the glory of God; and the firmament showeth his handiwork', and went on 'in them hath he set a tabernacle for the sun' whose 'going forth is from the end of the heaven, and his circuit unto the ends of it: and there is nothing hid from the heat thereof' (Ps. 19:1, 4, 6).
- Light is knowledge. It gives direction, guidance, insight, break-through. 'Thy word is a lamp unto my feet, and a light unto my path' (Ps. 119:105).

We can see how these three forms of light have their counterparts both in the sphere of common grace and in that which pertains to the gospel. Let's talk about common grace once again. There is the light of the sun. The sun gives light, provides heat and energy. This light is what gives knowledge, whether it is advanced technology or new forms of direction. But what does the light of the gospel do? The light of the gospel gives brightness and cheer to the soul, dispels gloom, chases away doubt and guilt.

Do you know what it is to feel guilty? Oh, the weight of guilt upon one's shoulders! What can deal with this? Advanced technology, knowledge of psychology? Never! Only the light of the gospel. But not only that, this same gospel is the power to defeat the devil, to resist temptation, to overcome sin. For the light of the gospel gives heat, light, power, energy and guidance. When you become a Christian it is not simply that God says, 'Now you are saved. I'll see you in heaven.' No, from that moment on you have knowledge of guidance in your life and understanding. The breakthrough of breakthroughs comes through the light of the knowledge of the gospel.

Paul prayed for the Ephesians 'That the God of our Lord Jesus Christ, the Father of glory, may give unto you the spirit of wisdom and revelation in the knowledge of him: The eyes of your understanding being enlightened; that ye may know what is the hope of his calling, and what the riches of the glory of his inheritance in the saints' (Eph. 1:17–18). This is what God does. Jesus said of the Holy Spirit, 'He will guide you into all truth' (Jn. 16:13). This is the breakthrough of breakthroughs. What does the Spirit do? He obeys the command of the Son of God who is seated at the right hand of the Father. This is why James could refer to God as the Father of lights, plural. This is what I believe James wants us to see, that there are two kinds of light – that of nature and that of the gospel. They are created light, that which issues in common grace, and uncreated light, that which is the gospel of Jesus Christ.

What is Uncreated Light?

Created light is good, but what can be said of uncreated light? It is perfect not only because it proceeds from God but because this light is God. 'God is light, and in him is no darkness at all' (1 Jn. 1:5). God is brilliant brightness.

Saul of Tarsus had a glimpse of that light. He was struck down and was blind for three days (Acts 9). No created light even begins to rival the light of the uncreated light of God. Not even the light from the highest voltage of human technology or the light from lightning, or the light of the sun at noonday comes close to the light that is God himself. For all light that we see is derived light. But God is light.

Isaiah had a glimpse of the throne and he saw the seraphim with six wings, two with which to fly, two with which to cover their feet and two with which to cover their eyes (Isa. 6:1–2). There is coming a day when God in the person of our Lord Jesus Christ will deal finally and irrevocably with all the evil that is in this world, and will split the skies. We are told that all evil, all wickedness, even the Wicked One, will be consumed by 'the spirit of his mouth' and destroyed by 'the brightness of his glory' (Heb. 1:3). He not only dwells 'in the light which no man can approach unto' (1 Tim. 6:16), but he is that light. He himself said that he was 'the light of the world' (Jn. 8:12). But men love darkness rather than light because their deeds are evil. Jesus himself is God's perfect gift, for Jesus Christ is light of light. God of God. Very God of very God. Begotten not created. And when he comes the brightness of his glory will dispense with all evil.

We are told the good shall pass away. 'Heaven and earth shall pass away, but my words shall not pass away.' It is God's word which is unchanging, which is permanent. When people put their trust in the good they trust in that which will decay. But if we are made partakers of

God's perfect gift then we worship God who is unchangeable. And what is more, one glimpse of the Son of God puts one irrevocably into God's everlasting covenant. You look at a man, a woman, a friend and you know you are looking at somebody who is changeable. We are all so limited. But God's perfect gift is himself. And when God gives himself it means that we are put in him. The reason we know that we who are brought into the covenant will never fall away is because we're in God. 'God cannot be tempted with evil, neither tempteth he any man.' When we partake of this perfect gift we are partaking of God himself. We enter into that realm in which there is no change. Where there is permanence. No disappointment. No temptation. No sorrow. No death. God will never let us go. This is how we know that we cannot fall. In him there is 'no variableness, neither shadow of turning.'

This expression of the Authorised Version, 'shadow of turning', is probably close to James' meaning, but not exactly right. The Greek literally means 'in God there is no shadow that is cast by turning'. Think about it for a moment. All created light is characterized by shadow. In light I can see the shadow, a bit of darkness caused by an object in the way of created light. A shadow shows the limitation of created light. The brightest created light still has a shadow somewhere. But 'God is light, and in him is no darkness at all.'

James is showing that the perfect gift is God himself. God's uncreated light comes from beyond time and space. Wherever it shines it leaves no shadows, because there is no conceivable object that can get in its way and bring about a shadow. For God's light comes from before and behind and all around.

John described how it would be throughout eternity: 'I John saw the holy city, new Jerusalem, coming down from God out of heaven, prepared as a bride adorned for her husband.' 'I saw no temple therein: for the Lord God Almighty and the Lamb are the temple of it.' 'The city had no need of the sun, neither of the moon, to shine in it: for the glory of God did lighten it, and the Lamb is the light thereof ... and the gates of it shall not be shut at all by day: for there shall be no night there' (Rev. 21:2, 23, 25).

Throughout eternity we will be dwelling in God's uncreated light. Even now we are in it by his grace. We know that we are kept by one who knows no change of moods, 'with whom is no variableness, neither a shadow cast by turning'. And we wait for the day we're in that city. What do we do in the meantime? In the words of one old song,

But until then my heart will go on singing,
Until then with joy I'll carry on,
Until the day my eyes behold the city,
Until the day God calls me home.

Nothing can happen to change that because God has made us partakers of himself.

13

The Word of Truth

James 1:18

Saving Grace

In this text James brings to a climax his theme of contrasts by expounding upon the perfect gift. Common grace, though given in various degrees, is nonetheless bestowed upon all. Saving grace, however, is particular and limited. James says, 'Of his own will begat he us' – us – 'with the word of truth' that we might be the firstfruits among many creatures. If God left us simply to the natural realm, then we would be, along with everyone else, like those described in Romans 1 who were on a downward trend ending in becoming reprobate. Indeed, Paul said the same thing in Ephesians 2:3: 'Among whom also we all had our conversation in times past in the lusts of our flesh, fulfilling the desires of the flesh and of the mind; and were by nature the children of wrath, even as others.' Others. There's the contrast. Common grace goes to all, but some become distinct when God steps in. This is the crucial distinction, James' ultimate contrast.

Every good gift comes from above, from God. But this is the perfect gift – also from God – his word of truth which brings us into being. Earlier, James spoke of temptation bringing forth sin, and sin bringing forth death. He uses the same word now, but in a positive direction. It is translated 'begat' here and means that by his word of truth God has brought us into being.

This is James' clear reference to new birth, to being born again. As Jesus taught, 'Except a man be born again, he cannot see the kingdom of God' (Jn. 3:3). And Peter said, 'Being born again, not of corruptible seed, but of incorruptible, by the word of God, which liveth and abideth for

ever' (1 Pet. 1:23). Paul's language was slightly different – he talked about
a 'new creature' (2 Cor. 5:17; Gal. 6:15), being 'God's workmanship'
(Eph. 2:10) – but it's exactly the same thing.

The Christian teaching is that something must happen to us. It is life
beyond the level of nature, produced by the light of the gospel. That heat
and energy which move our will and make us seek God. After all, 'There
is none that seeketh after God ... There is none that doeth good' but
'God, who commanded the light to shine out of darkness, hath shined in
our hearts, to give the light of the knowledge of the glory of God in the
face of Jesus Christ' (Rom. 3:11, 12; 2 Cor. 4:6).

We Cannot Bring About Our Own Salvation

What is obvious is that this is not something we produce ourselves. Can
anything be more ridiculous than the notion that we give birth to ourselves? I've met people with some pretty big egos but I haven't run into
anybody yet who thought they brought about their own birth. Jesus said
we must be born again. And Nicodemus raised the question of what we
must do. 'How can a man be born when he is old? Can he enter the
second time into his mother's womb and be born?' Jesus answered,
'Verily, verily, I say unto thee, Except a man be born of water and of the
Spirit, he cannot enter into the kingdom of God' (Jn. 3:4, 5)

In all the New Testament nothing is more obvious than that being
born again is as equally out of our own hands as was our natural birth. Jesus
taught it. The apostles affirmed it. In John's prologue he told us: 'As many
as received him, to them gave he power to become the sons of God.' But
then he told us what lay behind that receiving – 'which were born, not of
blood, nor of the will of the flesh, nor of the will of man, but of God'
(Jn. 1:12–13).

So much evangelism today masquerades as evangelical but shuts its
eyes to this obvious fact. My fellow Christians, we are made members of
the kingdom of God by God's sovereign will. Salvation, being born again,
is out of our hands. As Jesus said, 'No man can come to me except the
Father which hath sent me draw him' (Jn. 6:44). Or as James says here,
by God's 'own will begat he us with the word of truth'. We are dealing
with something that is out of our hands. When Christians despise this
truth they are not unlike those who hate their own creation and ask for
existentialism. If we get this wrong, if we fail to grasp this truth, then we
will invariably have a deformed form of Christianity, to use John Crustie's
expression. Here's the way Paul put it to those who despise this truth:

'Nay but, O man, who art thou that repliest against God? Shall the thing formed say to him that formed it, Why hast thou made me thus? Hath not the potter power over the clay, of the same lump to make one vessel unto honour, and another unto dishonour?' (Rom. 9:20–21).

At the bottom of human rejection of this truth is sheer self-righteousness, the insistence on following the natural way of thinking; the course of self-love thinking we are going to be right on this truth when we get to heaven. Why not now that we may develop an increasing knowledge? Otherwise we reside in a binding pocket of unbelief and cheat ourselves of great joy and freedom.

New Birth Comes About by Hearing

Don't be afraid of James' language: 'Of his own will begat he us.' James asserts an equally great mystery, namely, how new birth happens. Know that new birth is by the will of God. It does not come about apart from what the apostle Paul calls 'hearing'. 'Faith cometh by hearing, and hearing by the word of God' (Rom. 10:17). Paul said, 'It pleased God by the foolishness of preaching to save them that believe' (1 Cor. 1:21). Here is an analogy. Everyone in the world lives not by chance but by God's creation, yet also by natural procreative processes. And every person who is born again has heard God's word. Some days before Saul of Tarsus was struck down he heard Stephen preaching and saw Stephen's face shining like an angel. There must be a hearing of the word. Paul said, 'How then shall they call on him in whom they have not believed? and how shall they believe in him of whom they have not heard? and how shall they hear without a preacher? and how shall they preach except they be sent? as it is written, How beautiful are the feet of them that preach the gospel of peace and bring glad tidings of good things!' (Rom. 10:14–15).

In the natural procreative process a seed comes to the egg. Conception. The egg remains unfertilized without the seed. The seed does not produce an offspring apart from the egg. So, in the new birth, the seed is called the word of God. The egg is called the heart. Sometimes it is called 'good ground' as in Jesus' parable of the sower (Mt. 13). 'A sower went forth to sow.' He sowed seed. Some fell by the wayside, or among thorns. Some fell on good ground. In the parable Jesus referred not only to 'good ground' but also the 'heart': 'they which in an honest and good heart … bring forth fruit' (Lk. 8:15). Paul said, 'If thou shalt confess with thy mouth the Lord Jesus, and shalt believe in thine heart that God has raised him from the dead, thou shalt be saved. For with the heart man believeth unto righteousness' (Rom. 10:9–10). This is new birth. It is the result of the word of God coming to the heart and finding reception.

What happens in the heart? Is it random that some just happen to be converted? As not all eggs are fertilized though the seed comes to them, not all receive the word of God. Paul went on to say, 'But they have not all obeyed the gospel' (Rom. 10:16). And Isaiah said, 'Who hath believed our report?' (Isa. 53:1). Some believe, some don't. What makes the difference? The answer is that the heart has no power in itself to create or receive life. It is passive, utterly dependent upon something external to it. What is more, the Bible says that the heart is by nature filled with darkness. This is like creation. We are told that 'the earth was without form and void; and darkness was upon the face of the deep. And the Spirit of God moved upon the face of the waters. And God said, Let there be light: and there was light' in God's new creation (Gen. 1:2–3). 'For God, who commanded the light to shine out of darkness, hath shined in our hearts, to give the light of the knowledge of the glory of God in the face of Jesus Christ' (2 Cor. 4:6).

The heart itself is not even neutral when it comes to fallen creation. Jesus said that where your treasure is there will your heart be also (Mt. 6:21). 'And this is the condemnation, that light is come into the world, and men loved darkness rather than light, because their deeds were evil' (Jn. 3:19). Only God gives life. So something must happen to the heart. Have you ever thought about those words in Acts 16:14? 'And a certain woman named Lydia, a seller of purple, of the city of Thyatira, which worshipped God, heard us: whose heart the Lord opened,' – 'whose heart the Lord opened', '*the Lord* opened' – 'that she attended unto the things which were spoken of Paul.' In the words of the hymn writer,

> Lord, I was dead! I could not stir
> My lifeless soul to come to Thee;
> But now, since Thou hast quickened me,
> I rise from sin's dark sepulchre.

The Word of Truth

What determines whether the heart responds? We've said the Lord must open it, but insofar as the agency, the word of truth, is concerned, what does it? Is it the quality of the word of truth? Is it the persuasive power of the preacher? Is it the atmosphere of the preaching? Is it the degree of truthfulness in the words? Is it one's frame of mind? Is it one's religious, moral or emotional background? Is it one's sociological environment? What causes a heart to respond? Do not disconnect any of these from the mystery of conversion, for God works through these things. In most cases God works despite them.

Ultimately, it comes down to James' own words – and note the order of his language – 'Of his own will begat he us'. The underlying, first and final cause of new birth is the sovereign will of God. As Paul put it: 'He hath abounded toward us in all wisdom and prudence; having made known unto us the mystery of his will, according to his good pleasure which he hath purposed in himself: that in the dispensation of the fulness of times he might gather together in one all things in Christ, both which are in heaven, and which are on earth; even in him: in whom also we have obtained an inheritance' – and how did it come about? – 'being predestinated according to the purpose of him who worketh all things after the counsel of his own will: that we should be to the praise of his glory' (Eph. 1:8–12). The same language: 'Of his own will'. The word of truth does it.

Ultimately, the explanation why we, unlike others, really do believe is not that we are psychologically better, or cleverer, or that we've been prepared in a different way. It's not just random chance. It is 'Of his own will'. This forces us all to bow before him. For there is not the slightest way in which we can take credit for our new birth. There's a song which illustrates both sides of the coin:

> In loving kindness Jesus came
> My soul in mercy to reclaim,
> And from the deapths of sin and shame
> Through grace he lifted me.
> He called me long before I heard,
> Before my sinful heart was stirred,
> But when I took Him at His word,
> Forgiven he lifted me.
> Now on a higher plane I dwell,
> And with my soul I know 'tis well;
> Yet how or why, I cannot tell,
> He should have lifted me.

It's a mystery. James says, 'Leave it at this: of his own will begat he us.'

How Much Truth Is Needed for Conversion?

James says that conversion happens by 'the word of truth'. This is also a phrase Paul used. 'In whom ye also trusted, after that ye heard the word of truth' (Eph. 1:13); 'The word of the truth' (Col. 1:5). How much truth is needed to precipitate new birth? And is there a necessary order; must one hear this truth before that truth in order to be saved? Or, as some put it, need law come before gospel? How much must one know in order to be converted? James simply says, 'He begat us with the word of truth.' What matters is that the truth that is heard is believed. That the word of God, 'sharper than any two-edged sword, piercing even to the dividing asunder of soul and spirit ... and is a discerner of the thoughts and intents of the heart' (Heb. 4:12), penetrates and finds reception. That's all that matters.

I understand when people say to me, 'Look, I have a friend I want to bring to church this Sunday night but before I bring him, what are you going to preach? What I really want to know is, are you going to preach on hell? Because if you are I won't bring my friend.' Others say to me, 'Tell me when you are going to preach on hell because that's when I want to bring my friend.' To both I say, 'It doesn't matter.' It's the word of truth. One proof of conversion is that people accept later what previously they had not heard; they don't need to hear it all before being saved. By the word of truth, if it is believed, new birth comes.

Finally, James shows why God works like this. He says, 'Of his own will begat he us with the word of truth, that we should be a kind of firstfruits of his creatures.' We dealt with the subject of creation at length in verse 17 under the term 'common grace'. We saw that the 'Father of lights' there depicted God as Creator and Redeemer. Created light flows from God the Creator, uncreated light from God the Redeemer. Redemption does what creation cannot do. What is it that transcends creation? The word of truth. 'Heaven and earth shall pass away, but my words shall not pass away' (Mt. 24:35).

We Are the Firstfruits of God's Creation

James says that those who are born again are 'a kind of firstfruits'. In the Old Testament, firstfruits, whether of produce or animals, were holy to the Lord. They were sacrificed to him. In the New Testament we often have the expression 'firstfruit' and it can refer to the first convert in a particular area (Rom. 16:5). However, in James 1:18, firstfruits refers not to chronological sequence but to quality and honour. It is not that which is first in time but that which is first in prestige, in glory, in pre-eminence. This is what we are: firstfruits of all creation. Think about creation for a moment. Consider the sun, moon and stars, the sky and clouds, an English countryside, a waterfall in Switzerland, a sunset in the tropics – the glory of creation. 'What is man, that thou art mindful of him?' (Ps. 8:4). Humanity is the image of God. God created us in his own image. But James does not mean humankind when he refers to the firstfruits of creation.

Although humans are God's ultimate in creation and the psalmist did say, 'I am fearfully and wonderfully made' (Ps. 139:14), yet we must say that not one of all of God's creatures, none of creation, can sink so low as humanity. A flower may fade. Fruit may rot. Water may become stagnant. An animal may turn on its young. But what is so ugly as people in sin? What is so melancholy as a promising boy or girl who ends up in the depths of sin? The promising young man who ends up a dope addict or a drunkard in the gutter – he cannot emancipate himself. That lovely young lady who sells her body, goes into pornography and prostitution – what is so ugly as guilt and shame and disgrace?

Surely, then, humankind is not the firstfruits of God's creatures. This is not what James meant. What surpasses the sun and the stars in glory? What is lovelier than a placid ocean or a tropical landscape, a healthy body, or a brilliant mind? What is greater than success? James answers, 'The new birth. Being born again.' It cannot happen to a fly or to a tree. It cannot happen to an angel. It can only happen to a man, woman, boy or girl.

James' point is in this contrasting theme. He says there is something more wonderful than any suggestion that leads to temptation, more dazzling than any temptation that leads to sin, more marvellous than any sin that leads to death. Not only that, says James, there's something greater than the glory of abundant common grace, than the discovery of penicillin, than brilliant music or moving art, than the highest achievements of technology. It is that which aborts the downward progression from temptation to sin to death, which won't let sin finish, which defies death. It is that which takes away guilt and shame, which wipes away sin and which gives people dignity in this present world. If anyone is in Christ they are a new creature, a new creation. Old things are cast away, all things are become new.

But the question of questions is, how is all this possible? First, because behind new birth there is a person: Jesus Christ of Nazareth, God's only begotten Son. He's not called the firstfruits of creation, but 'the firstborn of every creature' (Col. 1:15). He's called 'the first among many brethren'

(Rom. 8:29), 'the first born from the dead' (Col. 1:18). We are the firstfruits of creation because God the Creator became God the Redeemer. Because created life was transcended by uncreated life. 'The Word was made flesh, and dwelt among us' (Jn. 1:14). He died on a cross. He rose from the dead and declared, 'Behold, I make all things new' (Rev. 21:5). Creation as we know it shall be dissolved. Heaven and earth shall pass away.

Is there then any continuity between the old and the new? There is, but only this: Jesus Christ shall remain, for he cannot die. We shall remain, for we cannot die. All the glimmer and the glory of the first order shall be brought to nothing and shall make way for the only survivors. And who are they? The firstfruits of creation. Those born again. This is all possible because of the word of truth that came nigh, that found a reception in our hearts. What is the most precious commodity in the universe? Gold, silver? By what happens in this world you would think so. The world focuses on the importance of the material. But what is the hope of the world? It's the word of truth. Our only hope is the gospel. 'Heaven and earth shall pass away, but my words shall not pass away' (Mt. 24:35).

14

Swift and Slow

James 1:19–20

How practical and timely are these verses when you consider the harm done to every relationship by speaking without thinking. Whatever walk of life you be in, I've got a word that can help you. It will jolt you. It might make you feel guilty although that is not its purpose. It can help you in your business, with your friends, your teachers, in your marriage. It can help you if you are in a restaurant, in hospital or in church. Wherever. Even if you meet a stranger. Only remember and apply these words: 'Let every man be swift to hear, slow to speak, slow to wrath.'

Not only is James a practical epistle, we have seen that it is an epistle of order. There's not an idle comment here. Many people, taking its words out of context, see James as being but a series of disconnected moralisms. To be fair, you can read it like that and still benefit. But I want us to see the richness of this word in the light of all that James has said before. Because these words come at a particular time in the epistle and at a most appropriate moment.

We need to see James' continuity. James has just concluded his first major statement, the most profound thing that could be said about God. 'God cannot be tempted with evil, neither tempteth he any man.' I marvel at that statement, which only a godly mind could have thought. But, I might add, only the one who has seen God's glory can receive this word. For it is precisely here, my fellow Christian, where the water hits the wheel in Christian understanding. All men and women sooner or later come to this crossroads, and where you go will determine whether or not you are going to be a believer. James knew the seriousness of this word. That is, when you are tempted, be careful never to say you are being tempted of God. And so in verse 16 he paused to say, 'Do not err, my beloved brethren.' It is at this point all of us either pass or fail.

The Most Common Complaint

Talk to your neighbour. Talk to somebody that you run into in the street. What are their most common complaints about God? It is the problem of evil. Everyone has this complaint ready. It is their justification for not believing in God. How can God escape the charge of cruelty if he's all powerful and could stop evil but doesn't? People look at God and say, 'Damn you for letting this happen!' This is the way that natural people think.

James knows that no Christian is exempt from the temptation to think this way. For there's not a week that passes in which you do not have the temptation put before you. All of us have been tempted to think like Job's wife, to look at suffering and blame God. 'Curse God, and die' she advised Job – it's all God's fault. When James now says, 'Let every man be swift to hear, slow to speak', it is an elaboration of his warning in verse 16: 'Do not err, my beloved brethren.' For our being swift in hearing, our having a slowness to speak, will be a way of making our calling and election sure, of testing whether or not we are going to be different from the masses.

What are the masses doing? 'Broad is the way, that leadeth to destruction, and many there be that go in thereat: because,' said Jesus, 'straight is the gate, and narrow the way, which leadeth unto life, and few there be that find it' (Mt. 7:13–14). Everybody you meet will have a ready-made objection to God. But James is saying to the Christian, 'Do not jump to the natural conclusion which the masses feed upon. Be different. Realize that there is further light to be had on the subject.' Natural people depend on created light, on logic. That is all they have. But the Christian depends on uncreated light that bypasses natural reasoning. James says, 'Wait for the further word on the subject. Be swift to hear.'

The Authorised Version translates this 'Wherefore, my beloved brethren'. It's all right to translate it that way but you ought to know that the Greek word is *iste*, which comes from *oida*, meaning 'knowledge' of a well-known fact, familiar knowledge. James is saying, 'Know this backwards and forwards. Have this knowledge firmly embedded in your heart. Let this be your habit, your lifestyle, your natural reaction.'

Be 'swift to hear, slow to speak, slow to wrath' and though you may not have all the answers you want, in the meantime hang on to this: what comes from below is not of God. Temptation, sin and death are not of God. What comes from above is from God. The good, the perfect are from above.

When it comes to diverse trials, God orders them and you count them all joy. James says it works. You have learned what can happen when you dignify trials, when you resist temptations. This workable thing in your life is the earnest that God is moving. Verse 19 is an epilogue to this major statement, is a warning not to spout off. You will be blessed in withholding your immature conclusion. It will save you needless indignation and wrath.

Practical Relevance

In addition to the knowledge of God's nature and our attitude towards God, this is relevant for the living out of the Christian life. We can never blame God, only ourselves, for falling into sin. Godly living, holy living is to be the norm for the Christian, an anticipation of the holiness we will have with God for ever and ever.

This is James' way of telling us how to resist temptation. The preceding verse talks about the word of truth. Being 'swift to hear' is connected to the word of truth that brought about our new birth. Our lesson at this point is that as faith was produced by hearing in the first place so, obviously, more hearing will produce more faith. Therefore 'be swift to hear'.

There Are No Exceptions

James imputes to every Christian the responsibility and the ability to be 'swift to hear' and 'slow to speak'. 'Let every man', he says. All of us want to claim to be the exception. We all say, 'Well, in my case God understands. God knows that I have this tendency, this particular weakness. I wouldn't advise it for anybody else but God and I have a special thing going.' We all think like that, so James says, 'Let no man say'.

It is not that people don't have their own peculiar temptations but that all temptations follow a definite order, and every Christian has been converted by a definite order – the word of truth. We must recognize that God has done something for us. The same word of truth that converted us will carry us through. There are no Christians who can blame their failure to be 'swift to hear' and 'slow to speak' on their own peculiar temperament or disposition. Not all of us have the same weakness but all have the same responsibility and the same resource: God's word – the word of truth. James calls upon every Christian to activate the same word that issued in their own conversion. It will be hearing that will save us from wrath and indignation.

This is an enormous responsibility: to dignify our birthright by doing ourselves what God at first had to do – produce hearing. Now he has produced it we have new life, new hearing. We must be jealous of it, guard it, guarantee that nothing comes in to block God from continually speaking to us. This ability to hear is a most precious gift. 'God was swift to unstop our ears', James says, 'you be swift to use them.' Avoid at all cost any degree of deafness.

Grieving the Holy Spirit

My fellow Christians, behind James' exhortation is what the New Testament teaches about grieving the Holy Spirit. All Christians have the Holy Spirit, and the Holy Spirit will never leave us. 'He which hath begun a good work in you will perform it until the day of Jesus Christ', says Paul (Phil. 1:6). Jesus said that when the Spirit comes he will abide with us for ever (Jn. 14:16). So it's not a question of losing the Spirit. That cannot happen. But you can grieve the Spirit.

Do you know that the immediate consequence of grieving the Spirit is the setting in of deafness? It is possible for the Christian who has been given a new pair of ears to become deaf. With human beings this deafness normally accompanies old age, but when it comes to the new creature in Christ deafness can set in much earlier.

The Cause of Deafness

Deafness is caused by falling into sin. How do we fall into sin? By flirting with, excusing or justifying temptation. By saying, 'God allowed the circumstances that brought about the temptation.' James says, 'Be careful about thinking that. You had better wait for the word that comes from him because God has said that isn't the case.' James means then for us to be 'swift to hear', remaining open to the voice of the Spirit. Flirting with temptation brings about a dullness of hearing. If God ceases to speak to us then we begin to hear other voices. And we think those are God speaking, like Balaam. The result will be confusion upon confusion.

But there's nothing more wonderful than a warm heart that is open to the voice of the Spirit. God wants to talk to us. God is more willing to communicate with us than we are with him. And James is warning us here not to miss out. As Paul put it: 'Be not deceived; God is not mocked: for whatsoever a man soweth, that shall he also reap. For he that soweth to his flesh shall of the flesh reap corruption; but he that soweth to the Spirit shall of the Spirit reap life everlasting. And let us not be weary in well doing: for in due season we shall reap, if we faint not' (Gal. 6:7–9). 'It is your Father's good pleasure to give you the kingdom' (Lk. 12:32). 'I will not leave you comfortless' (Jn. 14:18). God wants to speak but we must be swift to listen and sure that it is his voice.

James knows that we have an adversary, the devil, who understands just how to get us to grieve the Spirit. The devil wants deafness to set in. Balaam's sin was to teach Balak how to bring God's wrath on Israel by teaching Israel to sin. The devil will do everything he can to get us to grieve the Spirit so that God won't bless us and will withhold communication. The warm receptiveness to his voice becomes something else. 'Keep thy heart with all diligence; for out of it are the issues of life' (Prov. 4:23). 'Be swift to hear.'

How Not to Grieve the Spirit

Now James adds this word, 'Be slow to speak.' Later on we will come back to this matter of the tongue. But this is James' first word on it. There is a sense in which we never really grieve the Spirit until we open our mouths, and James knows it. This is his practical way of showing you how not to grieve the Spirit. The temptation comes for you to speak your mind, to say what you think when you are agitated, or when your feelings are hurt. James says, 'Discipline yourself to say nothing.' Because if you can say nothing you will have a great victory when you are mistreated. The devil tempts you to get even. If only you can get one word in or just say your piece, let the other person know that you know what they did. You say, 'Well, if I think it I might as well say it.' That's the devil talking to you now. Only children say what they think. In fact, some children have more wisdom than adults. Once you say it, it's too late.

What would happen if everybody began to reveal everything they'd ever thought about another person at one time or another. All hell would break loose. The devil would have the greatest victory since Balaam taught Israel to sin. Months and perhaps years would pass before things would ever be the same again. There is no doubt you can grieve the Spirit by what you think. This is especially true if you harbour a grudge. But the fact is, until you do say something you can deal with it. To heal wounds and consciences, to restore a weaker brother or sister after that may take days, months, sometimes years.

The devil loves to make you think that you are being godly or pious by going to another and saying, 'I must tell you that I have felt very wrong towards you for what you did but I forgive you now.' Or going to somebody and saying, 'I've said some awful things about you. I've asked God to forgive me and I'm asking you to forgive me.' 'Well, what did you say?' 'Oh, it's all right. Let's not talk about it. I just want you to know God forgives me.' Until that moment the other person may not have had a clue you felt like that, but in your relieving yourself you've crushed another. Things may never be the same again. Often when you go to another person and say, 'I forgive you', you do it because you haven't forgiven them. It's your way of getting at them. If you really have forgiven them, show it. You don't have to say it. Saying it often gives the devil a handle. Real forgiveness is when you are self-effacing about it.

James' good advice is to listen to God and keep your mouth shut whatever you may be feeling, however much you may be hurting or chafing on the inside. Until you speak there's still time to deal with your feelings without bringing down wrath and indignation.

What is Wrath?

Wrath is the devil's victory. For the devil throws a party in hell and the demons congratulate each other, 'We did it. He grieved the Spirit and now God isn't going to bless him.' When we speak without thinking it leads to a further loss of self-control. It may be that losing your temper causes another to lose theirs. Or you reveal to another your hidden feelings and then they reveal theirs. Or you might reveal something about someone's character and cause others to doubt them. This wrath is the kernel explosion of the heart that could have been avoided but for the opening of your mouth.

The odd thing is that at the time we are speaking we often fancy that we are doing what God approves of. Most sinning done by the Christian begins with the assumption it is the thing to do. One thing leads to another until eventually it is obviously sin, but you realize it's too late. This sinning James calls 'the wrath of man'. At first it seems perfectly natural, perfectly legitimate, perfectly justifiable. But grieving the Spirit is almost never done consciously. Wrath comes and the devil's won.

James isn't finished. One more thing he says – and remember this – 'The wrath of man worketh not the righteousness of God.' It means three things. First, speaking before thinking is proof that you are not demonstrating godliness. Losing your temper is not what we mean by the love of Christ. It might have seemed quite natural to you, but that isn't God's way of doing things. Your 'honesty' is just self-defence, an excuse to speak your mind.

That is not carrying out God's righteousness. Because whenever you are captive to your flesh you are not living God's way. You cannot vindicate yourself and have God as your vindicator at the same time. You cannot praise yourself and have the honour of God at the same time.

Second, your capitulating to the flesh will not coerce God to work for you. You cannot manipulate God. You can't get him to move by threatening to miss church or jump off the pinnacle of the temple. You say, 'All right, God, here I go.' God lets you go. You jump and you kill yourself. You may think you can blackmail God, but you can't. He sees through your motives. Would you like to have power with God? It's a wonderful thing to have. Just remember, trying to do it carnally won't work. 'The wrath of man worketh not the righteousness of God.'

Third, and I'm so glad I can say this, our wrath does not influence God against us. This shows how God is with us, how kind and good he is to answer our prayers. We may be angry with him for unanswered prayer, but if God answered all our prayers it would prove that he doesn't love us because our wrath doesn't move him.

On the other hand, if our carnality doesn't manipulate him it follows that our carnality does not dislodge us from his faithfulness and love either. In God there is no 'shadow of turning' (Js. 1:17). Once we are in God we inherit this awesome side of his nature by which he cannot be tempted with evil. His inability to be moved by sin. And we have the benefit of it.

Thank God he is not moved by our sin. Thank God he's beyond that. When I sin he does not take salvation away from me.

> The soul that on Jesus has leaned for repose
> I will not, I will not desert to its foes;
> That soul, though all hell should endeavour to shake,
> I'll never, no never, no never forsake.

This is all possible because God has not 'dealt with us after our sins'. He doesn't reward us 'according to our iniquities' (Ps. 103:10). This is so comforting to me when I think of how often I've spoken to him wrongly. Who among us is not ashamed of some ill word uttered that affected another's life? Our speaking without thinking may affect human relationships so adversely that there may be no healing possible. The greatest saint's righteousness is vacillating. We are affected by what others say to us. We are human and tempted by evil. But God isn't. He remembers that we are dust.

He can even forgive Job's wife for her rash statements just as he forgives our wrath, our weakness. Thank God for unanswered prayer, for his ignoring our ill-posed requests shows that he really does care for us. We have tried to blackmail him and we have disgraced him. All of us have sinned. We blush when we think how we have let him down.

God could use it against us and yet he can't because he doesn't even say it. He doesn't even know about it. He cannot be tempted with evil. Why is this? Because he sent his Son into the world. 'While we were yet sinners, Christ died for us' (Rom. 5:8). God gave his Son and established once for all an everlasting righteousness whereby all of us may know that we are forgiven and that salvation is a permanent gift. God's righteousness is not vacillating. He holds no grudges. He's a forgiving, magnanimous God.

> His love knows no limit,
> His grace knows no measure,
> His power knows no boundary known unto men;
> For out of his infinite riches in Jesus
> He giveth more grace and giveth and giveth again.

15

The Engrafted Word

James 1:21

James proceeds now to the practical application. The question comes, 'How can I be "swift to hear, slow to speak"?' Fortunately for us James stays on the subject and uses this word 'wherefore'. The Greek really means 'therefore'. Whenever you see the word 'therefore' in the New Testament, you can generally assume that a major conclusion follows with immense practical advice. The first thing James says in this connection is: 'Wherefore lay apart all filthiness and the superfluity of naughtiness.' His first advice is to refuse to dignify the shameful part of our nature. The Greek word translated 'lay aside' is *apothemenoi*. It means to 'put it aside', to 'put it away'. And this is following his 'therefore'.

Paul and James Taught the Same Things

When we think of a 'therefore' we often think of Paul because we are familiar with Paul's way of thinking. For example, there are the three great 'therefores' of Romans: '*Therefore* being justified by faith, we have peace with God though our Lord Jesus Christ' (5:1); 'There is *therefore* now no condemnation to them which are in Christ Jesus' (8:1); 'I beseech you *therefore*, brethren, by the mercies of God, that ye present your bodies a living sacrifice, holy, acceptable unto God, which is your reasonable service' (12:1). Paul's 'therefores' almost always follow his exposition of justification by faith. He says 'therefore' in the light of what God has done and how you are to be.

James has a 'therefore' too and, interestingly, he uses 'therefore' following the very same thing that Paul does. This is extraordinary. What Paul taught James also taught. They learned it from the same source but without talking to each other. Many people jump to the conclusion that James appears at the end of the canon to correct or balance Paul. Nonsense. James probably wrote this epistle, as I have said, before Paul ever wrote. This is probably the earliest book in the New Testament. Paul, who saw things clearly and espoused them in great detail, was preceded by James who said the same things.

I will prove it. What do you suppose is the Greek word used for 'the righteousness of God' when James says, 'For the wrath of man worketh not the righteousness of God' (1:20)? It's the same word Paul used in Romans 1:17: *dikaisune*. Paul said that human wrath does not move God. James says the same thing, 'The wrath of man worketh not the righteousness of God.'

Their vocabulary is amazingly similar. What James calls the 'word of truth' (1:18) Paul calls the 'word of faith' (Rom. 10:8). What James calls salvation by the will of God is what Paul calls sovereign grace in Romans 8 and 9.

Now what does James say when he comes to this word 'therefore'? He says, 'We lay aside all moral filth.' James and Paul are coming at the same truth. In the light of what God has done here's what we are to do. It's wonderful how the New Testament all fits together. How I delight that we are following an infallible Bible, that although the various men God used to write the Bible had different styles, everything that's said coheres.

The Christian's Life Should Reflect God's Grace

The point is, in the light of grace what manner of persons ought we to be? James says that the life of the Christian is to reflect the grace of God in us.

Incidentally, this Greek word *apothemenoi* is the same word used by Paul again and again. 'Put ye on the Lord Jesus Christ, and make not provision for the flesh, to fulfil the lusts thereof' (Rom. 13:14). In Ephesians he put it like this: 'Put off concerning the former conversation the old man, which is corrupt according to the deceitful lusts' (4:22); 'Wherefore putting away lying, speak every man truth with his neighbour' (4:25). And again in Colossians 3:8: 'But now ye also put off all these.' It's the same teaching. And the writer to the Hebrews uses the same word: 'Wherefore seeing we also are compassed about with so great a cloud of witnesses, let us lay aside every weight' (12:1). It's also what Jesus taught. 'If any man will come after me, let him deny himself, and take up his cross, and follow me' (Mt. 16:24).

It all comes to this. God does the big things. We do the little things. Before our conversion we were blinded by 'the god of this world' but uncreated light 'hath shined in our hearts, to give the light of the knowledge of the glory of God in the face of Jesus Christ' (2 Cor. 4:4,6). 'Of his own will begat he us with the word of truth.' We couldn't have done that. That was the will of God. We received him because we 'were born, not of the will of the flesh, nor of the will of man, but of God' (Jn. 1:13). The big thing is what we could not do for ourselves. That shows that God's grace overrules.

What is the little thing? The little thing is the truth, that we have received the word of truth by being 'swift to hear'. We prove that we have received the word by listening lest we grieve the Spirit of God who is in us. And we further prove our own listening by laying aside all moral filth. The proof that you do not believe you are being tempted of God is that you deny what comes from below. It is not just theory, saying to yourself, 'I know that God isn't doing this', you have to apply it. God has not done the tempting and you shoe that you believe that by the way you live. Temptation comes from lust. Therefore you deny your lusts.

You may be saying, 'That's not a little thing.' But it is. As Jesus put it: 'So likewise ye, when ye shall have done all those things which are commanded you, say, We are unprofitable servants: we have done that which was our duty to do' (Lk. 17:10). And as John put it: 'For this is the love of God, that we keep his commandments: and his commandments are not grievous' (1 Jn. 5:3). What is more, it's the best way to live. It spares us wrath and indignation. It keeps us from the sorrow and shame that follows from giving in to lusts. The result is great peace, joy, being motivated by love, power, a sound mind rather than a spirit of fear (2 Tim. 1:7).

What We Should Lay Aside

So if you want to know how to be 'swift to hear', James' first piece of advice is to lay aside every pollution and moral filth. This ought to encourage you, for James recognizes what we are like. The devil loves to get you thinking that you can't be a Christian if you think and act the way you do. But James says, 'You are like this.'

Perhaps you have come to see how corrupt and sinful you really are, through the conviction of the Holy Spirit or by reflecting upon yourself after you have sinned. Thank God you can see yourself as once you couldn't see, what non-Christians cannot see. If you thought that your moral filth would disappear simply because you are now a Christian you are wrong.

But James also says there is something you can do about it. Lay it to one side. Treat it with utter contempt. Refuse to dignify it. Loathe it. Because you are a Christian you are called the firstfruits of God's creation. It means this: you have life in you, life of the Spirit, and you can do this. As a Christian, the real you is in charge. Until you became a Christian you were not really the real you, you were under the dominion of sin, of the devil. You were blind. But now that you are a Christian you can no longer say, 'Sin made me do it', 'The devil made me do it.' You do it or you don't do it.

James admonishes you not to dignify that shameful part of your nature. For you have an opportunity to be a man of character, a woman of strength, to rise above your lust and corruption. This is what Paul calls rejoicing in oneself (Gal. 6:4). It will do you no good to say, 'Since I've got this corruption I cannot help it.' James says, 'You can help it.' And to say that you cannot is to treat with contempt God's life in you.

Two Common Maladies

Moral filth is not the only thing James tells us to put aside. He adds 'the superabundance of evil disposition'. The Greek is best translated 'super-abundance'. It's the same word used in Roman 5:17. The Authorised Version also says 'naughtiness'. It comes from the word *kakias* which means of evil temperament or disposition. James has combined our two most common maladies: moral filth and bad disposition. He has in one sweep touched the sensual and the violent parts of our nature.

Have you ever said to yourself, 'I've only got two problems: sex and a bad temper'? Do you know that's true of everybody? You're no different. James knows just what to say because if you take away these two facets of evil you have an almost perfect person. Keep in mind that this word refers not only to sexual corruption but to any immorality, lying, cheating, dishonesty. By dealing with these two words in one sweep James attacks what we all know to be our major weaknesses. We can make no excuses, James has a word just for you. James won't let any of us claim some peculiar, excessive weakness. The Christian life is to be lived in such a way as to reflect the perfection of God in us.

Dr Lloyd-Jones said (he said it from the pulpit in the early 1950s) 'The apostles lived the Sermon on the Mount. If you take the trouble to read the lives of the saints down the centuries and the men who have been most greatly used of God you will find that every time they have been men who have taken the Sermon on the Mount not only seriously but literally. This is how the Christian is meant to live.'

For James this means that as Christians we must keep on receiving the word of truth with meekness. If we don't receive the word of truth in this manner it won't come at all. We lay aside all moral filth, all evil disposition. And we don't do so grudgingly or in protest. James uses the word 'to receive', *dechomai*. It means 'to welcome', 'to receive with an embrace, heartily'.

The Engrafted Word

At this point James puts a new word into the discussion. What he called the 'word of truth' (v. 18) he now calls the 'engrafted word'. He uses the Greek word *emphuton*, meaning 'engrafted' or 'imparted'. Thomas Hooker, the Puritan who went to New England and founded the state of Connecticut, was famous for a series of sermons on preparation. One of his books was entitled *The Engrafted Word*. Hooker borrowed the phrase from James to show that the prepared heart is now indeed regenerate.

James, however, is talking to the believer who once received the word as truth. It is now implanted, engrafted. It's a way of describing internal new creation. Once the word of truth is in us it is there for ever. This is why the apostle Paul could say, 'For this cause also thank we God without ceasing, because, when ye received the word of God which ye heard of us, ye received it not as the word of men, but as it is in truth, the word of God, which effectually worketh also in you that believe' (1 Thess. 2:13). This effectuality of the word is that God, giving it to us, will never take it away. So Jesus could say, 'My sheep hear my voice, and I know them, and they follow me: And I give unto them eternal life; and they shall never perish, neither shall any man pluck them out of my hand' (Jn. 10:27–28). Jesus could also say to his disciples, 'Now ye are clean through the word which I have spoken unto you' (Jn. 15:3).

But why does James tell us to receive the engrafted word if it is already in us? The answer is that the real you must dignify your regenerate state. You must prove that you are a Christian by continuing to receive this word of God. You must prove that your conversion was not a mere emotional experience. Dignify your regenerate state. Make 'your calling and election sure' (2 Pet. 1:10). Again and again sanction what is true about yourself. We dignify this regenerate state. Of course, there is warfare between the flesh and the spirit, but allow the real you to win through. Where your treasure is there will your heart be also (Mt. 6:21). Paul wrote, 'Set your affection on things above, not on things on the earth' (Col. 3:2). 'Mortify the deeds of the body' (Rom. 8:13). Put away those things that are contrary to that new life that is in you. This is why James says, 'Receive it.' The word that is in you is Spirit, and it is possible to grieve the Holy Spirit.

One does not need to be reconverted in order to activate the engrafted word, because this word is already there. One need only lay aside one's moral filth and evil disposition, and with meekness set the word working. This is what the New Testament calls stirring up the gift that is in you (2 Tim. 1:6). Or as Simon Peter put it: 'Yea, I think it meet, as long as I am in this tabernacle, to stir you up by putting you in remembrance' (2 Pet. 1:13).

The fire of the Holy Spirit in us never goes utterly out, no matter how much one may have sinned. Like hot coals it can be stirred up, kindled and set ablaze. This ought to bring a special word of comfort to any backslider. You may have given up any thought that you could be a Christian. You haven't lived or behaved like a Christian. Those around you wouldn't suspect that you are one. And because of this you have just decided that you can't be one. But wait a minute. You may have grieved the Spirit a long time ago, but I've got a word for you.

I don't care how grievously you have sinned. I grant that you feel shameful and dirty inside. Put aside now all naughtiness and moral filth. There is life in you. Why do you think you care about it? The fire has not gone out. It's time now to come home and renounce the way you've been living. Remember this glorious promise: 'If we confess our sins, he is faithful and just to forgive us our sins, and to cleanse us from all unrighteousness' (1 Jn. 1:9).

How powerful is this engrafted word? 'Well,' says James, 'this powerful: it's able to save your souls.' What James does is to confront every Christian with the ultimate purpose and possibility of God's word that brought conversion in the first place. This word does what created light cannot do, not for your body, but for your soul. And that's what matters. The same word that brought your conversion, this uncreated light, will save your soul. What James has done is to describe the same word, the same work which is the essential work of the word of truth. Now that it is implanted he wants us to know it is no less powerful. Its abode is in your heart even though you are sinful. The extraordinary thing is that this engrafted word doesn't diminish in its efficacy. You have engrafted in you that word by which life was brought into the world. 'And God said, Let there be light: and there was light' (Gen. 1:3).

James says, 'Watch what can happen when you turn loose that word that is in you.' Rid yourself of all moral filth. Lay aside that hot temper. Swallow your pride. Say, 'I've been wrong.' Stop justifying yourself. Confess your sin. Come meekly before God. You will set loose within you the word that is able to save your soul. For that new life which once gave you joy will again be recognized. The voice of the Spirit – though you had forgotten what it was like, and had given up hope of hearing it again – will once more set you afire, kindle life, warmth and love. Thank God it's there.

How do we know this? 'Well,' says James, 'this word is able to save your souls.' We are not talking about the discovery of penicillin or new technology. The gospel deals with our souls. After all, if God's word can save you from death to life how much more can the same Spirit bring you into new vistas, new insights, new fields. You might be at the beginning of a new, unprecedented era in your life. 'Eye hath not seen, nor ear heard, neither have entered into the heart of man, the things which God has prepared for them that love him. But God hath revealed unto us by his Spirit' (1 Cor. 2:9–10). What would happen if all of us would with meekness receive this engrafted word?

During the Welsh Revival Evan Roberts went around from church to church with four principles. These don't guarantee revival – I'm sure they've been used a thousand times without success. But revival will not come without them.

- Be separate from all sin with particular emphasis upon forgiving others.
- Renounce all the doubtful things in your life.
- Be instantly and constantly obedient to the Spirit.
- Confess all that you have been made a partaker of. Confess the Lord Jesus.

That is receiving with meekness the engrafted word, a colourful word that can do anything if it can save your soul. And if God can save you he can save anybody.

16

Hearers or Doers?

James 1:22–24

James isn't yet finished with the ministry of the word, for he uses this word 'but'. 'Receive with meekness the engrafted word, which is able to save your souls. But . . .' But what? 'Be ye doers of the word, and not hearers only.' The implication is very clear. Having succeeded in not speaking without thinking, and in laying aside all moral filth, it is still possible to be a hearer only and not a doer.

Arrested Development

What a pity that one could grow in grace to this extent, and still be only a hearer. He succeeds in being a hearer. Despite receiving with meekness the engrafted word, it is possible for Christians to suffer an arrested development in their lives. This is precisely what James wants us to avoid. Let's be clear about this. We must not underestimate the degree of advanced spiritual growth which one has acheived in reaching this stage – an arrested development might come long before this but it is possible to go further.

Some Christians never move beyond what seems to them to be the normal Christian life: flirting with the world and temptation, blaming their temptation on God, on providence, on their own temperament, and imagining this is the way to live. There are Christians who think there is no other way to live but just by adding to the same old problems, succumbing to the same weaknesses, the same temptations. They experience this malady of an arrested development, but earlier, at the point of knowing nothing but wrath. They are rolled and tossed by everything that comes along and they think that this is quite normal. They never know the joy of being 'swift to hear, slow to speak, slow to wrath'. I think it is one of the most dreadful characteristics of the modern church that there is an undoubted majority of Christians who never move beyond putting up with the same old temptations. For too many today are not even real hearers of the word, much less doers.

We have to see here once again the importance of order in James' sentences. He never makes an idle comment. The order here is that one cannot be a doer until one's been a hearer. One cannot be a hearer until one has become 'swift to hear, slow to speak' and has laid aside all moral filth and evil temperament. You may say, 'I'll be glad if I could just be a good hearer, that would be the pinnacle of success.' If that is the maximum goal you have set for yourself as a Christian, you are not only underestimating the power of the word of God in you but are bordering on denying your own dignity as a new creation in Christ Jesus.

Keep in mind that James is not telling us to do what cannot be done. That you haven't done it is no excuse. Do not rob yourself of the kind of New Testament Christianity that the world deserves to see. We can live the Sermon on the Mount and show the world what authentic Christianity is. And the blessings that will be upon us if we do it are almost beyond description. We prove our love, we prove our waiting by our continued obedience. James calls obedience 'doing'. 'Be ye doers of the word' (1:22).

Being a Doer of the Word

A doer of the word is the living embodiment of all that the word of God is. It is the highest expression of Christian living. It is non-verbal Christianity. It is not having the ability to dispute on theological things. You may think you would like to be like Paul, theologically articulate. Paul's genius was not his learning, his education, background or credentials. He himself put it, 'According to my earnest expectation and my hope, that in nothing I shall be ashamed, but that with all boldness, as always, so now also Christ shall be magnified in my body, whether it be by life, or by death. For to me to live is Christ, and to die is gain' (Phil. 1:20–21). That was Paul's genius: that the Lord Jesus would be magnified in his body.

Flowers, trees and birds, they are not the embodiment of the word. They just reflect the glory of creation. They know nothing of redemption. The most brilliant scholars in the world, with the highest IQs, the highest levels of education, still can't destroy their own lust. But the crown of our redemption in this life is that Christ is manifested in our bodies. A non-Christian cannot be like Jesus. This is our task: to be like Jesus. However, that is a process. The words James uses to say, 'be ye doers' really mean 'become doers'. The Greek word is *genesthe*: 'become'. James tells us to become like Jesus.

We are told to be hearers as though the whole thing was in our hands. God gives the big things. He brings about our new birth by his own will. We do the little things. We prove that we have life and dignify our regenerate state. There's a sense in which we have only begun to live the Christian life when we are at the point where we become hearers. There's a sense also in which we've only begun when we qualify to become doers. For it is the creation of God's word in us that gave us new life. God did that of his own will, but we must receive this engrafted word with meekness, having laid aside all moral filth and evil temperament.

What we have, then, is the opportunity to prove the creative possibility under the redemptive hand of God. But, as James recognizes, this takes a bit of time, it is a process. We can see the wisdom of the way James' mind has been working all along. How did he start this epistle? 'Count it all joy when you fall into divers trials.' We actually become doers of the word by suffering. But we don't qualify for real suffering until we resist temptation. I call resisting temptation, suffering. And so it may seem.

I must tell you, you aren't truly a partaker of the divine nature until you have escaped the corruption that is in the world through lust. Until then you are not a true follower of Jesus. We are told that Jesus was tempted at all points 'like as we are, yet without sin' (Heb. 4:15) but that he was a man of suffering. We are commanded to be like Jesus.

One of the most extraordinary verses in the Bible is Hebrews 5:8. 'Though he were a Son, yet learned he obedience by the things which he suffered.' Or as we see in Hebrews 2:10, 'It became him, for whom are all things, and by whom are all things, in bringing many sons unto glory, to make the captain of their salvation perfect through sufferings.' The combination of becoming and suffering are pulled together in one process, that we may become 'doers of the word', the living embodiment of all that the word of God is.

But what is this suffering? Is it emotional or economic? Is it the frustration of our goals? It can be any of these. But the essence of this suffering is the continual reminder that we are not our own. We are bought with a price. Even Jesus said, 'I have not come to do mine own will but the will of him who sent me' (Jn. 6:38). Later he turned to his disciples and said, 'As my Father hath sent me, even so send I you' (Jn. 20:21). This is the essence of Christian liberty. 'For, brethren, ye have been called unto liberty; only use not liberty for an occasion to the flesh, but by love serve one another' (Gal. 5:13). For 'the Son of man came not to be ministered unto, but to minister' (Mt. 20:28). This ought to give you a hint as to what the great saints of the ages were put through to become what they were. Do you ever read the biography of a great saint and think, 'I'd like to be like that.' They didn't just get that way. They suffered. Suffering is key to true greatness in living the Christian life.

Three Kinds of Christians

Let's analyze where we are now. James has shown that there are in fact three kinds of Christians. First, there are those who flirt with the world, with temptation, who know no joy or resisting of the world, the flesh and the devil. Billy Sunday used to say that so many Christians fall into sin because they treat temptation like strawberry shortcake rather than a rattlesnake. Second, there are those Christians who succeed in resisting the flesh. They reach the point of receiving the engrafted word, but are hearers only. Third are those Christians who are doers of the word.

You can probably see what I'm thinking here. What if all of us were doers of the word and not unlike the greatest saints in history? If you think you can remain a second-class Christian James says you deceive yourself. 'But be ye doers of the word, and not hearers only, deceiving your own selves.' The Greek is *paralogizomenoi*. It means 'to misreckon', 'to miscalculate', 'to be deceived'.

What a pity if we just miss the honour that comes from God by thinking that being a hearer is as near to greatness as we will ever get. What a pity if you become a hearer of the word and don't move on, deluding yourself that that's all you can ever manage. This same Greek word is used in Colossians 2:4 of being deluded by false reasoning. Its root is *logizomai*, which has two meanings. One is 'intentionally to misreckon' or 'to cheat' in any way. And the other is 'to misinfer', 'to draw a wrong conclusion without any evil intent'. What James would have us understand in choosing this word, is that if you are a hearer only but not a doer, you are doing two things.

Deceiving Ourselves

First, you are missing God's will by coming to a false conclusion at this stage in your Christian life. Let's assume for a moment that all of us have become hearers of the word. We have received with meekness the engrafted word. We know something of communication with God and fellowship in the Spirit, a sense of his presence and guidance, the joy of hearing him speak to us. This is good. But when you reach this stage you have a new kind of temptation.

The temptation is once more to draw a wrong conclusion. We saw the temptation to say, 'When I'm tempted I'm being tempted of God.' You've passed that, but the temptation now is to conclude that you have made all the progress necessary. After all, you feel God's presence and are turning your back on the world, you come to church and God speaks to you.

The new kind of temptation is to think that hearing the voice of the Spirit is enough. You may even say, 'Well, I never thought I'd get this far. It's wonderful to know how much I've grown.' But to think that this is God's best for you is a false conclusion.

Second, James uses this word to show that if you're concluding this way then you are deceiving yourself. It is one thing to conclude wrongly, quite another to suffer for it. James is saying that we are the losers if we conclude wrongly.

But not only do we lose, everybody loses. For what good is our Christianity if we are mere moral examples to the world? Jesus came 'not to be ministered unto, but to minister'. When we are at the level of being hearers only we are still being ministered unto. Our own impoverishment is the inevitable consequence, an unhealthy introspection that becomes counterproductive for others and for ourselves.

If there's anything that the Bible teaches it is this: that God rewards obedience. 'Them that honour me I will honour' (1 Sam. 2:30). Being a doer is to learn the lesson that Isaiah sought to teach Israel hundreds of years before Christ. God wants us 'to loose the bands of wickedness, to undo the heavy burdens, and to let the oppressed go free, and that ye break every yoke' (Isa. 58:6). God wants us to be going about emancipating others, living for others, serving one another by love. What God has in mind for us, says Isaiah, 'Is it not to deal thy bread to the hungry, and that thou bring the poor that are cast out to thy house? when thou seest the naked, that thou cover him; and that thou hide not thyself from thine own flesh?' (Isa. 58:7).

The consequence of being a hearer and not a doer is that God may choose not to hear us. We're inferring what comes by being a doer. 'Wherefore have we fasted, say they, and thou seest not? wherefore have we afflicted our soul, and thou takest no knowledge?' (Isa. 58:3). It could be that what was once working for you and providing a great sense of the presence of God isn't working now. But you haven't done anything different. What has happened? You recall a time when God was so real when you prayed and read his word. But now it isn't quite the same. Isaiah's message was: you are fasting, you are praying, you are afflicting your soul and God is taking no notice. If God doesn't hear us it follows that we are not going to hear him. It doesn't mean that we are back to square one like the backslider. We have undergone an arrested development at the point of sinning and are hearers only. We have deceived ourselves.

This relates to large numbers of Christians in a rather painful way. They pray for revival, but it doesn't come because they are not doers. They spend their time praying. They prefer to be ministered unto. James has a rather humorous illustration of what such deceived Christians are like. They're 'like the man who looks at his face in a mirror and, after looking at himself, goes away and immediately forgets what he looks like' (NIV). In other words, they get deluded with their own pious progress. They proceed no further than admiring themselves all the time.

The Folly of Introspection

This shows the folly of endless introspection. It shows the vanity of spiritual pride. It points to the possibility of spiritual paralysis, soaking in the word like a sponge but keeping it to oneself. It's like being a miser. That's the way so many of us are. We gaze at ourselves in the mirror – our own religious admiration society. It seems never to enter our minds to give ourselves to others.

James, not a man given to idle comment, repeats himself. 'For if any be a hearer of the word, and not a doer . . .' In case you missed it he says it again. I have a deep-seated fear that this is one of the things that has given Christianity a bad name. For the world has the impression – an impression given by most Christians – that Christianity is nothing but morality. Outward appearance is all that's important, like those who constantly look in the mirror.

What happens to the person who miscalculates God's will by being a hearer only, who looks in the mirror all the time? They may not like what they see. We keep examining our hearts. We think eventually we are Hgoing to understand ourselves by looking at ourselves. But it doesn't change our appearance or our behaviour. Still, we can keep on looking. 'O Lord, pour out your Spirit upon us. Show us ourselves. Convict us of sin' we pray, and we never change.

This is the endless introspection of so much Christian piety. We keep on examining ourselves, feeling our spiritual pulses, going back and getting a thermometer, shaking it down – maybe we didn't get it right last time – sticking it in our mouths, seeing whether we're really normal. No, we don't ever change. Why? Because looking at ourselves won't change us. We fancy that we are after our hearts, but it's really the face we're after. This is little different from the Pharisaical piety that Jesus upbraided.

So when the world steps inside the church today, what does it see? It sees Christians looking into mirrors, primping and praying, Christians constantly wanting to be better by being ministered unto. The modern church is like the inside of a hairdresser's shop in which everyone is comfortably seated, being waited upon, trying to have their appearance improved. Are we like that? James says, 'Move on. If you are a hearer only you deceive yourself.'

Until we are doers we make no impact on the world at all: looking at our faces, primping and praying, being ministered unto while the world is going to hell. If only we all could learn the lesson as Isaiah put it: 'If thou draw out thy soul to the hungry, and satisfy the afflicted soul; then shall thy light rise in obscurity, and thy darkness be as the noonday ... and they that shall be of thee shall build the old waste places: thou shalt raise up the foundations of many generations; and thou shalt be called, The repairer of the breach, The restorer of paths to dwell in' (Isa. 58:10, 12).

What happens to those who are doers? They win. Everybody wins. They affect the world. And if that's you, 'The LORD shall guide thee continually, and satisfy thy soul in drought, and make fat thy bones: and thou shalt be like a watered garden, and like a spring of water, whose waters fail not' (Isa. 58:11).

17

The Law of Liberty

James 1:25

If we look into the mirror of introspection we will never change. But if we look into the mirror of the 'law of liberty' we will see what we are like in the eyes of God. It is that which shows us that we are emancipated.

Applying the Word

James desires that we might learn to apply the word. He assumes now that we have indeed with meekness received 'the engrafted word'. Application is the small thing that we must do. God did the big things. The danger is that we expect God to do everything. We thank God for saving us, but want him to do everything else as well when he is saying to us, 'Get on with it.' James calls this application 'being a doer of the word'. It is being followers of Jesus.

Jesus, though he did not sin, did suffer. James has called us to a life of not sinning, not one that is exempt from suffering. Peter said, 'He that hath suffered in the flesh hath ceased from sin' (1 Pet. 4:1). This is the burden of the New Testament. It is not a sinless perfectionism but it is a life that is clean. Being doers of the word presupposes that we have been made partakers of Christ's suffering.

A New Temptation

However, once we have begun to be followers of Jesus in this way we risk a particular kind of temptation, the proneness to look at ourselves rather uncritically. To imagine that all we are doing is Spirit led. The devil wants to abort all following of Jesus, to prevent us becoming doers of the word. How? By intelligently, craftily playing on our weakness and pride. He points you to your progress up to now, and says, 'This is what you wanted. Quit while you're ahead.' Thinking like that is the easiest thing in the world to do. It's easy to just be a hearer.

James works overtime to warn us that being a hearer only and not a doer is to make another mistake. What was the first mistake? To think that God is the author of evil. James realizes that if we have come this far we have abandoned that kind of thinking. But he knows that that does not make us invulnerable to other mistakes, like thinking that being a hearer only is sufficient. So James takes us to the mirror and the ridiculous man who cannot recall his own likeness.

When you look in the mirror you see yourself, warts and all. There's an analogy here with being in church. You hear the word of God and get convicted. God has a way of applying the word so that you think you're the only one it is meant for. You say, 'I must be different from now on. I will never be the same again.' Yet once you're outside the church door you forget all about it until the next time you're in church. Again God speaks and you think, 'I must change.' You are convicted and you're smitten. You go outside, go home and you forget all about it.

Deafness Sets In

The sad thing is that eventually you become immune to preaching. You no longer feel conviction. Instead, you begin to excuse yourself or find fault. You wonder why God is not speaking to you. You laid aside evil disposition that you might receive the Spirit. Then you were enjoying it so much that you just wanted to be ministered unto indefinitely. But you didn't apply the word. The result is that deafness comes in after all. You unconsciously suffer an arrested development at the point of being a hearer of the word only.

I'm speaking to an awful lot of evangelicals. Do you know the world's impression of evangelical Christianity? It is that we are nothing but pious people with morals. Looking into the mirror all the time, hearing preaching all the time and being ministered unto all the time results in our becoming dull within. You forget what you really are. What once bothered you doesn't any more. What used to convict you doesn't any more. Places that you would once not even go near you now go into.

A Different Mirror

James says, 'Stop gazing into the mirror and set your sight in a different direction. Look into a different mirror.' James directs our gaze into what he calls 'the perfect law of liberty'. This is an expression you might have thought had come right out of a Pauline epistle. Indeed, Paul did put it like this when he said, 'There is therefore now no condemnation to them which are in Christ Jesus ... For the law of the Spirit of life in Christ Jesus hath made me free from the law of sin and death' (Rom. 8:1, 2). Again Paul said, 'To them that are without law, as without law, (being not without law to God, but under the law to Christ)' (1 Cor. 9:21). And again, 'Bear ye one another's burdens, and so fulfil the law of Christ' (Gal. 6:2).

The term 'law' is not irrelevant for the Christian life. Which law? The law of Christ. The law of the Spirit. The interesting thing is that every time the term 'law' is used with reference to the new covenant it is what we are set free from and what we are set free to do. To be and to do. For the nature of Christian liberty is that we've been emancipated from something but also set free for something. James calls it 'the perfect law of liberty'. Why call it liberty? It is because of what regeneration does for us. We are emancipated from sin that we might explore the unlimited creative possibilities under God's redemptive hand. No longer are we in bondage, dead, lame or immobile. We are set free: free to be ourselves and to show what we really are.

Remaining seated in front of the mirror of introspection leads to a new kind of bondage. A different kind of immorality sets in. It is called 'the spirit of fear'. And yet we are told, 'God hath not given us the spirit of fear; but of power, and of love, and of a sound mind' (2 Tim. 1:7). The devil calls attention to every blemish that we see when looking into this mirror in order to make us think that we need a little more primping and praying, a little more attention before we're ready.

The easiest thing in the world is to gaze at the mirror of introspection. That, James tells us, is a pitfall in the Christian life. There is a difference between introspection and self-examination. Introspection is entirely subjective and egocentric. It breeds conceit and complacency. Self-examination, on the other hand, is objective and Christ-centred and it breeds hope and motivation. Looking into the mirror of introspection leaves us unchanged, useless and immobile. James says, 'Get away from looking into that mirror and look into this mirror.' As Paul put it: the mirror of seeing 'in a glass the glory of the Lord' whereby we 'are changed into the same image from glory to glory, even as by the Spirit of the Lord' (2 Cor. 3:18). James wants us to look at this perfect law of liberty.

To look into the law of liberty is to see what God has done for us and what we have been set free to do. The Greek word translated 'doer' can also mean 'maker'. As a matter of fact, it comes from a word that means 'to create'. This word becomes a tool in our hands, a word of power. It's the word, we recall, that was able to save our souls and can save others. Jesus gave the promise that through this word and by the Spirit 'greater works than these shall he do; because I go unto my Father' (Jn. 14:12). We are set free to be created with God's infallible word. The more that we look at this law of liberty the more we will see that it is perfect freedom. The Greek is *parakupsas*, meaning 'looking intently' into the law of liberty.

James wants you to throw away that mirror of introspection and look intently into the law of liberty. It says, 'You're free. You're okay. God's grace has made you that way.' James says we should look steadfastly into that law of liberty because it never condemns. It will never say, 'Well, you aren't quite ready yet. Don't look at me. Go back to the other mirror and get right.' James says, 'Look into this law of liberty and you will know straight away that you are wanted and accepted.' For this law of liberty is Christ.

If you look into the old Mosaic law what do you see? Justice, condemnation, wrath, every blemish, every sin, every shortcoming. The old covenant, the Mosaic law, is a merciless instrument of despair. It makes us cry out as Paul did, 'Who shall deliver me from the body of this death?' (Rom. 7:24). But that's not the mirror James tells us to use.

You may feel grossly inadequate. How could you ever be a doer of the word? You are just not ready yet. But James says, 'Look into that law of liberty. It says to you, "You're okay, I have redeemed you. Fear not. You are my child. Now get on with it. Be a doer of the word."' You may say, 'Very well. It may have been all right to do this once, when I first became a Christian. But surely not again and again?' James says, 'Whoso looketh into the perfect law of liberty, and continueth therein . . .' This law of liberty is not to be looked at only once but it is the very source of our strength. We never outgrow it. We never move beyond it, much less kiss it goodbye. We live by it. We dwell in it. And we become the very embodiment of it.

It must never enter our minds that we are not accepted by God. For if you look into the mirror of introspection you will always wonder. I can tell you this from pastoral experience: those who have the problem of not knowing whether they really are Christians are the ones who keep looking at themselves. James says, 'Stop it. Look to Christ. There you know you are accepted.' By the way, this is a part of doing. For doing is applying. Doing is seeing what the gospel is and saying, 'Yes, I believe it. God's word is true. I am his child.' Do you think you are going to get assurance by just listening all the time, having your soul fed and becoming introspective, being ministered unto? A part of doing is to believe God and believe what he has said. We know that we are loved with an everlasting love.

'However,' says James, 'while doing all this you must not become a forgetful hearer.' This is obviously a possibility or he wouldn't mention it. James' point is: accept your own forgiveness, quit dwelling upon your blemishes and get on with it. The devil will draw attention to the fact that everybody knows you and knows your weaknesses. But if God says, 'Look at me and be saved and get on with it', that's sufficient. It doesn't matter what people think. After all, do you want the honour that comes from God or are you wanting to be accepted by others? 'Who shall lay anything to the charge of God's elect? … Who is he that condemneth us? It is Christ that died, yea rather, that is risen again, who is even at the right hand of God' (Rom. 8:33–34).

One of the Devil's Greatest Lies

One of the greatest lies that the devil has perpetrated in the Christian church is that you are not ready to be a doer until you are perfect. The devil will say, 'You are not quite ready. You will be, but not quite yet.' And ten years later you will be in the same situation. The extraordinary thing about the apostle Paul is that right after he received his sight and was baptized, we are told, 'he was strengthened … And straightway he preached Christ in the synagogues, that he is the Son of God' (Acts 9:19, 20). Saul of Tarsus wasn't exactly the kind of man that met with everybody's approval, but he went doing anyway.

The fact is, God tells us we're okay. He always says 'Yes' when we look to him. In Jesus Christ the promises are yea and amen (2 Cor. 1:20). If God could use a Saul of Tarsus or a Peter or a Jonah, then God can use anybody. We must gaze in this mirror of liberty, continue in it and yet not be forgetful.

Becoming a Doer

We see in verse 25 a subtle shift of words, more so in the English than in the Greek. James has been talking about being a hearer of the word and a doer of the word. Now he says 'a doer of the *work*'. It is not a misprint, the

Greek words are quite different: *logos* is 'word', *ergon* is 'work'. James is saying that being a doer of the word is a verbal witness. But now, looking into this law of liberty, we become a doer of work. It is at a non-verbal level that we do the work with our bodies, with our hands. We become what Jesus was when he was on earth – we are to be little Jesuses.

The word of truth became the engrafted word. And now the doer of the word becomes a doer of work. For that which regenerated us became implanted in us and it is putting the word into non-verbal practice. James doesn't tell us at this stage what he has in mind and what he means by work. Nor does he need to.

I might say that when he does become more specific (v. 27) one should not take what he says in a mechanical, legalistic or restricted sense. James' burden is that we get our eyes off ourselves, off our personal piety and our own concerns, and that immediately following on the call to liberty is a call to serve. As Paul put it to the Galatians, 'Ye have been called unto liberty; only use not liberty for an occasion to the flesh, but by love serve one another' (Gal. 5:13).

What is this work? It is applying what we know even if we don't feel like it. What makes work work is that we resist it. Many of us simply want to be led by the Spirit. It's not work then, is it? Being led is not work. What makes work work is that you do it. You don't have to pray about it. Do you pray about whether you are going to get up and go to your job tomorrow? No, you just do it. You may feel led not to go but you go anyway. Should you take the work of God less seriously?

You don't pray about some things, you do them. If God is speaking to you today don't say, 'Lord, help me to do it', because if you start praying that then you will say, 'Lord, you didn't help me to do it. I guess I just wasn't supposed to.' Later on James says, 'To him that knoweth to do good, and doeth it not, to him it is sin' (4:17). The world is not interested in our morality or our piety or how much we feel thrilled by what we heard on a Sunday morning. The world wants to see something in us, in our bodies. Christianity is not just verbal, it's what we do, what we are.

James says, 'This man shall be blessed in his deed.' God didn't have to tell us we'd be blessed but he does. And, best of all, he keeps his word. How blessed? The blessing is greater than anything that can be said about it!

I can tell you this: although you may make another person happy by bringing cheer, help, aid and hope to them and you know that person is happy because of what you do, the truth is, you must be candid and say that you were the happiest. It did more for you than for them. You can't outgive the Lord and you can't outwork God. Do it and you'll be blessed.

I hope I have left you without excuse. But what is more important is that we leave the world without excuse, that they see more than just outward piety. And when they come into church they see more than those who are just being ministered unto. They see faces that they've seen before and they know that here are those who take their religion seriously by applying it once they get outside the door. Don't pray about it, do it.

18

Pure Religion

James 1:26–27

We Are Set Free to be Like Jesus

Since the law of liberty sets us free to be ourselves, we are to be like Jesus who was both the verbal and nonverbal witness of God. He went about doing good. We are in Christ. That is our justification. But Christ is in us. That is our sanctification.

James' terminology is 'being a doer'. Because of the common default of being hearers only, James says, 'If any man among you seem to be religious . . .' Why did he say this? Because those who primp and pray in front of a mirror think they are being religious. The Greek *threskos*, which is translated 'religious', means 'pious'. It is like those in Isaiah 58 who prayed, fasted, afflicted their souls, but took time to realize that God was not taking any notice.' James' point is that people like that only appear to be religious.

It is at this point that James once more brings up the matter of the tongue. He wants to make it absolutely clear that it is what you don't say that counts as much as what you do say. This being a verbal witness, a doer of the word, consists not only in applying the word of God to ourselves but in demonstrating that we have applied the word in such a manner that we are able to control our tongues. James is really more concerned about controlling our tongues than using them. Being a doer of the word requires the bridling of our tongues. However important gossiping the gospel may be, James puts equal if not more priority in being able to control your tongue.

Three Dangers

You may wonder why it is that James has so much to say about the tongue. (There's much more in chapter 3.) He is concerned about three dangers.

- The danger of jumping to a false conclusion. We saw this earlier. 'Let no man say when he is tempted, I am tempted of God.'
- The danger of grieving the Spirit by speaking without thinking. James said, 'The wrath of man worketh not the righteousness of God.' There is a sense in which we don't really grieve the Spirit until we open our mouths.
- The danger of our being a poor public witness. What James doesn't want is hypocritical piety. We all know about people who never miss church, know their Bible, can think theologically and they love to sing hymns, but lose their tempers at the drop of a hat. They're the ones who show that all that they believe hasn't affected the way they live. They're the last person to go to if you have problems.

James says three things about such people in this verse. First, they only seem to be religious, and making that impression is what they really care about. They are like those Jesus described in Matthew 6. When they gave alms they wanted everybody to know about it. Jesus said, 'All right. Everybody knows about it. That is their reward.' They are not going to get a reward from God but that doesn't bother them, they're concerned with what people think. James says a person like that only seems to be religious. All you have to do to make them happy is to tell them how spiritual they are, how godly.

The second thing James tells us about such people is that they have only succeeded in deceiving their own hearts. Their inability to control their tongues, or to receive God's honour, their anxious determination to let you know how religious they are: it all points to this. According to James it is the tongue that exposes the heart. Jesus said it first: 'Out of the abundance of the heart, the mouth speaketh' (Mt. 12:34). The grace to control your tongue shows that you are applying the word and are not a hearer only, that religion has reached your heart and is affecting the way you are living. 'Otherwise,' says James – and this is his third point – 'that person's religion is vain. Useless. Futile.' James didn't say, 'A person like that is not a Christian.' No, it's not a question of salvation. This is simply James' description of hypocritical religion.

Pure Religion

So far, James has been negative. He moves to the positive with this immortal statement – possibly the best known of the whole epistle – 'Pure religion and undefiled before God and the Father is this, To visit the fatherless and widows in their affliction, and to keep himself unspotted from the world.' That is James' definition of pure religion. Does that match what you would have said? He says not 'religion' but 'pure religion'.

Notice what James has done in this magnificent statement. He has killed two birds with one stone. In one statement he shows us that pure religion is being a doer of the work and a doer of the word. What is doing the work? Visiting. What is being a doer of the word? Keeping oneself unspotted from the world. With two adjectives James shows us two things about religion. One side he calls 'pure', the other 'unstained'. They're synonymous terms but he uses them to show that he's dealing with two things now. Being a doer not only of the word but a doer of the work as well.

It's very important to remember that in this verse James has not abandoned the notion of personal piety. It's simply that he wants us to be faithful in our witness and keep ourselves unspotted from the world. Therefore it's not an *either or*, it is a *both and*. If we are pious in abandoning worldliness but we are not faithful in caring for the widow and the orphan then our religion is not pure religion. On the other hand, if we are faithful in caring for the widow and the orphan but we abandon godliness and personal piety then it is not pure religion.

James wouldn't be very popular today. Professing Christians today generally prefer to make doing the work or the word an 'either or' proposition. For example, let's take the 'social gospel'. Those who uphold the social gospel love the first part of this verse. They even extend it to include issues of race, poverty and wealth. But they also often scoff at godliness, personal morality and piety. It doesn't seem to bother them one bit that they are not doers of the word. They want only to be doers of the work. They are not interested in laying aside moral filth to receive the engrafted word. They are not interested in doctrine. They justify their existence by their so-called works. They often pay no attention at all to the matter of salvation.

This is the folly of the ecumenical movement. They make doing the work the lowest common denominator for the basis of unity but forget the word: what God says to be and do, what God says about himself and his Son, about salvation and the church. Those who emphasize the doing of the work need to remember that James says, 'and to keep himself unspotted from the world'.

Most of us emphasize orthodoxy, sound doctrine and separation from the world. But we are weak when faced with non-verbal witness. In James' progression of thought there are three stages: being a hearer, then a doer of the word and then a doer of the work. If there is a temptation to stop at the point of hearing and not being a doer of the word there is also a temptation to stop at being a doer of the word and not being a doer of the work. There can be an arrested development at that point too.

How We Begin to be Like Jesus

You may want to ask, 'What on earth does visiting orphans or widows have to do with demonstrating God's grace?' It shows that we are beginning to be like Jesus. That we care about those who can't possibly do us any good. Have you ever thought about whether Jesus was selective with those people he healed, or cast demons out of? Do you think Jesus healed in Capernaum because it was a nice suburb with lots of middle-class families? He didn't heal the sick of any one class. Jesus was no respecter of persons. He did what he could for everybody who crossed his path.

When James mentions widows and orphans he uses them as illustrations to show those whose physical or material circumstances were without any hope or promise. A widow has no husband to support her or her children. Orphans have no parents or means of support at all. They can't help themselves or do us any good.

James' choice of vocabulary here is interesting and important. The Greek means not simply 'to pay a token visit' but 'to care for by inspecting', 'to get to the bottom of things'. You may say, 'I visit every six months, and everybody feels a little better.' Well, that's mechanical. You'd be like a Baptist church in Alabama that has one black member so they can say they are integrated. James won't let you off with that. This is the word used, for example, in Acts 15:36, 'And some days after Paul said unto Barnabas, Let us go again and visit our brethren in every city where we have preached the word of the Lord, and see how they do.' It's the word used in Hebrews 12:14–15, 'Follow peace with all men, and holiness, without which no man shall see the Lord: looking diligently'. It's the word used in Acts 7:22–23 when Stephen said, 'Moses was learned in all the wisdom of the Egyptians, and was mighty in words and in deeds. And when he was full forty years old, it came into his heart to visit his brethren the children of Israel.' Do you think Moses just went to say, 'Hi there'? No. Moses identified with his brethren, and he did for them what they couldn't do. He went to Pharaoh and said, 'Let my people go.' That's the way Moses visited. And that's what James means. Find out what is going on, whether there is any need. Get to the bottom of the matter.

James leaves us no room for mechanical, cost-free visiting. What is the golden rule? 'Do unto others as you would have them do unto you.' You find out what's going on as you would like somebody to find out about you if you were hurting. James means us to care for people. That may or may not cost us materially, but I'm sure it won't do to just put in 5 pence or £5 for the benevolent fund. James will not let us avoid a direct and personal involvement. There's no hint here that you ought to look for the one who might be worthy of your help. You don't say, 'Look there's potential there. We'll help that person.' There's not the slightest hint that you only do it for the so-called spiritual. When you do help you don't go to scold or moralize. Moses went to help the children of Israel because nobody else could.

What about matters of race and poverty? With regard to poverty you do what you can. When it comes to race I'm afraid we are left without excuse. If there's any non-Anglo Saxon, whether Pakistani, Indian, black or oriental, and you show priority to the Anglo Saxon you've sinned before God and are without excuse. You can grieve the Holy Spirit by withholding care and love from those whose culture or race is not your own. Who knows what Christianity might do for Moslems in Britain if we began to take James' word seriously?

Keeping Yourself Unspotted From the World

What does 'and to keep himself unspotted from the world' mean? When James says 'keep himself', it means 'guard yourself'. You don't say, 'I just couldn't help it.' Jesus said, 'Watch and pray, that ye enter not into temptation' (Mt. 26:41). That means that you apply will-power as though there were no Holy Spirit to help you. You 'make not provision for the flesh, to fulfill the lusts thereof' (Rom. 13:14).

James has just shown us that we are to be doers of the work. But now he says, 'Keep yourself unspotted.' We are back to 'pure religion'. It's the two things combined in one. As Jesus said to the Pharisees, 'Woe unto you, Pharisees! for ye tithe mint and rue and all manner of herbs, and pass over judgment and the love of God: these ought ye to have done, and not to leave the other undone' (Lk. 11:42). It's not a matter of deciding what we are going to do to feel religious or pious. Having been doers of the work we keep ourselves unspotted. As Isaiah put it: 'Here's the fast I've chosen: to give your soul to the one who is oppressed and remember your own flesh. Care for those who are in need and keep yourself guard yourself – 'unstained' (Isa. 58:6). This means that we are in the world, not of it. It's an old cliché, but it's true. You're in it but not of it when the charm of the world makes no impression at all on your thinking processes, no dent upon your character, your conduct, your motivation to live for God and exhibit godliness. It's when the world does not divert your affections from God, and doesn't squeeze you into its mould.

We remember Jude's word about hating 'the garment spotted by the flesh' (v. 23). We are not to pitch our tents near Sodom, to impute to ourselves more strength than we have. It is no sign of strength when you say, 'I can get right next to the world and it doesn't bother me one bit.' Greater strength is when you know what you are like and flee temptation. Don't fancy yourself to be the exception and see how close to the world you can get. Because, my friend, to the extent that the world gets its grip on us we cease to be hearers of the word, much less doers.

When James says, 'Keep yourself unspotted from the world', he's simply affirming what he's already said in verse 21, that we put aside all moral filth and evil disposition. Find out who is hurting, be there and keep yourself unspotted from the world. It's not *either or*, it is *both and*. This is 'pure religion'. Doing of the word, doing of the work, controlling yourself but maintaining demonstrable non-verbal witness. That's 'pure religion'.

Do we want this? You might want to say, 'Wait a minute. Surely what James is saying here is just an optional extra. Surely he's not serious?' Let me tell you how serious James is. This is something that he says you carry out before God. 'Pure religion and undefiled before God and the Father is this.' That is why it matters. The Pharisees didn't care about that. They just wanted people to think they were all right.

We have been grafted into the family by 'the word of truth'. We have a heavenly Father who cares for us, who supplies our need. Sometimes God uses another person to do that. He doesn't send an angel with white glistening wings to sit beside you and talk. No, it's another person who comes and says what you need. 'All right', says James, 'your heavenly Father is taking care of you in that way. It's now time for you to start doing it for somebody else.' Do this and guard yourself from the stain of the world. This isn't just religion, this is 'pure religion'.

A friend of mine used to say, 'One of these days somebody is going to come along, pick up the Bible, read it and believe it, and put the rest of us to shame.' I'm talking about a kind of religion that is exceedingly rare. Let's not wait for anybody else to come along. Let's pick up our Bibles, read them, believe them, and put the world to shame by showing we are different. It is something we do before God, and that matters.

19

Be No Respecter of Persons

James 2:1–4

It is all very well to profess openly to God how willing we are to serve him. But we don't really know how willing we are until we face the details that are involved in living the Christian life. James comes to the details now. And they can be most painful. So practical is this epistle that James even applies his own words, and therefore leaves us without excuse.

Pure religion is to care for the widows and the orphans as well as to keep ourselves unspotted from the world. Now James applies this statement with yet another illustration of what he means. 'My brethren, have not the faith of our Lord Jesus Christ, the Lord of glory, with respect of persons.' This phrase 'respect of persons' conveys a most astonishing truth that never ceased to amaze the Jewish Christians of the early Church because it was a truth they thought they understood. They didn't. But when they did understand it they never got away from it.

An Astonishing Truth

God is no respecter of persons. This verse is nothing new. It's an old truth. For example, 'For the LORD your God is God of gods, and LORD of lords, a great God, a mighty, and a terrible, which regardeth not persons, nor taketh reward' (Deut. 10:17). Again, 'Wherefore now let the fear of the LORD be upon you; take heed and do it: for there is no iniquity with the LORD our God, nor respect of persons, nor taking of gifts' (2 Chron. 19:7). Even one of Job's friends, Elihu, felt a need to get this over to Job: 'How much less to him that accepteth not the persons of princes, nor regardeth the rich more than the poor? for they all are the work of his hands' (Job 34:19). It is a fundamental teaching of the Bible that we hear all the time and yet don't understand.

Here is a word that Peter with his tradition ought to have known backwards and forwards before he ever went to the house of Cornelius. Yet we are told that when Cornelius was talking to him and demonstrated how God had visited him and had him send for Peter, Peter saw something for the first time. He said, 'Of a truth I perceive that God is no respecter of persons' (Acts 10:34). When the breakthrough does come there's a sense of awe and amazement but sometimes a little disappointment that it means what it says. We often delay grasping the truth simply because we don't want to believe what it says. It is so obvious. And we say, 'Well, it can't mean that.' Although this is a fundamental truth of the Bible, Peter was given an extraordinary type of preparation that he might understand it right. This shows the kindness and patience of God.

Why is it that it takes us time to grasp the most simple of statements? The answer is that years of tradition build up an immunity to the plain statements of Scripture. You remember how Paul put it to the Corinthians: 'But I fear, lest by any means, as the serpent beguiled Eve through his subtlety, so your minds should be corrupted from the simplicity that is in Christ' (2 Cor. 11:3). The problem is that our projections get in the way. The new Christian just picks up the Bible, reads it, believes it and puts the rest of us to shame. So many of us have reached so far, then have an arrested development and never move on. James and Peter both had to learn how true this is.

James' First Reference to Jesus

It is not surprising that both James and Peter would incorporate this truth in their own epistles. However James broadens the meaning of having no respect of persons to include every level imaginable, not restricting it to issues of racial or national prejudice. And he brings in this truth now with reference to the faith of Jesus. 'Have not the faith of our Lord Jesus Christ, the Lord of glory, with respect of persons.' This is the first reference to Jesus in James' epistle. It's also the last, at least explicitly. James refers to Jesus with mention of two things: the *faith* of Jesus and the *character* of Jesus (that he is the Lord of glory).

Why this expression: 'the faith of Jesus'? This is something that, unfortunately, so many contemporary versions of the Bible prefer to interpret rather than translate. The Greek is explicit that it is 'the faith of our Lord Jesus Christ'. This is a phrase Paul uses with regard to our justification. How does James use it? We have been seeing right along that James wants us to be like Jesus, but until now he has not said so explicitly. It is not until we have abandoned sin that we are really followers of Jesus, because Jesus never sinned. 'Now,' says James, 'we are ready, if we have abandoned our sinning, to follow Jesus.'

Two Kinds of Faith

In the New Testament there are two kinds of faith: saving faith and experimental faith. Saving faith is that which sinful humanity needs in order to have assurance of eternal life. Experimental faith is the application of faith; it is volitional, our wills are involved. It is important, not to prove that we are Christians – saving faith persuades our hearts of that – but because it is the faith that acts. This is what Hebrews chapter 11 is all about. Jesus had faith, but not saving faith. There is no mention of Jesus ever repenting because Jesus never sinned. However Jesus did believe. Hebrews 2:13 tells us that.

Again and again the New Testament tells us that Jesus was a man of perfect faith. That we have been given saving faith is proved by the fact that we are now in a position to imitate Jesus who went about doing good. He did things without respect of persons. Jesus did not do good to those who could do something for him. Love keeps no records. Jesus did what he did for people for their own sake.

James says, 'Have the faith of our Lord Jesus Christ ... without respect of persons.' Hold the faith. Paul uses this expression of the ground of our justification, James uses it as being the ground of our sanctification. With Paul it was our justification before God. With James it is our justification before others. Our Lord's perfect faith issues in our justification by faith. Nothing could be more incongruous than using his faith in a way he would not have done. Justification by faith, for example, cannot possibly lead to sin. In the same way the life of faith which our Lord lived before all, every class, every distinction, cannot be diverted for our own selfish ends. If justification leads to holiness, so sanctification shows itself in our being no respecters of persons.

The Lord of Glory

Notice how James describes our Lord Jesus Christ: 'the Lord of glory.' Jesus had total satisfaction with himself. He had no intrinsic need for extrinsic recognition, approval or glory. Our Lord wasn't impressed with another person's stature. Thus, whether standing before Herod or Pilate, the wealthiest in Judea or the poorest of the poor, Jesus gave as much time as anybody needed. James says, 'You be like that.'

Have not the faith of our Lord Jesus Christ with respect of persons because he is the Lord of glory. And if you have his faith then you are going to have total satisfaction within. Jesus found his satisfaction from doing his Father's will. He would say, 'For I do always those things that please him' (Jn. 8:29). That's all that mattered. This is why he could say to his disciples, 'How can ye believe, which receive honour one of another, and seek not the honour that cometh from God only?' (Jn. 5:44). 'Ye are they,' he said to the Pharisees, 'which justify yourselves before men ... that which is highly esteemed among men is abomination in the sight of God' (Lk. 16:15).

If we have the faith of our Lord Jesus Christ we will only want to please his Father – our Father – and want his glory, his approval. This means to have an intrinsic satisfaction that makes all earthly honour and recognition seem nothing. By the way, it is not likely that God will bless us until we are like this.

Judges of Evil Thoughts

The preparation for receiving this truth comes with a test. The test is how you treat those with human status who happen to come along to your services. The Greek is translated 'assembly', but it is obvious it is the synagogue. James is addressing Jewish Christians who were still going along to their synagogues, which is one of the evidences that this is a very early epistle, maybe as early as AD 40. They still went, for three reasons. First, they went if only to witness by claiming continuity with the Old Testament. They went to show they believed the Bible. Second, we know that they went to evangelize. Paul would go to the synagogue every Saturday because he knew that that's where the people would be to whom he could witness. Third, it could be that in some cases Christianity had completely taken over these Jewish places of worship.

James wants to show us how to treat all kinds of people who come in to our services. He uses as illustration an obviously rich person who comes in with rings of gold, wearing an expensive suit. You look at them and say, 'Wow! Are we glad to see you! You know you're going to like this place. Here's the best seat in the house. You're the type of person we've been waiting for. These other people around here are not what we like.

So good of you to come. Hope you feel welcome.' And then along comes a person who doesn't have any jewellery, who couldn't even afford to go to a church jumble sale. We look at them and say, 'Oh, it's you. Would you mind standing over there? Or if you must sit down, sit right back over here.'

James goes on to say that if you act like that, you've made a judgment based on outward appearance, a deliberate distinction. 'What is more,' says James, 'you have become judges of evil thoughts.' This phrase is best translated: 'You are like judges who are swayed by evil reasonings', and is the root of our word 'pornography'. It is the equivalent of turning the grace of God into lasciviousness. Justification by faith can never do that. If you make the faith of Jesus into something Jesus himself would never have done, it's hard to know which is worse: perverting the faith of Christ by which we are justified or perverting the faith by which we are to minister to other people. 'You've become like judges who are swayed by evil thoughts.'

The type of people who come into the congregation are not evil. James is not rebuking them at all. James takes for granted that all kinds of people from every stratum of society, with every type of personality, gift and career are to be expected. He neither condemns the people who come along, nor their appearance or the lifestyle which they represent. What is evil, where one goes wrong, says James, is our favouritism according to what they represent.

The Greek here means if you 'regard with partiality'. There is nothing intrinsically wrong with that word. For example, in Luke 1:48 it was used by the Virgin Mary who said, 'My soul doth magnify the Lord, and my spirit hath rejoiced in God my Saviour. For he hath' – and here's the same word – 'regarded the low estate of his handmaiden.' It's also used in Luke 9:38 when a man of the company cried out saying, 'Master, I beseech thee, look upon my son: for he is mine only child.' 'Show partiality to my son. Look upon him with favour.' The point is subtle but we need to see it. As well as these New Testament examples, this is a word used all the time by the Septuagint (the Greek translation of the Old Testament) to refer to God looking on people with favour. But when God does it, it is never in respect of what they represent or what their status is. He is being gracious or is showing mercy. There's nothing wrong with the word. The sin is treating people differently because of what appears to be their class or wealth.

God has looked favourably upon every one of us. 'By grace are ye saved through faith; and that not of yourselves: it is the gift of God: not of works, lest any man should boast' (Eph. 2:8–9). When the Bible says that

God is no respecter of persons it means that he never chooses or esteems on the basis of merit. So Paul could say that we've been chosen from before the foundation of the world 'not according to our works, but according to his own purpose and grace' (2 Tim. 1:9).

The burden of James is that it is unthinkable that we should negate God's grace, that having received it ourselves we could now pervert it when it comes to our disbursement of it. We are to be instruments of grace. We ourselves are being chosen not because of what we are or can become or because we represent anything to God. We don't know why he chose us. We may never know. We just know how his choice wasn't made on the basis of our works or anything that we could offer. We are objects of grace because somebody reached out, was indiscriminate. Somebody witnessed to them. Now it's come to us. Are we going to abort this continuity of God reaching some by witnessing to all? 'Nothing could be more unthinkable', said James. It is our responsibility to be indiscriminate towards those who come into our services.

Apparently in these synagogues there were choice seats. Everybody knew they were there and what they represented. We may not have choice seats in our churches but this is not a verse to be interpreted mechanically. Our danger is not where we seat certain people, but whether we welcome some and treat others with a benign neglect. This refers both to class distinction and to racial discrimination. As long as we delay coming to terms with this matter, God's blessing on us will be delayed.

A Divided Mind

There's one more thing. James raises a rhetorical question. He says, 'If you have respected people like this have you not become partial in yourselves?' This word means to be divided in your mind as a result of how you've acted. In chapter one he said, 'Let him ask in faith, nothing wavering ... A double minded man is unstable in all his ways' (vv. 6, 8). 'You have become partial in yourselves', really means that you 'become divided in your own minds'. Jesus used the same word in Matthew 21:21, 'If ye have faith, and doubt not . . .' It's also used by Paul: 'He that doubteth is damned if he eat' (Rom. 14:23). In other words, there must be a singleness of mind.

If you are showing respect of persons it backfires on you. You become divided in your thinking. The singleness of your mind and faith is split, shattered because you are trying to show a devotion to God on the one hand and giving in to a petty idea on the other. You can't have it both ways. James is touching upon a most profound principle. Treating people with partiality results in a divided mind, the inability to grasp what true wisdom is.

This division is not the warfare between flesh and spirit. It is more particular. It's the warfare of a mind so divided that we lose touch with what is good, the perfect will of God. Do you know what it's like as a Christian to be confused and unsettled, to lose touch with what is really right? 'Well then,' says James, 'a sure way to know that is to be partial.' You can't have it both ways. If you are going to serve God you must be one who has the faith of our Lord Jesus Christ.

You lose touch with the Spirit by showing partiality on the basis of outward appearance. When you do that you grieve the Holy Spirit from your own heart, though you may not be aware of it at the time. We have seen that you can grieve the Spirit by speaking without thinking. Here's another way – by being preoccupied with what others might do for us.

Leanness of Soul

The result of grieving the Spirit is a divided mind. By trying to endear ourselves to one we think might do something for us, we lose. What do we lose? Well, what do we gain? What do you gain if, let's say, you win over the person with the expensive suit and the gold ring? You get what Israel got. God 'gave them their request; but sent leanness into their soul' (Ps. 106:15). You are like Samson who did not know that the Spirit of God had departed from him (Jdg. 16:20).

Do you know what it is to succeed in life without the Spirit? Not a few Christians do. Even ministers of the gospel do, if they get to a high living or a good pulpit and take that to be evidence that God is with them. God may have had nothing at all to do with it, except at the level of common grace. Christians can take success to mean that God is with them and as a result they never bother to examine themselves. They are ruined and don't even know it.

Dr Lloyd-Jones once said, 'The worst thing that can happen to a man is to succeed before he's ready.' James wants us to be ready before we succeed. And the test is how we treat those who come into our assemblies. We must respect everyone indiscriminately. It does not follow that we do the reverse, treating the 'down and out' with great honour and snubbing those with social and economic status. Not only would that be contrived, but we would do the poor no favour at all because their attraction would be to us and not to the gospel. James' burden is that we refuse to win people at the level of nature but deal with all as souls who need the gospel.

James wants us to not be controlled by natural motivation. For if we become judges swayed by evil thoughts not only do we lose, the result being leanness of soul, but everybody loses. We send souls right on to hell by trying to win them over at a natural level. We do people the greatest honour, whether they are rich or poor, famous or unknown, Members of Parliament or lorry drivers, royalty or servants, when we treat them as they are before God: souls who will stand before their Maker and give an account of the way they have lived their lives.

If we have respect of persons, everybody loses. But if we are not respecters of persons we gain everything. First, we gain the honour that comes from God only – peace, joy and anointing of the Holy Spirit. Second, we gain the souls of God's elect because we give them the gospel, the only thing that can deliver them, that can give them victory over their lusts and peace of mind in a wicked age. If we are not respecters of persons, everybody wins.

20

Be Rich in Faith

James 2:5–7

A good summary of the epistle of James is: be like Jesus. That's the message of all the New Testament writers. Peter says, 'For even hereunto were ye called: because Christ also suffered for us, leaving us an example, that ye should follow his steps: who did no sin, neither was guile found in his mouth' (1 Pet. 2:21–22). Paul says 'Let this mind be in you, which was also in Christ Jesus: who being in the form of God, thought it not robbery to be equal with God: but made himself of no reputation' (Phil. 2:5–7).

Now in order to be like Jesus we have to not only grasp the glory that comes from God alone, but also exercise our wills in carrying out his commandments. Application. Here James puts our responsibility before us in such a way that we must go against what is natural to us. This is not the first time that James talks about rich people and it isn't going to be the last. With each point James raises we need to apply ourselves, to exercise our wills. At the moment James' point is the matter of class distinction. He shows that being partial backfires on us.

Three Questions

In this light James raises three questions. First, 'Hearken, my beloved brethren, Hath not God chosen the poor of this world rich in faith, and heirs of the kingdom which he hath promised to them that love him?' Obviously the answer is yes. Second, 'Do not rich men oppress you, and draw you before the judgment seats?' Again, the answer is obviously yes. Third, 'Do not they blaspheme that worthy name by the which ye are called?' Unfortunately, the answer to that question is also yes.

James knew who he was talking to and their specific situations. He reminds them again that the gospel was ostensibly designed for the poor of this world. Remember that when Jesus was in the synagogue and read from the book of Isaiah? He read, 'The Spirit of the Lord is upon me, because he hath anointed me to preach the gospel to the poor', then closed the book and said, 'This day is this scripture fulfilled in your ears' (Lk. 4:17–21). Jesus saw his mission as giving the gospel to the poor. Just look at the people who were attracted to his ministry, those who felt welcomed by him. When John the Baptist dispatched messengers to Jesus asking 'Art thou he that should come, or do we look for another? Jesus answered and said unto them, Go and shew John again those things which ye do hear and see: The blind receive their sight, and the lame walk, the lepers are cleansed, and the deaf hear, the dead are raised up, and the poor have the gospel preached to them' (Mt. 11:3–5).

Christianity was the first movement in the history of the human race that had anything to offer the poor. Every civilization has been class conscious. Certainly ours is! Whether class distinctions are based upon education, breeding, money or whatever, it's always the same – nobody favours the poor. But the gospel is ostensibly designed for the poor.

The Appeal of Marxism

The only thing since Christianity that has had anything for the poor is Marxism. It should not surprise you that Marxism has thrived in the poorest countries of the world, where capitalism has been abused. No wonder the people have responded. Marxism appeals to our natural instinct. It wants to reduce everybody to the same level. But it ought not to be Marxism that is penetrating the inroads of poor society. Christianity ought to be doing that.

James says, 'You know the kind of people that were attracted to Jesus, don't you?' 'Hath not God chosen the poor of this world . . .' This word 'chosen' comes from the Greek meaning 'to pick out', 'to elect', 'to choose'. This is the word used in the New Testament for the doctrine of election. But it does not mean that all the poor are God's elect. Neither does it mean that only the poor can be saved. It simply shows that God gives special attention to the poor. And it ought to be our hint that if we are not growing it is because we are being selective. We are not giving the gospel to those for whom it was ostensibly designed.

The New Testament shows us that the church should, by and large, be made up of poor people. Paul said to the Corinthians, 'You see your calling, brethren, how that not many wise men after the flesh, not many mighty, not many noble, are called' (1 Cor. 1:26). Whether it be socio-economically or intellectually, Christianity is for poor and simple people. James sees a dangerous possibility on the horizon, that although the gospel is offered indiscriminately to all, the church might become selective in its evangelism picking out certain types of people. Once the church does that it is finished.

We can call for intense prayer for revival, but if we discriminate, selecting those to whom we offer the gospel, we mock God. It may be true that one effect of Christianity is to make one better oneself. And hence Christianity does become a sort of middle-class phenomenon – it will make a tramp want to take a bath, will make a drunk look after the family. But that is an accidental effect of Christianity. The fatal danger is when we make Christianity a certain thing on purpose, looking for the effect rather than sticking with the message. The way to avoid this, says James, is to refuse to become a respecter of persons.

James adds that the poor are chosen to be rich in faith. Marxism appeals to the poor because it appeals to their natural instincts. But it does not make one rich in faith. Marxism is purely materialistic. But God has not chosen the poor of this world to be entrepreneurs in finance or big business, or to start climbing the social ladder. The foolish error of the social gospelists and certain neo-evangelicals is that they think the church's task is to feed the world. God has chosen the poor to be rich in faith.

If the Bible teaches anything it teaches that the rich – by rich I mean those who trust in their riches – have pleasures in this world only. The genius of the poor is in their deaths if they're Christians. The folly of the rich is in their deaths.

Being Rich in Faith

It means three things to be rich in faith? First, it means that you are successful in that which eludes most people: to have it both ways. You have the best of this world and you die well. You live through this life without guilt or shame but with a sense of dignity, whatever your status. And, as John Wesley put it, 'Our people die well.'

Second, to be rich in faith means that you make regular deposits in the bank of heaven, not in the Bank of England. As Jesus put it, 'Lay up for yourselves treasures in heaven, where neither moth nor rust doth corrupt, and where thieves do not break through nor steal' (Mt. 6:20).

How do you 'lay up for yourselves treasures in heaven'? Well, every time somebody slaps you, you turn the other cheek. Every time somebody says something naughty about you, don't defend yourself. When tempted to lust, turn your eyes. When tempted to murmur, refuse, when tempted to listen to the devil, don't. Every time you are tempted and you say no – more treasure in heaven.

To be rich in faith means, thirdly, that you've put all of your eggs in one basket. You have abandoned earthly glory and postponed vindication until you get to heaven. One of these days you will go to heaven's chief accountant and say, 'How much have I got in the bank?' And you'll cash in for all eternity. As James puts it, the poor are those who are made heirs of the kingdom.

This interpretation of the kingdom was in Jesus' ministry. The Jews missed the Messiah because they had preconceived ideas as to what he would be and do which didn't fit. The Jews were looking for another Moses, another David, an earthly kingdom to end all kingdoms. But Jesus came using language like this: 'My kingdom is not of this world' (Jn 18:36). He would say, 'The kingdom of God is within you' (Lk. 17:21). And, 'Except a man be born again, he cannot see the kingdom of God' (Jn. 3:3). Language like this went in one ear and out the other. They didn't want to hear it.

But Pentecost proved that the messianic kingdom had come. Jesus was a prophet like Moses, another David, the son of David. And his was the kingdom to end all kingdoms with one King, one Priest, one Prophet. For John said, 'We shall reign on the earth' (Rev. 5:10). 'We are joint-heirs', said Paul, 'in this kingdom' (Rom. 8:17). Though there is one King we are all kings, one Priest we are all priests. Every one of us is a prophet in our own right. That is our heritage. We shall judge the world. We are heirs of the kingdom.

The gospel is this: 'the last shall be first, and the first last' (Mt. 20:16). 'That is our heritage', says James. We may not be received by the world, outclassed by worldly people, outwitted by the ungodly. We may have battle after battle with those who scoff and laugh. We may lose battles but we will win the war. We're heirs of the kingdom. That's what matters. So John could say, 'The seventh angel sounded; and there were great voices in heaven, saying, The kingdoms of this world are become the kingdoms of our Lord, and of his Christ; and he shall reign for ever and ever' (Rev. 11:15). That is our heritage. The last shall be first.

Faith Is Grounded in Promise

The proof of this comes in James' promise: 'Hearken, my beloved brethren, Hath not God chosen the poor of this world rich in faith, and heirs of the kingdom which he hath promised to them?' Faith is grounded in promise. Not in empirical, tangible, material proof, but in promise. Not in sight, conjecture or projection, but promise. We believe *that* he promised and we believe *what* he promised. After John's vision was complete he got another command from the Lord, 'John, write this down. All these words are faithful and true. God shall wipe away all tears. There shall be no more death or crying. Neither shall there be any more pain.' (Rev. 21:4–5). Those who trust in their riches know nothing of this. They don't live by a promise but by pleasure, prestige, class superiority, worldly recognition. But those who are rich in faith, who are heirs of the kingdom, live by promise. We believe his word.

James does, however, qualify this statement. 'God hath chosen the poor of this world rich in faith, and heirs of the kingdom which he hath promised to them that love him.' The gospel is to the poor *ostensibly*, but not to the poor *unconditionally*. The gospel is offered to all without distinction, but not to all whether or not they believe. The proof that either the poor or the rich qualify is whether they live by the promise; whether they are rich in faith; whether they love God so much that they want more than anything to see him; whether they live ready for Jesus to come, and are thrilled at that prospect. If there is that in you that would delay the coming of Jesus, you betray that you are too attached to things. It came time for Paul to die and he could say, 'I have fought a good fight, I have finished my course, I have kept the faith: Henceforth there is laid up for me a crown of righteousness, which the Lord, the righteous judge, shall give me at that day: and not to me only, but unto all them also that love his appearing' (2 Tim. 4:7–8). You prove your love for God if you love his appearing and you say, 'Thy kingdom come. Even so, come, Lord Jesus.'

Despising the Poor

James is now ready to go to his second question. He knows those he is writing to and their situations and he puts before them a most serious accusation. He says, 'Ye have despised the poor.' The Greek word means 'dishonoured'. They held the faith of our Lord Jesus Christ in a way that our Lord never would have done, and James rebukes them for it. He's going to have more rebukes for them. And it would appear that their troubles began because they were class-conscious in choosing their friends and did their evangelizing with discrimination. The most grievous thing to be said of any church is: 'You've despised the poor.' This doesn't mean that a church doesn't take up a little collection once in a while. No, it means that when the poor come in they don't feel welcome.

We've not yet come to James' ultimate point, for he raises now two more questions. 'Do not rich men oppress you, and draw you before the judgment seats? Do not they blaspheme that worthy name by the which ye are called?' Why does James ask these questions? Is he saying, 'Look here, you've been good to them, what have they done for you?' That isn't his point, and yet it is a pragmatic test.

His point is this: 'You've dishonoured the poor and been especially nice to the people of status.' But has it worked? No. 'Not only did you not win them to the gospel,' says James, ' but they now treat you as dirt under their feet. What is more they continue to oppress you. Your being partial backfired on you spiritually, and you've even lost materially. Not only have your efforts failed to win them or their respect, but now they scoff at what you believe.'

Favouritism

James is saying that they've actually lost on three counts. First, they didn't win the rich by showing favouritism. Second, they didn't even get special treatment. Being nice to the rich hasn't made them be nice back. 'And worst of all,' says James, 'your witness has been so bad that these people now blaspheme your Lord.' In other words, even though they were trying to show the rich respect, so little do they think of the church that they now even speak contemptuously about what it believes.

Nothing can be sadder than learning that the person you were so anxious to meet and win doesn't have the slightest hesitation in blaspheming all you hold to. Why? Because you turned the faith of our Lord into something it was never meant to be. They always were profane, venal, profligate. But now they blaspheme your Lord: the name by which you are called.

James is not referring to effectual calling. The Greek here means how you are known, what people call you. You're known as a Christian. What do people think of Christianity now that they've got to know you? I would hope that there is such a manner of life, such a way of thinking, such a behaviour that they will respect the name of Jesus, that they even want to know him. But as James shows, behaviour can work the other way too, it can give people leave to speak against Christianity without the slightest feeling of guilt.

James' description of these Christians, I'm sorry to say, has been repeated many, many times. It happens whenever we try to win others at the level of nature, by compromising, by being like the world, by hoping that the world will be partial to us. And it can happen to anyone. You put your convictions to one side hoping that that will make a name for you. But it doesn't work. For people will treat you as dirt. They will despise with greater vigour than ever all that you stand for. Why? Because they see it as worthless and you as no different from anybody else.

My fellow Christians, we do them the greatest favour and pay them the highest honour when we treat all people without discrimination. If you seek to win another by natural motivation you have destroyed the faith of Jesus. You have laid your integrity aside and, worst of all, you leave the name of Jesus open to shameful contempt. 'Hearken, my beloved brethren, hearken.' Can you think of anybody who thinks less now of Christianity because of you?

What Matters

What matters is that we are rich in faith, and this shows itself in that we're like Jesus. 'For ye know the grace of our Lord Jesus Christ, that, though he was rich, yet for your sakes he became poor, that ye through his poverty might be rich' (2 Cor. 8:9). What matters is to remember that there is one reason that we are saved. Because the gospel came to us without discrimination. We would never have believed if we thought we might not qualify. We were not won at a natural level but at a spiritual level. If James' words here can capture us then we will become again the salt of the earth. We will be the light of the world. All who know us will glory in the name of Jesus. 'And thou shalt be called, The repairer of the breach, The restorer of paths to dwell in' (Isa. 58:12).

21

The Golden Rule

James 2:8–12

The Royal Law of Scripture

At this point James brings in the principle of loving our neighbour as ourself, which he calls 'the royal law' of Scripture. The Greek word translated 'royal' here is almost like the word for 'kingdom'. In verse 8 we're told to fulfil the royal law in light of what James has said in verse 5: 'Hath not God chosen the poor of this world rich in faith, and heirs of the kingdom?' The royal law is that which governs this kingdom.

The kingdom is offered to all indiscriminately, but it is governed by one royal law that governs all laws. If you fulfil this law on purpose, you will fulfil all of the commandments accidentally. James says, 'Ye do well.' How well? Love your neighbour as yourself and you're going to keep the whole law.

You may ask, 'Why bring in law at all?' In 1:25 James referred to the 'law of liberty', which is the ground of our justification and our assurance and the motivating cause of our obedience.

The royal law is the ground of our sanctification, the standard of measurement by which the Christian faith will be judged. It is possible to love your neighbour as yourself because of the law of liberty. Jesus lived this way. So can we. In my opinion, the most powerful doctrine of the Christian faith is that Christlikeness is a real possibility. And yet it is this teaching that has most successfully eluded the Christian church.

James says, 'If ye fulfil the royal law ye do well.' That's a big if. But it's a possible if. James isn't dangling an unattainable carrot in front of us. He is putting before us the standard of measurement by which all will judge what we believe. He puts before us the real possibility of being like Jesus.

This is assuming, of course, that we have followed his way of thinking all along – we're not ready to talk about loving our neighbour as ourself if we haven't managed to quit our sinning.

Jesus did not sin, but he did suffer. 'And if we suffer in the flesh', said Peter, 'we have ceased from sin' (1 Pet. 4:1). If we have begun to suffer, if we have laid aside all that is commensurate with the flesh and know what it is to cease from sin, we're ready now, if only for the first time, to follow Jesus. You may say, 'Surely that is not possible.' My answer: if it is not possible to follow Jesus, then his own words are sheer mockery. Jesus said, 'Verily, verily, I say unto you, He that believeth on me, the works that I do shall he do also; and greater works than these shall he do; because I go unto my Father' (Jn. 14:12).

There are two reasons why the modern church is powerless, void of the miracles and signs that Jesus said would follow those that believe. One is that we haven't quit our sinning; the other is that we haven't taken seriously, much less literally, Jesus' own words: 'The works that I do shall you do also.' Paul said, 'Eye hath not seen, nor ear heard, neither have entered into the heart of man, the things which God hath prepared for them that love him. But God hath revealed them unto us by his Spirit, for the Spirit searcheth all things, yea, the deep things of God' (1 Cor. 2:9–10). Until we obey the simple commands of Jesus we will not be the church which he himself envisioned. Before we see the power of God in demonstration we must first fulfil the royal law: love your neighbour as yourself.

Short Cuts to Power?

There are always those who want the short cut to power. We can pray and fast for revival from now till doomsday, but until we love our neighbour as ourselves we will remain powerless. In the main there are two ways the church has been guilty of trying the short cut to power. One is to bypass the importance of Christian doctrine, the other to bypass holiness.

Christian doctrine is vital. It is here that I query the 'charismatic movement'. I don't mean to be critical, but the charismatic movement unduly emphasizes power and the gifts of the Spirit. However, a person cannot have Holy Ghost power and deny the substitutionary death of Jesus or the great Reformation. The fact that one or two may be blessed or converted no more justifies the charismatic movement than it does us. Because we're not what we ought to be either. And I'm not justifying us against them. For 'judgment must begin at the house of God' (1 Pet. 4:17). And most of us are rendered speechless by this royal law of Scripture.

Yet it will do no good to pray for power and despise the theological principles of Scripture at the same time.

The second short cut is to bypass holiness. This is even more incriminating and indicts us all the more. For many of us want to take refuge in our faithfulness to sound doctrine. Nothing is more abhorrent, more paralysing, more counter-productive and more self-righteous than taking refuge in our theological soundness. What is more, nothing carries with it a safer guarantee of the delay of revival. For God is serious about holiness.

The acceptable doctrine before God is the law of liberty. The acceptable holiness before God is to love our neighbour as ourselves. If you can't imagine loving your neighbour as yourself you are still in sin. Have you quit saying, 'My temptation is of God'? Have you laid aside all moral filth and evil disposition? Have you taken seriously the enterprise of aiding those in distress as well as keeping yourself unspotted from the world? Then love your neighbour as yourself.

Who is Our Neighbour?

James brings in the royal principle now because whoever fulfils this royal law will never be a respecter of persons. I hope you know that your neihbour is never only who you hope it is. Jesus asked, 'If ye love them which love you, what reward have ye? do not even the publicans the same? Be ye therefore perfect, even as your Father which is in heaven is perfect' (Mt. 5:46, 48). Jesus did not say, 'Love your family, friends or fellow Christians as you love yourself.' We may wish that he had. The Greek word means *everybody* and *anybody*. Rich, poor, black, white, American, English, Indian, Pakistani, Christian, non-Christian. Furthermore, we are talking about an *agape* love. The Greek word *agape* used in 1 Corinthians 13 is used here. It is an unselfish love. It is not *philia*, the Greek word meaning 'brotherly' or 'family love'. It is not *eros*, the Greek word that means 'physical love', lest you think you're going to win the opposite sex to the Lord by romance. But it is *agape*, a love that seeks the highest good without the respect of persons. 1 Corinthians 13 is the ultimate commentary on the kind of love that is intended here.

This royal principle is not only that by which the world will judge the Christian faith, it is also the principle that will hold homes together, that will hold your marriage together. A marriage cannot be held together by *philia* love or *eros* love. It may fall apart if they are absent, but they will not hold it together. It must have *agape*, an unselfish, mutual love. The royal law is: love your neighbour as yourself.

Not Self-Love

When it is added 'as you love yourself', it is not a divine sanction for self-love. Quite the opposite. Self-love is precisely what lies behind being a respecter of persons. For self-love will invariably lead you to respect the one who will respect you, the one you think will do you a favour some day. It is self-love that leads to sexual sin. Any sex outside marriage is self-love. And self-love will invariably backfire if relied upon in Christian witness. The principle of self-love works fine in worldly relationships, in business, politics, salesmanship. But as a Christian testimony it will not work. For it is like putting new wine in an old wineskin and it will burst every time. Thus when it comes to Christian behaviour one must stay in the realm of consistency, of congruity.

What is it then to love yourself? It means that you would treat another as you want others to treat you. We call it 'the golden rule'. 'Therefore all things whatsoever ye would that men should do to you, do ye even so to them: for this is the law and the prophets' (Mt. 7:12). You want to be treated with respect, dignity, honour, care, thoughtfulness, unselfishness, and without manipulation. So do the same for others.

The royal law does not say: love your neighbour more than you love yourself. Many people, driven by pseudo-guilt, try – they can't, it's an impossibility – to go to this extreme. But that would entail denying both your personality and your being. Jesus did not love others more than he loved himself. He often, of necessity, would have to get away from the multitudes and from the Twelve. Jesus called Herod a 'fox' and the Pharisees 'hypocrites', 'vipers'. Jesus had a special love for Simon Peter but once had to say to him, 'Get thee behind me, Satan' (Mt. 16:23). Our Lord lived to please his Father. Jesus was a man. When he grew tired he slept. When he got hungry he ate. To love oneself means to respect oneself.

Understanding *agape* is again important here. You must *agape* love your neighbour, so what is being sanctioned here is an *agape*, unselfish love for yourself. The Golden Rule assumes that we love ourselves that way. We treat our bodies, our minds, our time with an unselfish love, with a certain reverence. And thus we do the same for others. This is why if you fulfil the royal law on purpose, you will keep all the commandments accidentally. James himself lists certain commandments as illustrations of this: 'do not commit adultery', 'do not kill' (v. 11). He is saying, 'If ye fulfil the royal law ... ye do well.' You keep the rest of the law without realizing it.

This is why the Christian does not need the ten commandments as a moral guide. Not only that, the ten commandments will put a ceiling on our righteousness. They are restrictive. They limit how righteous we can be. If the ten commandments become your cue for holy living you will never move beyond them. But with the royal law there is no ceiling. There are no outer limits.

James says, 'If indeed you fulfil the law' (for some reason the AV doesn't include the 'indeed' of the Greek), meaning 'if indeed you keep it', 'if you really keep it', you do well. Not only do you keep the commandments without trying but you have begun to follow our Lord. 'But if ye have respect to persons, ye commit sin, and are convinced of the law as transgressors.' Our Lord's sinlessness is further manifest by this verse – if Jesus had ever shown respect of persons he would have sinned, but he never did.

How to be Kept From Being a Respecter of Persons

There are three reasons why loving our neighbours keep us from being respecters of persons. First, because our neighbour is anybody and everybody. Second, because we treat all people according to the golden rule. Third, because fulfilling the royal law ensures and produces positively what the Mosaic law ensures negatively and inadequately.

The Mosaic law, especially the sixth, seventh, eighth and ninth commandments, sought to achieve the protection of others by fear of punishment. The forbidding of murder, adultery, stealing and lying are negative admonitions to protect others. But they could never produce a love for people. The best that the law could do was to provide a guarantee against abuse. But only some sorts of abuse.

James says, 'If you are showing favouritism you sin.' How? Because you are abusing people. What is more, you are even convicted as transgressors of the Mosaic law. It should be beneath your dignity as a Christian ever to be convicted of sin through the Mosaic law. After all, the law was not made for righteous people. How did Paul put it? 'Knowing this, that the law is not made for a righteous man, but for the lawless and disobedient, for the ungodly and for sinners, for unholy and profane, for murderers of fathers and murderers of mothers, for manslayers, For whoremongers, for them that defile themselves with mankind, for menstealers, for liars, for perjured persons' (1 Tim. 1:9–10). This is why the law was made. 'But,' says James, 'if you are a respecter of persons you, as a Christian, have sunk so low that even the Mosaic law can uncover you.'

What Happens When we Despise Others

These Christian Jews were in danger of being like the Pharisees whom Jesus rebuked over and over again. For Jesus showed that sin was in the heart and these Pharisees thought that they never sinned. They thought they were quite moral, thank you. But Jesus said that if you lust after a woman you've committed adultery in your heart (Mt. 5:28). If you hate you've committed murder in your heart.

James says to these Christian Jews, 'Ye have despised the poor.' He didn't say, 'I have a theory you might start despising the poor. I have a fear that you're going to dishonour them.' James knew what he was saying. By respecting persons they had abused the poor, bruised their consciences, broken their spirits, destroyed their very souls. They had made the poor think that Christianity had nothing for them. If that is not murder, pray tell what is.

Not only had they abused the poor, they had abused the rich by showing partiality to them. They'd driven the rich away, sent them right to hell. If that is not murder, what is? They'd made the rich think that Christianity is a status symbol, that Christianity treats people the way the world treats people. 'That never wins the rich', says James. 'You make them think that Christianity is essentially a here and now phenomenon. But these people have all they want in the here and now. So they're not interested at all.' Consequently, the rich both cease to respect Christians and blaspheme Christianity too.

How We Shall be Judged

Although we may be exposed by the Mosaic law, thank God we're not judged by it. For if we were judged by it, all of us would be doomed and damned throughout eternity. But James says in verse 12 that we'll be 'judged by the law of liberty'. The law of liberty shouts, 'You're okay. Go on, be a doer of the word. You are free.' Let's live lives that show rich and poor, black and white, that there is a God in the heavens. He's a God who cares, who is not a respecter of persons, who has forgiven us despite the fact that we all stand condemned and are rendered speechless. 'God so loved the world, that he gave his only begotten Son, that whosoever believeth in him should not perish, but have everlasting life' (Jn. 3:16).

22

Who Do You Think You Are?

James 2:10–13

This is one of the most interesting, thrilling sections of this epistle of James. It concludes the discussion that has been going on since the beginning of this second chapter. We see how James' mind works and how, in his own way, he comes to the same conclusion about conviction of sin as do both Paul and Jesus.

An Inherent Weakness

James knows his readers personally. He knows their nature and shares their heritage – important as he's dealing with a pastoral manner at this point. We all, because of our various backgrounds, have certain unique weaknesses, different from anybody else's although they still come within what is common to humanity.

The inherent weakness of these Christian Jews was a tendency to be self-righteous. Everybody has that weakness, of course, but these Christian Jews were especially prone to it because, being brought up on the Mosaic law, they had been spoon-fed from birth with the notion that their race made them special in God's eyes.

Paul recognized that we all have particular weaknesses when he said to the Corinthians, 'The Jews require a sign, and the Greeks seek after wisdom: But we preach Christ crucified, unto the Jews a stumbling block, and unto the Greeks foolishness' (1 Cor. 1:22–23). Many of those James was addressing were like the Pharisees that Jesus had to put down so many times. Pharisees, outwardly speaking, never really sinned. They wouldn't think of sinning. And many of these Christian Jews believed they did not sin. They were highly moral people. Of course, they experienced conviction of sin. But it is possible to know conviction of sin and yet not sin in deed. We can be so aware of sin, yet outwardly appear as people who really reflect the grace of God in our lives. The danger then is that we begin to think that we are sinless, and a self-righteous spirit takes over before we know what is happening.

These Christian Jews were like Paul who said, 'Touching the righteousness which is in the law, blameless' (Phil. 3:6). Paul thought he was blameless. James knew how to deal with people like that. He turns the law right back on them, showing that they had degenerated to the place where even the law – which had been made not for the righteous but for sinners – could expose them. In these verses James shows them that they have sinned and become immoral by what they have done. And the way he does this has far reaching sociological and even psychological implications. James has to show them that sin is in the heart, but can be revealed through the totality of the law. 'Whosoever shall keep the whole law, and yet offend in one point, he is guilty of all.' An apparently total morality is rendered void by the law itself. If there is the slightest inconsistency in anyone, they fall on all counts, despite appearances and despite their delusions of righteousness.

Mastering One Sin Is Not Enough

Jesus showed that the Pharisees had sinned by showing their hearts. James showed these Christian Jews they had sinned by comparing one commandment with another. Here's what lies behind all of this. The easiest thing in the world for anybody to do is to think they haven't sinned because they've mastered one element of their sinful nature. We all have what we think is our gross weakness. The feeling among many of us is that if we conquer that we need not worry about anything else.

Let us say that my weakness has always been lying. Finally, I master it. I feel so good about it that I think that nothing else really matters. But James simply says to me, 'What about the commandment: thou shalt not steal?' My danger would be to think that I have kept the law due to one success over my gross weakness. But James says, 'You've only begun.' If you have quit lying but you still steal, you are guilty of sinning against the whole law. For if stealing has never been your weakness you're going to think that if you do steal it's not going to be so bad. You work on a malady that bothers you and neglect what doesn't. It just shows how deceitful the heart is.

To these Christian Jews James is saying, 'Indeed you don't commit adultery. Good. But if you commit murder you become a transgressor of the law and that is precisely what you have done. For abusing the poor and the rich is tantamount to murder. You stand convicted for showing partiality to those of a certain socio-economic status. That makes you grossly immoral.'

Have we thought ourselves perfectly righteous simply because we've mastered one area of Christian living, not realizing how ridiculous and how abhorrent we appear to others? Many Christians fancy themselves totally godly because they don't smoke, drink or go to cinemas. They don't have a clue how ridiculous they look to the world. The world sees their self-centredness and their self-righteous spirit. Our problem is that we gag on a gnat and swallow a camel. It's like sending a missionary to Africa or to India while refusing to sit next to Blacks or Asians in church. Or, we give to Tear Fund but avoid face-to-face contact with the poor.

Jesus said, 'Woe unto you, Pharisees, for ye tithe mint and rue and all manner of herbs, and pass over judgment and the love of God: these ought ye to have done, and not to leave the other undone' (Mt. 11:42). It is easy for us to fall here too. For living the Christian life encompasses the whole. It is a life of discipline in every area, not mastering one and thinking that you are a total success. James says that these Christian Jews had done the unthinkable. They had dishonoured the poor. It seems not ever to have entered their minds that having respect of persons and neglecting the poor was committing sin.

Jesus Cared About the Poor

It reminds us of when the rich young ruler came to Jesus. 'Good Master,' he said, 'what shall I do to inherit eternal life?' And Jesus said unto him, 'Why callest thou me good? none is good, save one, that is, God. Thou knowest the commandments, Do not commit adultery, Do not kill, Do not steal, Do not bear false witness, Honour thy father and thy mother.' And he said, 'All these have I kept from my youth up.' Now when Jesus heard these things, he said unto him, 'Yet lackest thou one thing: Sell all that thou hast, and distribute unto the poor' (Lk. 18:18–22). 'What about the poor?' says Jesus.

The apostle Paul's writing to the Galatians, told about the first time he ever met James. They didn't get on too well at first, but did manage to get together. And Paul says James only had one request: 'that we should remember the poor' (Gal. 2:10). 'And this,' Paul says, 'we were glad to do'.

Isn't it remarkable that the apostle Paul would make that comment about James: 'that we should remember the poor'? James was a man who practised what he preached. The poor, according to James, are the status heroes of the gospel. James could say, 'Hearken, my beloved brethren, Hath not God chosen the poor of this world rich in faith?'

The rich young ruler thought he was blameless. These Christian Jews thought they were blameless. James shouts, 'It won't do. You should speak and act in light of the happy condition that you are under. Realize that you, though exposed by the law and though worthy of punishment, shall yourselves be judged by a higher principle.' The law of liberty.

The Law of Liberty Never Condemns

Our Lord Jesus Christ, who had no respect of persons, fulfilled this law and it therefore pronounces you free. The law of liberty accepts you because it supercedes the Mosaic law. For the law of liberty is the ultimate demonstration of the triumph of mercy over judgment. It declares us just, righteous, never condemns or shames us. The law of liberty simply judges us by the righteousness of our Lord Jesus Christ.

'Well,' says James, 'as our Lord Jesus Christ showed no favourites – it was his faith and his works that enabled you to be free – how can you yourselves do otherwise?' If there had not been an indiscriminate offer of the gospel *you* never would have been saved, would you? How can *you* then turn around and be discriminating? If God had discriminated and selected to save on the basis of works, you would be condemned. 'Now, how can you who have been chosen apart from your works turn around and be selective in your evangelism?'

Law, Mercy, Grace

What James is doing is fighting with all of his might for the free offer of the gospel. For if it offered to a certain class only, then it ceases to be the gospel of our Lord Jesus Christ. Verse 12 summarizes the first chapter of James. 'So speak ye, and so do.' What we have in verse 13, the concluding statement of this section, is a succinct commentary on the strictness of the Mosaic law, 'He shall have judgment without mercy, that hath shewed no mercy', and the glory of the law of liberty – 'mercy rejoiceth against judgment'. The first part of verse 13 deals with the whole of verse 11. The second part of verse 13 deals with the whole of verse 12.

James is showing that under the old law, with which his readers were so familiar, every social abuse received judgment without mercy. For there was no excuse if you committed sin. The law had no compassion, however great the temptation might have been, however justified one may have felt in sinning. Refusing to commit murder, refusing to commit adultery, is to show mercy. You may be tempted to kill but instead you show mercy and withdraw. Or you may be tempted to commit adultery but you stop and you show mercy to that person. For indeed not to commit sexual sin is showing mercy to that other person. Your greatest kindness to another person is not to let them sin.

According to Mosaic law, if you did not show mercy then God would show none to you. As the writer to the Hebrews put it: 'He that despised Moses' law died without mercy under two or three witnesses' (Heb. 10:28). 'How would you like it if it were that way right now?' says James. 'You people who have thought you were so moral, so clean and upright, how would you like it if the Mosaic law were in force? For your conduct to the rich, to the poor, is reprehensible. However, you blessed people, you won't be going to hell, for mercy triumphs over judgment. Therefore treat others the way the law of liberty is treating you.'

Here's James' accusation: 'You are behaving in a manner ominously like that of the Pharisees.' The Pharisees liked that verse: 'An eye for an eye, and a tooth for a tooth' (Mt. 5:38). They operated on a 'you be good to me, I'll be good to you' basis and took judgment into their own hands. If that's the way you're going to treat people, then how would you like it if you were brought to justice in light of your own behaviour? The trouble with you,' says James, 'is you want to act according to nature but be judged according to grace.'

God's Judgment

'But wait a minute,' says James, 'you've already been judged for this. Have you not noticed that the whole practice has backfired on you? What do you think lies behind the way you've been oppressed by the rich? That's nothing but God's judgment. And it's exactly like Jesus said it would be.' For James 2:13 is a commentary on Matthew 18:33–35. 'Shouldest not thou also have had compassion on thy fellowservant, even as I had pity on thee? And his lord was wroth, and delivered him to the tormentors, till he should pay all that was due unto him. So likewise shall my heavenly Father do also unto you, if ye from your hearts forgive not every one his brother their trespasses.'

'God has shown mercy to you,' James goes on, 'He's cancelled the debt. You're judged by the law of liberty and yet what are you doing to show your gratitude? Not much. You're showing favouritism and you've rendered yourselves immoral by such conduct.' 'But has it worked? Has that rich person you were buttering up been nice to you? No. And this should not surprise you. Jesus warned you of this. And now you are paying for your folly, after all.'

In his parable of the unforgiving servant Jesus had shown the senselessness and the injustice of those who have been forgiven a great debt but refuse to forgive others smaller debts. Jesus said the forgiven man who would not forgive would be delivered to his tormentors till he should pay what was due to him. 'And so shall my Father do to you.'

The Law of Liberty Supercedes the Law of Moses

Does this mean that our failure to forgive renders our own forgiveness null and void? No, thank God. Or our forgiveness wouldn't last very long. Because mercy triumphs over judgment the law of liberty supercedes the law of Moses. 'But,' says James, 'that does not mean that you will not pay for your conduct.' Indeed they had paid, they had been delivered to their tormentors. It was God's judgment. 'You are so impoverished', says James. 'You're double minded. You're incapable of coming to truth. You can't see clearly. You've failed to impress the rich. In fact, they exploit you. And, worst of all, they use the name of Jesus in vain because they don't see anything in you that is any good.' Neither they nor we can live like that and get away with it. God will humble us to the dust. He'll bring us to rock bottom, make us recognize our folly and turn back to him.

James can talk like this because he believes he's talking to those who will take heed of his warning. He knows they're Christians. Like them, many of us have to learn by walking through the fiery furnace of God's chastening. We ourselves will be saved though 'as by fire' (1 Cor. 3:15). We will have paid.

God will not use us until we honour his word. Mastering one sin is not enough. We must present our 'bodies a living sacrifice, holy, acceptable unto God which is our reasonable service' (Rom. 12:1). God will not tolerate our beginning to feel good about ourselves because we've mastered one area. The whole law will convict us if we do.

Do you want to know what the sin of twentieth-century Christianity is? The desire for status. We're like Israel who demanded a king so that she could be like other nations. The church is mad for science, to show that we can believe in evolution. The church is mad to say that the Bible can be understood like other literature, just as you'd understand Shakespeare. We're trying to show the world that we're learned and that we're philosophical. Has it worked? No. Look at the churches emptying right and left. It has not impressed the world. We have paid. God, grant that we will have learned our lesson, for our own sakes and for the sake of the world.

23

Faith and Works

James 2:14–16

We now approach the best known and most controversial, but what could be the most rewarding, section of this epistle. Faith and works. It is this section that put Luther off James. He was so obsessed with defending the doctrine of justification by faith that he felt compelled to speak against anything that threatened that view. It's a great pity that Luther did not see what an ally he had in James. Luther is a lesson to all of us. If Scripture threatens us, it shows our insecurity. It shows how much we have to learn.

The Threat of Scripture

We must adopt the principle that if what we believe is right then any threatening passage will bolster all we believe once we understand it. But if what we believe is wrong then we must be willing to abandon it in light of Scripture. For it is our task to follow truth wherever it leads. We have a chance to show whether we believe the truth and want it by following Scripture. We must never have an emotional reaction to any threatening passage or we will miss its meaning.

Although we moved on slightly, we must remember to read this section in context. James has not changed the subject. What we have here is an illustration to show how the law of the kingdom, the 'royal law', works. You may wonder why James put this famous illustration that deals with faith and works here. The answer is firstly, because of the poor man and secondly, because of that glorious law of liberty. The tragedy of Luther's blindness is that he did not see that James brought in this section on works simply because we are saved apart from works.

If we got our entrance into heaven by works James would never have had to say this. These Christian Jews were not worried one bit about their own salvation. Neither was James. It was because of the law of liberty that they became negligent about works. We are saved with no strings attached. Because of this, the most human, easiest thing in the world is to forget works. After all, the doctrine of justification by faith is most vulnerable to the charge of antinomianism. In fact, until our doctrine has this charge it is likely not understood.

Paul actually had to make the same point James does here, to Titus. 'This is a faithful saying, and these things I will that thou affirm constantly, that they which have believed in God might be careful to maintain good works' (Tit. 3:8). Again, Paul said, 'Likewise reckon ye also yourselves to be dead indeed unto sin, but alive unto God through Jesus Christ our Lord. Let not sin therefore reign in your mortal body, that ye should obey it in the lusts thereof. Neither yield ye your members as instruments of unrighteousness unto sin: but yield yourselves unto God, as those that are alive from the dead, and your members as instruments of righteousness unto God' (Rom. 6:11–13).

Sanctification Comes by the Exercise of Our Will

Holiness as a fruit of justification is something that is produced by the most careful fertilizing of the soil. For the doctrine of sanctification, or of good works, comes by struggle, by the exercise of our will. The will may be effaced in conversion, but not in sanctification.

James now puts this argument in a positive way to show what the responsibility of the Christian is. In the preceding verses he has argued negatively to illustrate their folly. Now he turns to a pragmatic, positive argument. He says, 'What doth it profit, my brethren'. 'Profit' – that's the Greek word that also means 'utility', 'advantage', 'gain'. 'What doth it profit ... though a man say he hath faith, and have not works?' James has the conviction that Christianity is something that works. But these Jewish Christians had given little indication of this. They have, for instance, despised the poor, and James is not happy with them.

He says, 'Though a man say he hath faith', *if* he says he has faith. If they hadn't made the claim to faith nobody would know. 'But you've made the claim,' says James. 'Everybody knows what you are. You've been baptized. You've confessed Christ. But if you say you have faith and don't have works, treat the poor like you do, what is the advantage?'

Someone might say, 'Well, the way to get out of that is not to claim to have faith so I won't be judged.' This was the way Constantine, that curious figure in church history, got out of it. We don't know whether he was really a Christian, but he said he was. He put off his baptism until he was very old because there was then a common view that if you sinned after you were baptized you fell into the category of Hebrews 6:4–6 and you couldn't be renewed.

That will not work because, as Paul put it, 'With the heart man believeth unto righteousness' but 'with the mouth confession is made unto salvation' (Rom. 10:10). Avoiding the open declaration of your faith won't do, for then you will be in danger of losing your soul.

James boxes us in. We're forced to admit that we're Christians but equally forced to show it by the way we live. Every single soul who confesses Christ is then and there on open display in the world, whether old or young, single or married. After all, the world has a right to judge us. Nothing in the world claims for itself what Christianity claims. We don't have the right to turn Christianity into something that it is not. We may not save everybody, but we must leave all without excuse. How? By allowing the world to see in us a character, strength, manner of life, way of living that is so different that they are rendered without defence, speechless. For men and women in this world know they're not going to see such a life anywhere else, and if they don't see it among Christians where will they see it? It is our responsibility.

Someone once asked Voltaire – the famous French atheist who loved to speak against Christianity and constantly called attention to the hypocrisy in the church – 'Did you ever see anybody that you thought was really a Christian according to the Bible?' Voltaire responded after thinking a bit, 'I once met a man by the name of John Fletcher.' John Fletcher of Madeley was an early Methodist, a contemporary and friend of John and Charles Wesley, a godly man. One Sunday morning someone was walking for miles to hear John Fletcher preach and, passing a farmer, was asked 'Where are you going?' The reply: 'I am going to see John Fletcher preach.' Several hours later, on their return, the farmer asked , 'Well, did you see John Fletcher?' The reply: 'No, I didn't. I saw Jesus Christ and him crucified.'

Faith Without Works Delays God's Blessing

James' burden is that we live lives that render non-Christians defenceless. Nothing is sadder than the claim to have faith that has not works. Nothing is more calculated to guarantee the delay of God's blessing upon us.

Do you ever wonder why it is that a new convert can be such an effective soul winner? Most new Christians don't have a clue about theology, but others see the change in the way they live. It is not articulate doctrine that saves souls, it is works. How many people, spinning their wheels trying to be orthodox and sound, haven't won a single person to Christ? What convinces people? Works. James knew this. You may not like his pragmatism, but here it is. 'What profit is there when a man says he has faith and has not works?' No profit at all.

James follows with the question: 'Can faith save him?' It is here that Luther got into a muddle. Others following Luther have thought that this meant that the absence of works renders one's own faith void. But James is not questioning the salvation of the Christian who does not have works. He does not say, 'Will he himself be saved?' He doesn't say, 'Can faith save himself?' The Greek is accusative, not a reflexive pronoun. 'Can faith save him?' The other person. James is talking about the utilitarian value of the word 'profit'. What is the profit? It is for the other person's good. This has been the burden of James all along – the abuse of others by despising the poor (2:2, 6). The 'him' of James 2:14 refers to the *poor man* (Gr. *protochon* – accusative singular, meaning the poor man as translated by the New English Bible). In other words James 2:14 is referring to the poor man of James 2:6.[1]

Not only that, when James says, 'Can faith save him?' he actually uses the definite article. In the Greek it is: 'Can the faith save him?' In other words, what we believe has no value in abstraction. Faith must be concrete. It must be apparent at the empirical level. Those people you meet every day are not interested in your doctrine. They want to see you. Are you able to overcome temptation? Can you resist sin? Do you have a lifestyle that is different from anybody else's? That's what impresses them. Are you unlike anybody else they're going to meet? That's what saves another.

---

[1] Many readers may object to my view of James 2:14 on the grounds that (i) the 'him' refers to something too far back in the text, and (ii) the change in the meaning of the word 'him' is thought to be unexpected. I would direct the reader to see the linguistic comments of M.A. Eaton, *James: Preaching Through The Bible* (Sovereign Word), chapters 13 and 14.

Dr. Eaton not only confirms the view taken in this book, but shows in detail how a verse thought to be unexpected or referring to something too far back in the text is far from unprecedented in the New Testament. The 'him' of James 2:14 connecting to the 'poor man' of James 2:6 is the only thing that makes sense of the whole section and shows Paul and James do not contradict each other and how wrong Luther was.

If the faith which you describe so eloquently is not backed up by a difference in the way you live, what is the advantage? Can faith save? 'No, it never will', says James. And he says to these Christian Jews, 'Look at what you've been doing. How many have you been saving lately? Have you not noticed? You're the ones that have turned people away from the church. They see the way you carry on and they say, "Why should I be what you are. You're no different from me." They're put right off Christianity and may never be saved.'

We Are To Be Instruments of Salvation

What on earth is sadder than this? We are to be the instruments of salvation, not damnation. James shows the seriousness of not living up to what Christianity claims for itself. Most of the people that we're going to meet have some idea of what Christianity is supposed to do for a person. And they want to see if you measure up. We send others to hell if we do not reflect the face of our Lord Jesus Christ who himself was beyond reproach.

But now to the heart of James' pragmatic illustration. He says, 'If a brother or sister be naked, and destitute of daily food' – a likelihood, by the way. Who is the brother or sister? Is James simply speaking of Christians? If so, we might want to ask, how could they be without clothes. The Psalmist said, 'I have been young, and now am old; and yet have not seen the righteous forsaken, nor his seed begging bread' (Ps. 37:25). Perhaps it's a temporary state, a time of urgent need? If so, other Christians ought to be there ministering. But Christians are normally those who go begging. Maybe James means fellow Jews. Or Christians and Jews? No, I'm quite sure James means literally anybody and everybody. He's already said that the royal law of Scripture is to love your neighbour as yourself, and we know that 'neighbour' means anybody. James is not telling us to take notice of the regenerate in need, but anybody without clothes and daily food. And it is unrealistic to think we're not going to come across people like that. 'For ye have the poor always with you', said Jesus (Mt. 26:11).

James gets more specific. He says, 'If any one of you says unto them, Depart in peace, be ye warmed and filled; notwithstanding ye give them not those things which are needful to the body; what doth it profit?' Not only is it no good, it is tantamount to insult to say, 'Go. I wish you well' and then do nothing for them. James is commenting further on what he has called 'pure religion and undefiled' back in 1:27.

Be Willing To Be Used

Pure religion is never to let another person suffer if you can help it. It is not enough just to say, 'God bless you'. James says, 'If you have the faith of the Lord Jesus Christ you will keep your eyes wide open, asking questions if necessary, to be sure you are doing everything you can to help other people. That's what Jesus would do.' For the work James demands is Christlikeness and nothing less. It not enough to say, 'God bless' to the needy. How do you think God might choose to bless them? Cause money to grow on trees? Or have a fatted calf come wobbling down the road and up to their door? Do you hope God will send some *other* person to bless them? James' rule is, never say 'May God bless you', unless you are willing to be *the one* God will use to bless them. Be careful about throwing that phrase around – 'God bless'.

Things which are needful to the body.' If only James had said 'soul'. That would let us off the hook and we could just say, 'The Lord help you, give you spiritual grace and strength'. But no, James said 'body'. Why? Because there's a world out there that knows nothing but the level of nature. They're only interested in material things. James warns us that we must begin where people are. William Booth, the founder of the Salvation Army, said, 'There's no use talking to a man about his soul who has an empty stomach.' How did Paul put it? 'To the weak became I as weak, that I might gain the weak: I am made all things to all men, that I might by all means save some' (1 Cor. 9:22). He didn't say 'save all' or 'save many'. But he wanted to save some. When you meet people on their level you have been to them the hand of God.

There's a song that goes: 'God has no hands but our hands'. Most of us could pick that line to pieces, but there's far more truth in it than many of us dare admit. For it is our responsibility to be God's hands to others. We are the nearest they're ever going to get to God.

James uses the word 'give'. 'Notwithstanding ye give them not those things'. It's not a loan or a contract. There are no strings attached. James has but one aim, and that is that you be so good to them, so Christlike, that you leave them without excuse. He doesn't ask us to give money to support the habit of the alcoholic or drug addict. We do no one a favour if we prolong their wickedness or postpone their deliverance. James talks about giving those things which are 'needful to the body' – food, shelter, clothing.

If we don't meet those needs, but just say 'God bless', we might actually be encouraging them to curse God. When you say, 'God bless' in one breath and disappear in the next you've brought them face to face with God and then you've backed off. You've brought God into the picture and then made it seem he doesn't care. How will that make them view Christianity? James is using this illustration to touch every nerve, every avenue of Christian living. Suppose you are the only Christian that the people you know will see. And suppose others form a permanent impression, a permanent judgment of what Christianity is because of you. Do you leave them without excuse or do you tempt them to 'blaspheme that worthy name by the which ye are called'? What does it profit if you say you're a Christian but don't live like it?

Cain, the first murderer, defended his action with a question: 'Am I my brother's keeper?' (Gen. 4:9). With that question Cain condemned himself. My fellow Christian, it will do us no good to be defensive about our actions or about our lack of good works. For if we get defensive we condemn ourselves.

One more thing. Neither must we avoid our responsibility by praying about it. Prayer is the greatest enterprise in the world for passing the buck. There are some things you don't pray about. You do them. The law of liberty shouts back, 'You're okay. You've got grace. Put it to work. Do it now.'

I'm talking to *you*. Stop waiting for somebody to do this to you. You start it. You will surprise yourself, and this surprise will be God's grace upon you. The greatest surprise of all will be the power of the witness that you leave on other people. You will leave them without excuse, rendering them defenceless. In the meantime you will save some. You won't save all. You may not save many. But you will save some.

24

Faith Without Works?

James 2:17–18

Behind the Moral Problem was a Theological Problem

We surely see by now what an ally James was to the apostle Paul and even to Luther, although he was never able to see it. James' concern is the influence upon others of those who are saved, particularly when it is bad.

James continues to chide his readers, showing them that behind their moral problem lay a theological problem. This should not surprise us. There is an inseparable connection between the way we live and treat others and what we think about God. James describes their theological problem like this: 'Even so faith, if it hath not works, is dead, being alone.' They didn't understand the nature of faith.

Three Theological Issues

Their theological problem had three characteristics. First, these Christian Jews thought that their own personal salvation was the only thing that mattered. Neither they nor James questioned their salvation, and the law of liberty was nothing new to them. Their problem was that they were guilty of being hearers only. How did James put it? 'Be ye doers of the word, and not hearers only.' We are saved by hearing and it is the word of God that saves us. But, as James makes clear, faith alone is not enough.

Christianity *is* salvation but it is *not only* salvation. Christianity aims to do two things: to save us from our sins and to help us live as examples of grace. The purpose of Christianity is to make us fit for heaven and to make us fit for earth – in that order. You're not ready to live until you're ready to die. Jesus, the second Adam, came to restore what the first Adam lost. But in doing this by his death on the cross, he also left us an example that we should walk in his steps (1 Pet. 2:21). We are therefore to be as Jesus was to all the offspring of Adam. But these Christian Jews had never moved beyond the assurance of their own salvation.

The second characteristic of their theological problem was that they thought their personal faith was by itself a sufficient witness to others. After all, they had confessed Jesus of Nazareth as Son of God, Messiah – a scandalous thing in the eyes of other Jews, as was in being baptized. They had made themselves vulnerable, but James asks, 'What doth it profit, my brethren, though a man say he hath faith, and have not works?'

James' message was this: *faith works with God but not with people.* With God, works count for nothing and faith counts for everything. But with other people, faith counts for nothing and works count for everything. This is the way people are. James says, 'Live in the real world. If you say you have faith what does that do? That is something between you and God but what does it mean to anybody else?'

Dr R.T. Williams used to warn those he was ordaining to 'Beware two things in your ministry: sex and money; because if you are involved in a scandal in either of those, God will forgive you but the people won't.'

It is a wonderful thing to be forgiven, but it doesn't mean anything to anybody but you. The psalmist said, 'There is forgiveness with thee, that thou mayest be feared' (Ps. 130:4). And to show that you fear God is to demonstrate it before others. These Jewish Christians felt it but they didn't show it. Faith may save you but it won't save others.

So arrives James' strongest assertion yet: 'Even so faith, if it hath not works, is dead, being alone.' Some have taken this verse to refer to temporary faith, the sort found in Jesus' parable of the sower. But that is not what James is about here. It was the influence and testimony, not the salvation of these Jewish Christians that was in question.

Somebody will say, 'Wait a minute. Surely if faith is not joined by good works it proves that the faith is not saving.' That may be valid, but it's still not James' concern. The New Testament does teach that true faith produces good works. But it also teaches that these works contribute nothing to salvation. If you think that the lack of good works nullifies faith then you are either a Roman Catholic or an Arminian. Roman Catholics always interpret this passage as proof that salvation is contingent upon works. Consequently assurance of salvation was never a possibility in Catholic theology. But James isn't talking about salvation or the assurance of it. Rather his concern is with what influence the gospel has upon *others*.

He desires to show that faith has no way of speaking to others if that faith is not backed up by the kind of obedience which Jesus demonstrated, by Christlikeness in all of us.

The third characteristic of their theological malady, which lay behind the pitiful influence of the Christian Jews, as that they didn't think that works had any bearing upon their own relationship with God. This is a very subtle nuance of the Christian faith, and perhaps one of the most neglected teachings in Protestant Christianity. It is that one may have the assurance of salvation and still have a defective relationship with God. It is possible to have a right relationship with God and a bad relationship with God at the same time. For the relationship may be right in that one has personal faith but wrong in that there are no works by which to glorify God. It is an unchangeable, eternal and rewarding truth that our own personal works glorify God. This is why Jesus said, 'Let your light so shine before men, that they may see your good works, and glorify your Father which is in heaven' (Matt. 5:16).

It is precisely because works glorify God that they actually strengthen your faith. If you are a hearer only you will never move beyond mere assurance. There are Christians whose only concern after twenty years is that they're not sure they're Christians. And they never grow. Others get to assurance and they think, 'Well, that's it.' And they never grow. If you think like that you are deceived. You are a hearer of the word only. They thought that faith alone pleased God. But James says, 'Faith if it hath not works is dead, being alone.' Why? Because it makes no impact on others.

Obedience Is Always Rewarded

There are things which we do by faith which in turn build up and perfect our faith. Do them. Don't pray about them, do them. And you will feel a strength and a sense of God's presence that will surprise you. You will know what you have been missing out on. Obedience is always rewarded. God delights to bless those whose faith is not merely about their own salvation but is demonstrated outwardly by conduct that proceeds from an inward character that is transparent and pure.

Why does James say, 'Faith, if it hath not works, is dead, being alone'? Because faith is no more useful than a dead body if it doesn't have works. It is not going to be useful to another person, to God or to yourself. The Greek word is that used for a dead body, utterly and absolutely useless to anybody. It's the word used by Paul in Romans 6:11: 'Be dead ... unto sin.' It means be useless to sin. Faith without works is just as useless, not at

all the useful and pragmatic reality that Christianity is supposed to be.
Christianity works. But not by faith alone.

Faith can do absolutely nothing without works. Nothing is more
scandalous than faith without works. It is like a drunkard passing out
Christian tracts in the street. It is like a whoremonger witnessing to a
prostitute. It is like a wife-beater trying to win his children. 'Such a faith
is as useful as a dead body', says James.

Having a faith without works means you will never know God more
intimately than you did in your first moment of conversion. It means to
worship the transaction between the Father and the Son and no more.
You'll be like the converted thief on the cross though you live for another
twenty years. If I have faith but no works it is like my singing in the
congregation, 'My Jesus, I love thee' and then going out and denying
him. Or singing, 'O Jesus, I have promised to serve thee to the end' and
keeping my faith secret from the world. Or praying for the lost but never
speaking to them. That's faith without works. It's never to know the joy
and the strength that comes from being a doer.

God is trying to show us that we must put our Christianity into
practice. It is not enough to say, 'I have faith.' There's a sceptical world
out there that is saying, 'Show me. Prove it.'

At this point James anticipates a reaction from his readers. He knows
they will say, 'You have faith, I have works.' There's no inference here
that some claimed to have works without faith. It is simply that they
believed there were two kinds of Christians: those who had faith but no
works and those who had both faith and works. But is there such a thing as
a Christian who does not have works? What about those countless people
who have professed Christ but never come to church? Or those Christians
who don't tithe their income? Or those who never witness to their
neighbours? Are these people really Christians? Mind you, it is possible to
do all these things and not be a Christian. But James is not dealing with
that issue. Oddly enough James raises the question but doesn't really
answer it. His answer, such as it is, is just, 'Shew me thy faith without thy
works, and I will shew thee my faith by my works.'

We must look at this very carefully. James does not say that faith
without works is an impossibility, however much we may wish he had.
If you are honest, however much you deplore widespread hypocrisy,
you will be pleased to know that he doesn't rule out the possibility of
faith without works. After all, was there not a time in your Christian life
when you were not what you ought to be? Were you not a Christian
back in those years when you were not tithing, you were not faithful,
you were not witnessing, you were not reading your Bible and praying

as you ought, you were not resisting temptation as you should? What James does say, in a very heart-searching manner, is 'The onus is on you to prove to me that you are a Christian if you don't have works.'

Works Demonstrate Faith

The Greek gives us some clues here. 'Show me' means 'demonstrate to me'. It is the word that Jesus spoke to the leper, 'See thou tell no man; but go thy way, and shew thyself to the priest' (Mt. 8:4). Demonstrate your healing. It's also the word used in Acts 10:28, 'God hath shewed me that I should not call any man common or unclean.' This is a word that means 'prove it.' James says, 'You say you have faith. How would anybody ever know? Show me this faith. Prove it's real.'

James' point is not that faith without works is impossible, rather he demonstrates the folly and impossibility of *proving* that you have faith without works! It cannot be done. These Christian Jews claimed faith and great morality. What James does first, then, is a gigantic job of excavation. He shows them that they are immoral. Then he shows their faulty theology. Not only that, he shows the utter folly of even claiming to have faith without works to prove that faith is there.

'Look at what has happened to the reputation of Christianity because of you', James says. 'The onus is on you to prove to me that you have faith. In the meantime, I will prove my faith to you by my works.' That's the only way that you can show another that you really have faith. The sun will set a thousand times while you are trying to convince me that you are a Christian if you are not godly. 'But as for me,' says James, 'I will show you my faith by the way I treat my neighbour, by the way I conduct my life.'

He has three reasons for making this bold claim. First, he cares what God thinks. James wants more than anything else to please and glorify God. Do you know the prayer, 'Against thee, thee only, have I sinned' (Ps. 51:4)? That is the prayer of the godly person who knows that when they sin they have grieved God, the last thing they want to do. Second, James cares what people think. Not what they think about him, but what they will think about Christianity having met him. James vows never to put another person off Christianity. Third, James cares about his own spiritual growth. He knows that works both confirm and strengthen faith. Works are a great encouragement, their absence impoverishes us spiritually.

We Should Leave Others Without Excuse

If you are characterised by obedience, godliness, Christlikeness, sanctification and good works, you will please and glorify God. You will also render others defenceless, without excuse. They will never blaspheme because of you. They will know that there is something to Christianity because they'll see in you the kind of person they never thought they would see on this earth. All this will do something for your faith that nothing else will do, nothing but works can do. 'Thus,' says James, 'to be a hearer and not a doer is simply deceiving yourself. But to be a hearer and a doer is self-enriching.'

It's a pragmatic world out there. People ask questions. They have a right to. For no enterprise on the face of the earth makes the claims for itself that Christianity does. The problem that we face today is that most people have a vague idea of what Christianity is. They know just enough to render us without excuse. I ask you, are you like a dead body, useless to others, to God, to yourself?

Amazingly, God has put us on our honour. He hasn't threatened us with the loss of salvation if we don't become doers. We are not motivated to good works by that fear. God doesn't work like that. And that's just one more reason why we should give to him everything that we have: our bodies, our minds, our time.

25

The Devil's Faith

James 2:19

This is one of the most frequently quoted verses from James. It is an epistle that makes us feel most uncomfortable and yet very comfortable at the same time. What makes this epistle so remarkable is that James could motivate us without making us feel that we're not Christians – he does not threaten us with the law. Never does James hint that, 'You could not be Christians and act like that,' a weapon used frequently throughout church history. He never moralizes, nor even espouses a certain doctrine of assurance.

Four Interpretations

Generally speaking, the whole epistle, and this section about faith and works in particular, has been interpreted in one of four ways. One is that James is saying that we're saved by works. Another is that James is saying that we're saved by faith and works. The third is that James is saying that we're saved by faith but that faith is not valid unless there are works. And the last is the view that James is saying that we can have no assurance that we're saved if there are no works – that we're saved by faith but assured by works.

If that fourth option is true, it follows that there is no hope of salvation if you don't have works. And the result of that is that you get your assurance and your joy from your works. That becomes your preoccupation. That was the major error of Puritanism (with the exception of John Cotton), why so few in that movement felt assured. They were never sure they had repented enough. There are those to this very day who will not come to the Lord's Table because they are afraid they have not repented enough.

But James never says, 'The trouble with you people is you're just not saved', though he might well have been justified in doing so. Motivation like that never works. Or if it does, it usually does so with somebody who is not a Christian. The non-Christian or backslider might say, 'I'll do a little better', and then change for a week or two.

How God Motivates People

James believes that God motivates people first by accepting them, and then by chastening them. And in both cases God wants us to know that we are his. As far as James is concerned, the question of assurance ought never to come up. But there are people who say, 'Look here, if you are going to motivate people, don't let them think they're saved or they won't do anything.'

Thank God he doesn't play petty, manipulative games like people do. Nor is he fickle. Nor does he play games with the blood of his Son. Nor does he create faith in us only to have us doubt whether we have faith. God does not want us ever to doubt his Son's work generally or particularly. As when James shows us, he gives us the law of liberty and says, 'That's the way you are going to be judged. Live like it.'

Faith Does Not Speak for Itself

Mind you, just as God can be ruthless in chastening us, so too could James be ruthless. He now gives his most serious indictment of his readers thus far. 'Thou believest that there is one God; thou doest well: the devils also believe, and tremble.' Only the true Christian will be smitten by language like that. James' point is that faith does not *speak* for itself.

Faith is an intangible. It means absolutely nothing to someone who is living at the level of nature. The only thing that is going to convince them is the way you live. They must see something so different about you that they are compelled to recognize there is a God in the heavens.

'But', says James, 'you must recognize that if what you believe can be sanctioned by the devil, then faith without works is dead.' He is not concerned with whether they are saved so much as whether what they believe has utilitarian benefit. A dead faith does no good at all for others.

If you're going to claim to have faith without works, the onus is on you to prove your case. With that in mind James drops this bombshell upon them. Remember that he drops it in the context of what he's already said. He has told them, 'You have sunk so low that you have even become exposed by the moral law.' And 'Faith without works is dead.' Now he says to them, 'You say there is one God, that God is one. You do well. The problem is the devil believes that too.'

We saw that these Christian Jews took refuge in their sound theology. They didn't know they had a moral problem. But James pulls them up short: 'Your witness at the moment is so bad that it doesn't even go beyond that which the devil could condone.' It's a pretty sad day when the devil can match you in faith. And an even sadder day when faith has a greater effect on him than it has on you. If that Satan can affirm all that we believe and do then our witness clearly poses him no threat.

Are you aware of the devil's purposes for this world? He wants to destroy all God's people that the world might be his totally. 'The one thing,' said Edwards, 'that the devil cannot duplicate in man is to destroy Satan's interest in the world.' Do you have any reason to believe that you are a threat to the devil?

Monotheism and Trinitarianism

Why did James select this particular proposition: you believe God is one? There were hundreds of theological statements that he could have put to his readers, knowing they would say they believed them too. He chose this one, not because the belief that God is one is by itself necessarily saving faith – every Jew under the sun believed that, and it is essential – but because this was the boldest and most offensive Christian expression that could be made in a Jewish community. When Christians said that God is one they at once brought in the deity of Jesus. For a Christian Jew to say that God is one was to make Jesus of Nazareth and Jehovah one. For a Jew to say this was blasphemy so far as Judaism was concerned.

The classic objection to Christianity by a Jew was, and still is, that Christianity is idolatry for it breaks the law. 'Thou shalt have no other gods before me' (Ex. 20:3). Yet that Jesus is God is essential to Christian belief. The Jews would say to Christians, 'You cannot hold to the deity of Christ and monotheism at the same time.' Therefore for a Jew to say, 'Jesus is God' but also to say 'God is one', is to look ridiculous. The Jew would say to the Christian, 'If you want to be trinitarian go on and be trinitarian, but don't say that you believe God is one.'

Maintaining that Jesus is God and God is one was a powerful confession and offensive testimony in these circumstances. But that was the Christian Jews' faith, and they thought it ought to count for something. After all, it was costing them a lot. It separated them from their friends and brought them persecution. Holding to it endangered their future, their lives. James does not take their confession lightly, indeed he says 'Thou doest well.' He compliments them for sticking to their guns. 'But', James adds, 'I have to tell you that the devils believe this too.'

It is well known that Jesus got his most violent reception when he was around demon-possessed people. We're told in Mark 1:23–24 that 'there was in their synagogue a man with an unclean spirit; and he cried out, saying, Let us alone; what have we to do with thee, thou Jesus of Nazareth? art thou come to destroy us? I know thee who thou art, the Holy One of God.' In Matthew 8:28–29 Jesus 'met him two possessed with devils, coming out of the tombs, exceeding fierce, so that no man might pass by that way. And behold, they cried out, saying, What have we to do with thee, Jesus, thou Son of God? art thou come hither to torment us before the time?' James knew that the demons affirmed the oneness of God and the deity of Jesus at the same time. That doesn't make the belief wrong, but if the best you can do is hold to a confession that the demons affirm, then something is not right.

Consider the devil. The devil was once Lucifer, son of the morning, cast out of heaven. We know that the devil is wickedness, evil, the lie. He hates the people of God with an icy hatred. He is the arch enemy of Jesus of Nazareth and he knows who Jesus is. 'To think that your own witness', says James, 'has not even gone beyond what the devil could endorse. There's something wrong about that.'

The Faith of the Devil

What about this matter of the devil's faith? We must be careful about this. The devil's 'Faith' is a certain kind of knowledge, not trust in God. The Greek word comes from a root which means 'to persuade'. It is not a solely theological word. A person can have faith in something which is not divinely given. We can have faith at the level of nature. I have faith that in the summer it will be slightly warmer, in the winter slightly colder. I have faith that sun and rain will make the flowers grow. I am persuaded of that. So in Satan's realm there is obviously knowledge that is taken for granted. The devil who was cast down from heaven has great anger, for he knows his time is short (Rev. 12:12). And so the devils cry out to Jesus, 'Have you come to torment us before our time?'

There are things the devil knows. There was the time when those who were amateurs in casting out devils tried to do it in the name of Jesus, but only a voice came out, 'Jesus I know, and Paul I know; but who are ye?' (Acts 19:15). This is the devil's faith. He knows certain things and what he knows he knows well and it makes him tremble. It is a sad thing that James has to add this. 'All that you believe the devil believes, but he outdoes you. It makes him tremble. The devils are more affected by this same knowledge than you are. You feel that this confession has cost you. Satan could not only sign your confession of faith,' says James, 'but he outdoes you with respect of affection. For what has your faith produced? The same confession is something the devil has taken more seriously than you have. You say to people, "May God bless, be warmed in the fire", and that's as far as it goes. You feel that in the meantime you can be let off the hook because you affirm that God is one. The demons, the devils, the enemies of Christ, your enemies believe this and tremble.'

Trembling Produces Action

This trembling, so far as the devils are concerned, produces action. It keeps the devil aware that his time is short and, as a consequence, he works day and night. His only desire is to discredit the Christian message. Whenever you hear of Christians who have renounced their faith mark it up, the devil has just got another victory. Whenever anybody says, 'Well, if that's Christianity I don't want it', the devil has just got another victory. Whenever you do anything that gives the non-Christian reason to distrust all that you believe, it's another victory for the devil. If people judge Christianity by what you are and by the way you live and they now say, 'I don't want anything to do with Christianity', it is another victory for the devil.

Two things will bear looking at here. First, James shames these Jewish Christians by showing them that the unregenerate faith of devils produced stronger responses, results and works than the confession which they made. James has shown how disgraceful these Christian Jews had been – making blasphemers of people because they were status conscious, interested in their own prestige, wanting to make Christianity a respectable religion. It didn't work. This is perhaps the greatest put-down to any Christian community by a New Testament writer. Its only rival is what Paul said to the Corinthians about incest in the church (1 Cor. 5:1).

'But', says James, 'the devil is damned. He knows it and he shows it. You are saying you know it but you don't show it. The devils' faith which cannot save has a greater effect on them than your faith which does save has on you. The shame is that you should be judged by the law of liberty. You have nothing to dread. You have every reason to rejoice, but you do nothing to show this.'

Second, the faith of devils will do no good, neither for them, nor for anybody else. It's a faith without works. James' great indictment of his readers was the they had developed a witness like the faith of devils. James says, 'If you have faith without works, not only is your confession that which the devil can sign but so is your witness as well.'

James shows that these Christians' faith was making a similar impact to the knowledge and response of demons. If our witness in the world is no more than our faith, which doesn't speak for itself, and is actually what the devil can sanction, then obviously, he's sanctioning our influence as well. 'For', says James, 'you've put all of your eggs in one basket – faith alone.' That's the devil's faith and inasmuch as you are doing no works, Satan affirms you entirely. You're not threatening the devil much because of what you believe. The devil is more threatened by what you do, when you make an impact on others by a godly, upright life, a life that cannot be criticized for lack of love. Faith without works is not only the faith of devils but Satan himself could do no more harm than these Christians had done.

We sometimes use the expression, 'With friends like these, who needs enemies?' If these Christian Jews were the friends of Jesus Christ, what enemies did he need? Who could have done a better job for Satan? Who could have made Christianity look as bad? The devil loves it when people use the name of God in vain, when they blaspheme Jesus or speak ill of the church. All imagine the demons of hell could not have selected better instruments of evil than these Christians who succeeded in precisely those ends. Surely there is no more astonishing fault.

Serving the Devil's Interests Unwittingly

There follows but one lesson. Unless our total living cannot be sanctioned by the devil, what we believe and do leaves us vulnerable to being his unwitting agents in God's world. Can you think of anybody who might be put off Christianity because of you? Or anybody who would be surprised if they found out you were a Christian? There may be much confusion in this generation about what Christianity is, but most people do have a vague idea of what a Christian isn't supposed to be like.

Are you taking refuge in the fact of what you believe? You want it to count for something. As long as you're making no impact in the world the devil is quite happy. For if all that we believe is that which the devil could affirm, even though it makes him tremble, then we have no sure sign that our witness threatens his interest in the world. Could I have put my finger on our problem? You tell me.

26

Justification by Works

James 2:20–24

This is the single most controversial verse in James. 'Was not Abraham our father justified by works?' That's the question, the issue that has caused many to think that James opposed the apostle Paul.

Justification by Faith

Let's look very quickly at one of Paul's comments on this. In Romans 4 Paul said, 'If Abraham were justified by works, he hath whereof to glory; but not before God. For what saith the scripture? Abraham believed God, and it was counted unto him for righteousness. Now to him that worketh is the reward not reckoned of grace, but of debt. But to him that worketh not, but believeth on him that justifieth the ungodly, his faith is counted for righteousness' (vv. 2–5). Paul is clearly saying we're not justified by works at all, but by faith. James says, 'Was not Abraham our father justified by works?' Not only that, 'Pure religion and undefiled before God and the Father is this, To visit the fatherless and widows.' But Paul says that works will not glorify one before God.

It is this kind of thing that has caused many to say there must be a contradiction between James and Paul. But is there? As we have seen, James' term for what Paul calls 'justification by faith' is 'the perfect law of liberty'. What James meant by that clearly matches anything Paul himself said.

Why then did James say 'Was Abraham not justified by works?' We need to understand first of all that the doctrine of justification by faith is not something that came along later. It is often taught that Paul came up with justification by faith around AD 52–54, a rather late development. But this is utterly wrong. What Paul was to call justification by faith,

Peter had termed 'remission of sins' as early as the day of Pentecost (Acts 2:38). The same thing, different terminology. And, of course, the first Christians, being forgiven their sin through the blood of Jesus, were so thrilled, so electrified, that they knew exactly what Paul would later talk about. They experienced it from the very beginning.

We need to understand that James was not trying to get the church to focus its efforts on social concern. Some have recently used verses from James to justify what is called the social gospel. That is a prostitution of the epistle of James, a hasty conclusion that hides the real meaning of its message. You may think, because I happen to be an exponent of reformation theology, an admirer of Luther and Calvin, that I'm going to sugar-coat this matter of being justified by works. But we're going to see that when James said that we are justified by works he meant exactly that. In fact, so staggering and astonishing is James' teaching that I hope we'll wonder how we could ever have missed it.

Faith Without Works Is Useless

In verse 20 James seems to repeat verse 17, where he showed that faith without works is of no profit to others. When he said, 'Faith without works is dead', the word 'dead' is the Greek word that means a dead body. And a dead body is useless. When James now says, 'Wilt thou know, O vain man, that faith without works is dead', this time the Greek word is one which means 'useless'. James' point is that faith cannot speak for itself because faith is an intangible, it has no way of making any impact on the world by itself. Questions of personal salvation, or the assurance of it, do not even come into the picture. James' readers thought that salvation was all that mattered, but he is saying, 'There is something else.'

James raises the point again now, having just established that their Christian confession – something they considered sufficiently powerful to be their whole witness to the world – was no more than the devils could affirm. Right on the heels of that sobering thought, he says, 'But wilt thou know, O vain man, faith without works is useless?' By this James dramatizes how serious he is about the reputation of Christianity.

Christianity Is Essentially Evangelistic

Are you aware, my fellow Christians, that Christianity is essentially evangelistic? These Christian Jews were winning nobody, just like most of evangelical Christianity today. Calvin came up with a threefold formula for the true church. The true church is where the word of God is preached, the sacraments are administered and discipline is exercised. 'Wherever you have those three,' said Calvin, 'there you have the true church.' Many of us have just accepted that. But I think that Calvin was wrong. I don't think he went far enough. I would like to add a fourth thing, that the true church is also where people are being converted to the Lord Jesus Christ. Because if people are not being regularly converted it shows that God's glory has shifted to some other spot. How many churches are there that self-righteously go to the Lord's Day service from week to week, stiff-necked and saying, 'We are the true church', yet they're not seeing blessing and it doesn't seem to bother them?

These Christian Jews had in effect developed a bad theology, that what you believe is all that matters. James says to them, 'The devil can affirm everything that you are.' They had robbed faith of its ability to become what it was ultimately designed for, namely, to make us like Jesus. The law of liberty is the ground of Christian hope, and these Christian Jews knew that it was by that they would be judged. But James shows them there's something else the law of liberty ought to do. 'Whoso looketh into the perfect law of liberty, and continueth therein, he being not a forgetful hearer, but a doer of the work, this man shall be blessed in his deed' (1:25).

These Christian Jews had failed to produce a 'pure religion and undefiled before God'. They had come to think that the law of liberty was the only thing that mattered. James is trying to show them that Christianity ought to perfect us, to develop the finest specimens of humanity on the face of the earth. So he asked the question: 'Wilt thou know?' as if he's saying to them, 'Don't you see by now that faith without works is useless?'

What the Devil Cannot Affirm

There are two things in this repetition of the question which James hadn't said before. He says, 'Wilt thou know?' It must be a part of their sure knowledge. It must be a knowledge that exceeds what can be known in the satanic realm. The devil cannot affirm a knowledge that desires the glory of God, that aspires to defeat his own interest, that will affect our own wills.

To say that God is one requires an orthodox confession of faith, but it is something in the *mind*. When James says, 'Wilt thou know?' he uses the Greek word that touches the will. He's calling for a voluntaristic, volitional knowledge, a knowledge that affects the will, what we are. What one believes confessionally is in the mind or the heart (used interchangeably in the Bible). The heart is the intellectual faculty of the soul. For we see in the depths of our being that Jesus Christ has done everything required of us. And we believe that Jesus has been raised from the dead. We believe that in our hearts and it affects our salvation. 'But', says James, 'it's also got to affect the will if you're going to threaten the devil.'

Our Obedience Threatens Satan

Satan is not threatened by what we believe unless we believe also that we must do. The devil doesn't mind how articulate are your claims to knowing the Bible or understanding theology. The faith that threatens the devil is your obedience, how you live, whether people see Jesus in you. When your very manner of life, your transparent character, your conversation, your words, your spirit, your attitude, are such that the world sees you are different, you leave them without excuse. What threatened the devil in Revelation 12 was not only that 'they overcame him by the blood of the Lamb, and by the word of their testimony' – their salvation and their confession – but that 'they loved not their lives unto the death' (v. 11).

Do you know what will stir the devil? When you start obeying, doing things that the word of God says to do, setting your alarm clock a little earlier to pray. You say, 'Well, everything goes wrong when I do that.' Of course. The devil will fight you, trouble will come, but they should show you something. Unfortunately, most of us take any kind of hindrance as God's way of saying, 'You weren't supposed to do that.' We do not see that it's the devil working. Paul could say to the Thessalonians, 'We would have come to you once and again; but Satan hindered us' (1 Thess. 2:18). That isn't the way most of us talk. We say, 'God didn't allow it. We were providentially hindered.'

The reason why church attendance has fallen and why people are not excited about Christianity is that every hindrance is taken to be of God when we ought to see it's of the devil. When we become committed to what God wants and are determined to let nothing stand in the way, then we are threatening the devil. This is the kind of knowledge James is calling for. 'Wilt thou know, O vain man?' The Greek word means 'empty'. 'Empty Christian', you thought you could exist just by what you believe.

So much of today's 'empty' Christianity has the devil for its architect. Faith without works? 'Useless', says James, 'it makes no impression at all on the world'. But now comes the bombshell. 'Was not Abraham our father justified by works, when he had offered Isaac his son upon the altar?' The answer, of course, is that he was.

What Works Do

Using Abraham as an illustration, James proceeds to show five things that works do.

- Works justify. The Greek means 'to make righteous' (the same word Paul uses in Rom. 3:20, 24, 28; 4:2; 5:1).
- Works perfect or complete faith. 'Seest thou how faith wrought with his works, and by works was faith made perfect?'
- Works fulfill the promises about faith. 'And the scripture was fulfilled which saith, Abraham believed God, and it was imputed unto him for righteousness.'
- Works bring an intimate relationship with God. Was not Abraham 'called the Friend of God'?
- Works show that there are two kinds of justification. 'Ye see then how that by works a man is justified, and not by faith only.'

Abraham Is Our Father

James refers to Abraham as 'our father'. But in what sense? At a natural level he can only be such to Jews. And James no doubt meant at least this – he was talking to Christian Jews. But Abraham is also a spiritual father. And thank God for that. For without it Gentiles could never be saved. It is faith alone that establishes the spiritual continuity to Abraham.

These Christian Jews were tied to Abraham both naturally and spiritually. What James disputed was that their spiritual tie to Abraham was the only one that mattered. They had forgotten that Abraham was actually made righteous by his works.

When James says, 'Abraham was justified by works', he means this literally. He means first of all Abraham in his physical person. Abraham was personally righteous and just by what he did. That even made him righteous in God's eyes by God's standard, else God wouldn't have said it. What James is talking about right now is not an imputed righteousness, a declared righteousness. Abraham was in and by himself righteous.

Notice carefully, what James does not say Abraham achieved by this. He simply says, 'He, Abraham, was justified by works.' Many people fail to see the life of Abraham as a whole. This is where so much confusion sets in. The question is, *when* did Abraham achieve righteousness? When was he justified by works? Abraham's was a long life, and there's a lot to know about him. Does James have a specific event in Abraham's life in mind as he says Abraham was justified by works? Was it, for example, when God said, 'Get thee out of thy country, and from thy kindred, and from thy father's house ... and I will make of thee a great nation'? (Gen. 12:1, 2). No, that's not when it was. Might it be when God promised Abraham offspring like the stars (Gen. 15)? Abraham believed and 'it was imputed to him for righteousness'. Although Abraham was declared righteous by believing God at that moment, that is *not* what James selects to show that Abraham was justified by works. Crucially, James selects an event that took place years later, *after* Abraham had been justified by faith! He was justified by faith in Genesis 15 but the event James selects took place in Genesis 22.

Paul using Abraham to build his doctrine of justification by faith alone, selects Genesis 15, 'It was imputed to him for righteousness' (Rom. 4:3). And James also quotes Genesis 15:6, 'the scripture was fulfilled, which saith, Abraham believed God and it was imputed unto him for righteousness' (Jas. 2:33). That is James' point. He is trying to show them that Abraham believed that there was something important other than personal salvation, that Abraham himself became an obedient man, 'the Friend of God'. This justification by faith which Abraham knew in Genesis 15 had such an effect upon him that he became an obedient servant of God. Abraham was so grateful that he said, 'I'll do anything you say, God'. God took him seriously and began to try him. And Abraham just kept on believing and following, living in such a blameless fashion that it could be said that he was even made righteous by his works.

Faith Leads to Obedience

So when James quotes Genesis 15:6, he does so to show that faith was designed to do two things. One, to give salvation on credit. Two, to produce a life of obedience. Faith leads to obedience. You need to see, then, this definite order. Faith first, obedience second. When it comes to salvation throughout eternity it is faith alone. James calls that the 'perfect law of liberty'. Paul calls it God's righteousness, God's justice being satisfied. But the point James is trying to make is that obedience must follow. One must be justified by faith first, but then also by works. We should live lives that are blameless so that even God can sanction our character, conduct, thoughts and words, so that God is actually pleased with us, with our own goodness and integrity.

We can see that salvation is having the justice of God satisfied and its imputation of righteousness being given on credit. But there is a righteousness that God is asking of us and it's a very high standard. It's to be like the Lord Jesus. Too many of us in our heart of hearts have thought that standing for the faith in this awful day is all we are required to do. We hold fast to a faith that is no more than the devil could affirm, and we make no impact on this world.

There's a lesson to be learned here from church history. For the past four hundred years protestant Christianity, by and large, has had both Arminian and Calvinist movements. My background is Arminian. I was brought up in a church that emphasized holiness of life. They believed that as strongly as most of you believe in justification by faith alone. An extraordinary thing: since I've become a Calvinist I haven't converted one Arminian to the way I believe. I've tried, late into the night, day after day, but with no success.

I would be embarrassed, however, for some of my old friends to be around, some that I have had fellowship with in the last twenty years, to see the frivolity, and bent toward worldliness that is true among us. It's because we don't take real holiness seriously. If you want an idea of what I mean by holiness you ought to read some Arminian literature. You can say, 'Well, they weren't right on the doctrine of justification.' I say, 'You're not right when it comes to holiness.' I've got a theory that the world has yet to see Christians who are committed both to justification by faith alone and to living lives that would make you think they would be justified by their works.

If all that we are is just a confession which the devil can affirm, we're no threat to Satan. But if we would take seriously James' conviction that Christianity is designed to produce those who're like Jesus, and begin to be like him, then the world would have to take notice. You can expect the devil to be angry. If you begin to pray more and witness more, expect things to go wrong. But 'resist the devil, and he will flee from you' (Jas. 4:7). He's a conquered foe. It is time that we move on. There's a dying world out there and we are not reaching it. But we can do. And we begin by not just holding to our doctrine but by the way we live and talk.

27

Abraham's Righteousness

James 2:21–24

Justification by Works

We are right in the middle of the most controversial part of this epistle, and have seen that James' acknowledges both justification by works and justification by faith. The big point James makes is that Abraham was justified by works when he offered Isaac upon the altar. It shows the possibility of an obedience so complete that God himself approves. That takes some doing because God is holy and jealous, his eyes are so pure they will not look upon sin.

Obedient Abraham

Abraham had not always been so obedient. There were blemishes on that man's life. There was the time when he went into Egypt and lied about Sarah being his wife. And the time when Sarah and Abraham got impatient and decided to fulfil God's word themselves by Abraham sleeping with their servant girl, Hagar. Abraham lived to regret that. Even when God said, 'You're going to have a son through Sarah', do you know what Abraham did? He laughed. Not something to be proud of.

God stays with us despite our blemishes. Despite Abraham's sins, God did not drop him. God stayed, and there came a time when Abraham's obedience was so exact, deliberate and meticulous that he was justified by his works. We're told, 'Was not Abraham our father justified by works, when he had offered Isaac his son upon the altar?' That was the moment when he was indeed righteous.

Abraham is not the only man of whom this could be said. I daresay we could go through the eleventh chapter of Hebrews, the great faith chapter, and also make it the works chapter as James is doing right here. Take, for example, the Psalmist. He could actually say, 'Let integrity and uprightness preserve me' (Ps. 25:21). This is not an imputed righteousness. It is a real, actual righteousness. And he could say, 'Judge me, O LORD, for I have walked in mine integrity' (Ps. 26:1). This is the real righteousness that James is calling for.

For these Christian Jews in that second generation of the church had let their standards slip so much that the world was laughing. Those that they were running into had become blasphemers of Jesus' name, because these Christians thought their orthodoxy was sufficient. What James is trying to produce in these Christian Jews is a real righteousness, not only because they're going to be justified and saved by the law of liberty, but that they might also know that intimate relationship with God that Abraham had, be God's friends.

How We Are Justified By Our Works

What, then, is the standard of righteousness that God owns and affirms in his own people? When *do* works justify? The answer is demonstrated by Abraham's offering of his son Isaac. We can see five principles in this story that I hope we will apply to our hearts. The need of the hour is not a refinement of our theology or a reaffirmation of our orthodoxy. The need of the hour is for Christians who are justified by works. To find out how to be justified by works we turn to the original account of when Abraham offered Isaac (Gen. 22).

The Test

Principle number one is that *what God asks of us never makes sense at the time*. God asked Abraham to give back what was beyond doubt most precious to him, his son Isaac. Isaac was most precious to Abraham at two levels. At a natural level, consider Abraham's fatherly love for his son. You cannot dismiss Abraham's emotional trauma when told to offer his son.

If such natural affection between parents and their children is normal, how much more might God ask us to abandon anything that becomes a substitute for the joy of the Lord? It might be your most natural or legitimate pleasure. It could be your children, your studies, your job. It could be good eating or the most wholesome kind of entertainment. God is a jealous God, and however much you want to justify those natural feelings or normal affections, God wants to be first. He wants to be your joy and your praise.

This was something that Abraham had to recognize at a natural level, but also at a spiritual level. For God even asked Abraham to abandon his only tangible link between promise and fulfillment. Abraham had believed God's promise years before, and so was justified by faith. Despite years of uncertainty and the shameful arrival of Ishmael, God finally kept his promise in the birth of Isaac. The word was: 'In Isaac shall your seed be called' (Gen. 21:12). So the request, 'Give Isaac your only son upon the altar' involved something precious to Abraham at a spiritual level too. The promise was to be through Isaac. Abraham might have been tempted to argue with God. 'Surely not. You're the One who gave me Isaac. You're the One who said, "Count the stars. So shall thy seed be." Isaac is only one person and you want me to give him up, the only link between promise and fulfilment?'

This is the way God deals with us. You may be one of those who says, 'Well, look, I've only got one gift I can give to God. If he takes that away I've got nothing left. I've given him everything else. Surely God wouldn't want me to give this up?' Even your gift must be abandoned to God. It may make no sense to us, but we cannot know God's mind or plans. The first principle in any time of testing is that what God asks is always that which makes no sense at the time.

Faith Perfected

The second principle in Genesis 22 is that *faith is never perfected without suffering*. God asked Abraham to give what was most precious, in a way that was most painful. I don't know why suffering is necessary for the perfection of faith. But the writer to the Hebrews says of our Lord Jesus Christ that 'it became him, for whom are all things, and by whom are all things, in bringing many sons unto glory, to make the captain of their salvation perfect through sufferings' (Heb. 2:10). Again, 'Though he were a Son, yet learned he obedience by the things which he suffered' (Heb. 5:8).

Think about it for a moment. Our Lord did not need to have righteousness given to him on credit. He was perfect righteousness, he sanctified himself. And yet he learned obedience through suffering. How much more do we who have been given righteousness on credit, who have a sinful nature and the flesh to fight against, need a baptism of suffering? Jesus said, 'Strait is the gate, and narrow is the way, which leadeth unto life, and few there be that find it' (Mt. 7:14).

I don't know what suffering will be in your case, what it will take for God to bring you to a level of obedience where you are justified by works. It may be natural suffering: physical, financial, keen disappointment, frustrated dreams, the withholding of vindication, loneliness. It could be spiritual suffering: being forbidden to speak out when mistreated, having to forgive an adversary, being faithful without any reward. Whatever it is, I can tell you this, the suffering that is required in order for faith to be perfected is a level of consecration and righteousness that is far beyond what most of us have experienced.

I think the time has come when we who are serious about wanting to please God must tiptoe into the Wesleyan camp to see what they were doing that was right and godly, which God honoured. We may not like all their theology, but anybody who won the souls John Wesley did, or produce the hymns that Charles Wesley did, couldn't have been all bad. We must see what they did that was right. Wesley would say, 'Our people die well.' There was a quality of life among those men and women of which the world was not worthy. They had a standard of self-denial and consecration that was so exact that until it was there, as they put it, 'the fire would not fall'. They used to sing the song: 'I was all on the altar when the fire fell.' This standard requires self-denial until you've got no pride left. No gifts to offer. No resentment. There's nothing left of you and that's when God can use you. This is exactly what Peter meant when he said, 'Forasmuch then as Christ hath suffered for us in the flesh, arm yourselves likewise with the same mind: for he that hath suffered in the flesh hath ceased from sin; That he no longer should live the rest of his time in the flesh to the lusts of men, but to the will of God' (1 Pet. 4:1–2).

Trust God

Principle number three is that we *obey the Spirit without knowing the details of his will*. God kept the details of his will in suspension. He said to Abraham, 'Go to the land of Moriah and offer him there as a burnt offering upon one of the mountains which I *will* tell you of.' Our trouble is that we want God to give all the details now. This is why witchcraft and divination are regarded as works of the flesh (Gal. 5:20). It's human nature to want to know where we're heading, what's going to happen. But we are not God, we must give up the desire to know the end from the beginning. 'One step at a time', God says. We may have a general idea of what God is doing, but the details are kept until his time.

We're told that 'on the third day Abraham lifted up his eyes, and saw *the* place afar off' (Gen. 22:4). How did Abraham know that was the place?

God told him that he would know. We're not told precisely how Abraham knew, only that he saw it and knew. When God deals intimately with us he brings us to the place that we know in our heart of hearts is right. There's no use arguing, postponing or deliberating about it.

When the Holy Spirit puts his finger on something in your life you will know it. Respond. What matters is what you do when you see the place, when God puts his finger on something in your life. It could be that nobody else will understand. Abraham knew there was no use explaining to his servants where he was going. He just went on with Isaac. A chief part of your consecration is not allowing others to see what you see, lest you get self-righteous and say, 'This is what you've got to do also.' No, that's for you. Are you willing to suffer it alone?

The Worst Is Yet to Come

Principle number four is that despite what you've already been through, *the worst suffering of all may lie in the future* (although the worst is almost always just before the end). Genesis 22:7–8 is one of the most heart-rending scenes in all the Bible. 'Isaac spake unto Abraham his father, and said, My father: and he said, Here am I, my son. And he said, Behold the fire and the wood: but where is the lamb for a burnt offering?' I don't know how Abraham could stand that.

If your suffering becomes almost unbearable, it's a good sign! You're nearly in. You're near the point where God can affirm your righteousness on the one condition that you don't murmur. I suspect that all heaven was watching to see what Abraham would do. He was coming to the critical moment when the most heart-rending of all suffering would be put before him. Isaac says, 'Dad, I don't understand. I see the fire. I see the wood. Where's the lamb?'

Here was the moment for Abraham to murmur. Had he done so the whole trial would have been aborted. God will give you a trial that requires your bearing it without murmuring. What did Abraham do? He said, 'My son, God will provide himself a lamb for a burnt offering: so they went both of them together.' The greatest suffering may lie in the future. And until you pass that test, don't look for any other.

It Is Not Enough to be Willing

The final principle, number five, is that we are not justified by works until we have actually *carried out the ultimate request God makes of us*. James says that Abraham was 'justified by works, *when he had offered Isaac ...* upon the altar'. James did not say Abraham was justified by works when he believed God, when he went down into Egypt with Sarah, when he paid tithes to Melchizedech. It was not until he offered Isaac on the altar and had the knife hot in his hand that God stopped him. Because offering Isaac was not just what Abraham had to be willing to do. He actually had to do it. The works which justify are what you do. You may pray from now till doomsday saying, 'Lord, make me willing.' While you're praying like that God will be dealing with a thousand others and passing you by. Abraham was justified by works *when* he offered Isaac. You may ask, 'Why did Abraham have to do it? If he was willing shouldn't the will count for the deed?' The answer is threefold. First, Abraham had to do it so that his faith would be perfected. He was willing to be willing all along. But he had no way to know he would do it until he did it. 'The heart is deceitful above all things, and desperately wicked' (Jer. 17:9). We can all talk about how willing we are, but the only way to know really whether you're willing is to do it. Abraham's faith was not perfected until he did it.

Keep in mind that James is concerned about the testimony of these Christian Jews. They were willing and they thought their confession of faith was sufficient. You may be willing but the world cannot see what you're willing to do. While the world goes to hell are you going to feel good about yourself because you're willing?

But the chief reason Abraham had to do it was not just for his own faith or for the sake of how it would appear, but because of what it meant to God. The works that justify us actually do something to God. The angel of the Lord came to Abraham and said, 'Lay not thine hand upon the lad, neither do thou anything unto him: for *now I know* that thou fearest God' (Gen. 22:12). God is waiting for us to obey him in such a manner that he can affirm us by saying, 'Now I know.' Our faith being perfected pleases him. That's why it matters. You are deceiving yourself if you are a hearer only and not a doer. Most of us have not pleased God because we haven't *done*.

By doing it Abraham not only pleased God, but enabled God to give his life back to him. Jesus said, 'Whosoever shall seek to save his life shall lose it; and whosoever shall lose his life shall preserve it' (Lk. 17:33). God delights in giving our lives back to us. And yet I think the sweetest thing of all that comes out of this is that our works bring us into a most intimate relationship with God. Abraham, from then on, was called 'the Friend of God'. That didn't come because of his justification by faith. It came because of his justification by works.

How many of us are God's friends? What a test. How wonderful if God is dealing with us in such a manner that we have opportunity to pass the test, to become God's friends. Abraham had given God every reason to drop him. He had sinned and done foolish things and was now a hundred years old. You may feel that you're too old to do anything that pleases God. You may think that your life is such that all you can do is just hope to die. But wait a minute. Abraham was a hundred when God gave him his finest hour.

Who knows what God will do with any of us if we will make our calling and election sure by a selflessness, a self-denial that the world does not see in people? Two questions. Have you been justified by faith? Do you know what it is to believe God and have righteousness given to you on credit? That's how you go to heaven. That's how to know you're saved. Second question: have you been justified by works?

28

Friends of God

James 2:21–24

We proceed in our study of the most controversial and difficult part of James. One of the things that makes any part of God's word difficult is reading it defensively. Many times when we come to a difficult passage of Scripture, the best way to deal with it is to take it most seriously indeed, even literally, and it is amazing how it coheres with everything we thought at first it might not.

Growth in Grace

Keep in mind what James is saying. 'Be ye doers of the word, and not hearers only, deceiving your own selves.' The doctrine of justification by faith alone was nothing new to these Christian Jews. But they were deceived in that they deprived themselves of truly knowing God by allowing an arrested development at the point of their conversion. They thought that their justification which provided imputed righteousness was all that mattered. They needed to see the importance of growth in grace.

They were much like the famous antinomian Puritan of the seventeenth century, Tobias Crisp. He taught that imputation is all that matters, that God cannot see past the blood of Jesus. He can't see your sins but neither can he see anything good you do. Therefore there's not going to be any chastening for disobedience or blessing for obedience. Our relationship with God is entirely based upon the transaction between the Father and the Son. There's no spiritual growth beyond that you achieve in the moment of your salvation. Tobias Crisp was a godly man of such unimpeachable character that nobody could find fault with him. But that is a very dangerous and manifestly unscriptural doctrine. To say that there is going to be no blessing on the basis of our obedience is wrong.

Faith Is Not Enough

What these Christian Jews did not have was love. That is why James had to bring in what he called the royal law of scripture: if you love your neighbour as yourself you do well. Not only that, James says that God wants to bless us because of what we do. 'Surely not', says someone. 'Surely all we can do is but filthy rags.' James says, 'Was not Abraham our father justified by works, when he had offered Isaac his son upon the altar?' You might wish that James had said, 'Was not Abraham assured by works?' But he didn't mean that. And obviously he didn't mean that Abraham was saved by works. But there is a justification by works.

There is what Paul calls a 'faith which worketh by love' (Gal. 5:6). James calls it a righteousness or justification by works. Keep in mind that the words 'righteousness' and 'justification', while used interchangeably in English, are from the same Greek word. Justification, then, has a double meaning. There is an imputation of righteousness owing to our faith (what Paul makes most of in his epistles). But there is also a righteousness manifested in us owing to faith and works, and this is what James makes most of. The doctrine of imputation is not absent in James, neither is the doctrine of personal righteousness absent in Paul (see Romans 12:1, for example), but he they can each have their emphasis.

To show these two points – imputation and personal righteousness – James uses two illustrations, Abraham and Rahab. Rahab's righteousness was of the sort that the world could see. Abraham's righteousness, however, was that which God himself affirmed. James might have selected someone other than Abraham, or a different event in Abraham's life (as did the writer to the Hebrews 11:8). But I think I know why he chose Abraham's offering of Isaac. It was because God said to Abraham, 'By myself have I sworn, saith the LORD, for because thou hast done this thing, and hast not withheld thy son, thine only son' (Gen. 22:16). God affirmed Abraham's action. Not only do our works matter to the world, they matter to God. Nothing can motivate me more than to know God notices what I do.

In verse 22 James shows what lay behind Abraham's deed. It was faith and works simultaneously combined in that which God could affirm. 'Seest thou how faith wrought with his works, and by works was faith made perfect?' It shows the co-operation between faith and works.

The word *sunergei* is used. It's a common word in the Bible, but it does appear in one of the most famous verses of all: 'We know that all things *work together* for good' (Rom. 8:28). It shows faith and works together. Why would James even bother to say 'faith'? Why didn't he just say 'actions'? James wants us to know that what Abraham was doing was by faith. Abraham's offering Isaac could have been described as faith alone. You wouldn't have to bring in works if you didn't want to. In fact, the writer to the Hebrews did just that. He simply said, 'By faith Abraham, when he was tried, offered up Isaac: and he that had received the promises offered up his only begotten son, Of whom it was said, That in Isaac shall thy seed be called: Accounting that God was able to raise him up, even from the dead; from whence also he received him in a figure' (Heb. 11:17–19). But James says, 'Wait a minute. Can't you see that in faith Abraham was *doing* something? He believed God so much that he obeyed. He took God seriously and he did a marvellous thing. So the whole time faith was working together with works.'

When Abraham offered Isaac by faith, was that a saving faith? No, because Abraham was already saved. His saving faith was demonstrated in Genesis 15 when God said, 'Count the stars; so shall your seed be.' Abraham believed and it was accounted to him, or imputed to him, for righteousness. But now we're told that by faith he's doing something. What kind of faith? The wonderful thing about Abraham's faith was that it did not end with imputation of righteousness. That was only the beginning. Abraham continued on.

We've seen that there are two kinds of faith: saving faith and experimental faith. Faith has a double meaning, just as righteousness or justification has a double meaning. There is a saving faith when we lay hold of all that Jesus has done for us on the cross. By believing what he did we're given a righteousness on credit by which we know that we are eternally saved. But faith does more than that. This is what Hebrews 11 is all about: for these great men and women of faith had, over and above their saving faith, an experimental faith. And this is what James is saying now. 'You see then how faith co-operated with his works and by works faith was made perfect.' The Greek means 'complete'. It doesn't mean a perfect faith. It means a faith not left unfulfilled.

Faith Makes us Whole

Faith not only assured Abraham, it made him a whole person. The wonderful thing about the gospel is that it makes us real persons in the world. Christianity aims to produce the manner of people the world cannot see except by God's grace. This is what James is pleading for: that we'll not only be saved but have something about our lives that is so different that it compels the world to recognize the difference being Christian makes. Christianity not only fits us for heaven, it equips us for service on earth and it makes us do wonderful things.

James says, 'By *works* faith is made complete', not 'By *faith* faith is made complete.' In other words, he does not say that more assurance, knowing more about the Bible or coming to church and singing hymns makes your faith complete. Here's the awesome thing: there are no shortcuts. Works, what you do, are what make your faith complete. So, in James' words, if you are 'a doer of the work, this man shall be blessed in his deed' (1:25).

There's only one way to bring faith to its fulfillment and that is *obedience*. Saving faith, then, is believing God. Experimental faith is believing God by obeying him. If faith is deprived of fulfillment, is not allowed to become complete, the consequences are melancholy indeed. Do you remember Augustine's comment? 'Thou hast made us for thyself and our souls are restless until they find their rest in thee.' The same thing can be said of faith, for faith is restless if not allowed to reach maturity, to grow and to proceed. And restlessness becomes ruthlessness. There's an expression we all know: hell hath no fury like a woman scorned. The same is true of faith. Faith demands to be fulfilled and if that is not allowed, it will backfire.

It backfires in your adverse testimony in the world and by making you what James calls 'double minded'. This is why there's nothing sadder on the face of the earth than a disobedient Christian. You may not even know whether you are a Christian if you are disobedient – its result is a confused mind. You can't think straight. You are bewildered. Nothing is right with backsliders. They look at the world through a jaundiced eye, blaming everybody, confused. There's only one way, and that is to obey. Faith demands fulfilment, and if it doesn't get it you will suffer. For the double minded show that they have a defective relationship with God. Faith demands works. It reflects the character of God who will admit no rival. If faith is not complemented by works and by obedience it will take its toll. The world will blaspheme. James asked, 'Do you see how by faith working together with works, faith was made complete?' Do we see it?

The Scandal of the Gospel

It is equally important to know that there are happy consequences if faith is allowed fulfilment. And James proceeds to show two. First, the Scripture is fulfilled. He says, 'And the scripture was fulfilled which saith, Abraham believed God.' That's the fulfillment of Genesis 15. Abraham believed and God said, 'You're saved. I give you a righteousness on credit. You didn't earn it. You're whole. You are righteous for ever.' But James says, 'Look here. That scripture was fulfilled.' How? Remember who Abraham was when God called him. He was not a godly man. He was an uncircumcised sun worshipper. Not promising material. The scandal of the gospel is that Christ always justifies the ungodly, that God gives a robe of righteousness by faith. The most ungodly and wicked person can be given righteousness on credit. The blood of Jesus washes away all your sins. You don't have to earn it, work up to it, prepare yourself for it. Just believe the promise.

That's what happened to Abraham. Look at this sun worshipper now. God says, 'Offer your son.' Abraham doesn't understand that, but though the orders were painful and made no sense, he did it. Abraham had become a godly man across the years. 'Look at him now', says James. 'Was he not justified by works when he offered his son?' He had accounted that 'God was able to raise him up, even from the dead'.

This is the wonderful thing about the gospel. It gives righteousness on credit, the only thing that will ever make us godly. The biggest surprise of all is that any of us could have an affection for God and could want to please him. But it all began because God gave us a righteousness on credit. 'But', says James, 'the scripture was fulfilled.' God hadn't misfired. God sees the end from the beginning. Someday God is going to present the saints, all of us, blameless.

Even while Abraham was on this earth there was an obedience about him that God noticed. His obedience was an earnest of his glorification, a righteousness that vindicated God. God declared him righteous when nobody could see any hope in him. And thirty years later … It takes time. Some of us are slow. But God has a way of bringing us to a place where he can say, 'Look at Abraham. Try him. He's my friend.' And the Scripture was fulfilled, the Scripture which said, 'God imputed it unto him for righteousness.'

Remember Augustine's four stages? One, that God made humanity able to sin. Two, after the Fall humanity was unable not to sin. Three, through faith humanity was able not to sin. This is where we are now, we're able to obey. Four, one day humanity will be unable to sin. In other words, faith is allowed to be complete it justifies God for declaring us righteous because we eventually become righteous. In addition, Abraham's obedience actually did something to his relationship with God, after that he was called 'the Friend of God'. God does not let our obedience go unnoticed. 'God is not unrighteous to forget your work and labour of love' (Heb. 6:10). God can elevate us to a higher realm. Our relationship with him can be enriched to such a degree that we're called friends of God.

Friends of God

Saving faith assures us that God is our friend. But James is saying that we can be God's friends. That's different. Surely no more wonderful thing can be said about anybody than that they are a friend of God.

What are the ingredients of genuine friendship? I think there are two things. One, loyalty in the face of apparent disloyalty. Abraham could not have understood why God told him to offer Isaac as a sacrifice. Isaac was the promised child. God must have appeared to be disloyal, to have broken his word. But Abraham did what God said. It made no sense and was most painful, but Abraham did not question God. Abraham knew there must be an explanation. And, as the writer to the Hebrews tells us, he trusted that God would be able to raise Isaac 'even from the dead'. 'That's what God's going to do', said Abraham. 'It's okay. God isn't going to break his word. I don't know what God's thinking but he said, "In Isaac shall thy seed be called." That's good enough for me.'

True friendship imputes a hidden explanation to one's motives, so what Abraham did was to impute something to God. The word used in Hebrews 11:19 'accounting that God was able', is *logisamenos*, which means 'imputing'. What the writer to the Hebrews is saying is that Abraham imputed to God an integrity that didn't match appearances. God appeared to be being disloyal. 'No,' said Abraham, 'he's not disloyal. He's doing something else. I know what he's going to do. He's going to raise Isaac from the dead.'

James uses the same word when he says the Scripture was fulfilled that Abraham believed God and 'it was imputed unto him for righteousness'. The sweetest picture emerges. Why should God impute to Abraham righteousness when he was a sun worshipper? There's no reason why he should do it. But then, why should God save any of you? Why are you justified? What kind of bargaining power did you have? It just doesn't make sense. But that's what God did. You believed him; he imputed righteousness to you. Abraham said, 'I'll do the same thing with God. I don't know why this is happening, but I impute to him an integrity.'

God gave to Abraham a righteousness he didn't deserve. Abraham gave to God an integrity that he didn't understand. Abraham knew that when he was given a righteousness on credit it was something he didn't deserve. He never got over it. And now he just said, 'It's all right. If God wants to take my son he can have him.' This is the way the saints have always been. We don't always understand the way God is leading us but, after all, you can't understand why he would have saved you. He imputed righteousness to you. All right, you impute righteousness to him, integrity.

Shadrach, Meshach and Abednego didn't know what was going on. But they said, 'Our God is able to deliver us from the burning fiery furnace but if he doesn't we're not going to bow down' (Dan. 3:17). And there was Polycarp, the second-century martyr who, while being tied to the stake, was told, 'All you've got to do is pray to Caesar and deny your Lord.' Polycarp replied, 'Eighty and six years have I served my Lord and he hath done me no wrong. How can I deny him now?' That is the response of the obedient children of God. That's what friendship is. That's why Abraham was called the friend of God. Abraham didn't understand but he went on.

The second thing about true friendship is the acceptance of another's deepest secret. God had a secret he wanted to share with somebody. God had been longing to share his desire to have a people for himself. He knew how Abraham looked at everything. He knew the way Abraham interpreted the word 'seed' back in Genesis 15 – 'So shall thy seed be'. And now that Isaac was born he knew that Abraham would think that seed meant the natural procreation of the race. God wanted Abraham's seed to be the people of God, but not at the level of nature, not by natural procreation. So God decided to share with Abraham his deepest secret: that Abraham's seed would be continued not by procreation but by regeneration. There was only one way to get this secret over to Abraham and that was to make him offer Isaac. Abraham would have to give up Isaac, kiss him goodbye. Abraham did. And Abraham got him back, we're told, 'in a figure' by the writer to the Hebrews. Isaac could never be looked at the same again. Abraham had learned God's secret.

As the Psalmist put it, 'The secret of the Lord is with them that fear him' (Ps. 25:14). And Paul said, 'But we speak the wisdom of God in a mystery, even the hidden wisdom, which God ordained before the world unto our glory … as it is written, Eye hath not seen, nor ear heard, neither have entered into the heart of man, the things which God hath prepared for them that love him. But God hath revealed them unto us by his Spirit: for the Spirit searcheth all things, yea, the deep things of God' (1 Cor. 2:7,9–10).

So intimately did God deal with Abraham that he did not conceal his delight when Abraham obeyed. He said, 'I have sworn … because thou hast done this thing … in blessing I will bless thee, and in multiplying I will multiply thy seed' (Gen. 22:16, 17). God was able to share his great secret with Abraham. And this is the way Jesus was with his disciples. 'Henceforth I call you not servants; for the servant knoweth not what his lord doeth: but I have called you friends; for all things that I have heard of my Father I have made know unto you' (Jn. 15:15). Friend of God. What a privilege we have. Not only is God our friend, God invites us to be his friends. We must be loyal, even when we don't understand what he's doing, and let him teach us his greatest secrets. James says, 'Ye see then how that by works a man is justified, and not by faith only.'

There are two kinds of faith: experimental faith and saving faith. There are also two kinds of justification: one that is given on credit, one that is a visible righteousness which God affirms. When I realise that God will bless me in my deed, in my work, that makes it worthwhile. You may feel when the going gets rough that you just want to give up, but remember God is looking down from heaven, saying, 'There's my friend.' Jesus said, 'If ye love me, keep my commandments' (Jn. 14:15). John says, 'His commandments are not grievous' (burdensome) (1 Jn. 5:3). That means they're not demoralising. God has a way of dealing with us and if we'll wait we'll understand what was going on. He'll reveal the secret and he'll call us 'friend'.

29

The Harlot's Example

James 2:25–26

This is the conclusion of this second chapter of James. We squirmed in chapter one but it got worse in chapter two. Wait till you get to the third chapter! We all feel keenly the intensity of God's word, whatever the subject is.

James wants us to see that we should take sanctification as seriously as we do the doctrine of justification by faith. He doesn't use the words 'sanctification', 'holiness' or 'godliness'. He calls it 'justification by works', meaning by that to carry out the obedience that God gives us. As John says, 'We love him by keeping his commandments but his commandments are not grievous' (1 Jn. 5:3). So James is showing that there is an obedience that is pleasing to God, that he affirms. It is called 'justification by works'.

Righteousness

We have seen that 'justification' has a double meaning and that James brings out both aspects. There is a righteousness that is given to us on credit, and another that is produced when faith works alongside deeds, completing faith. As he puts it, 'how faith wrought with his works, and by works was faith made perfect'. For James, imputed righteousness makes possible the perception of faith. Without it Abraham would never have developed into a godly man. God begins with us where we are. Christ justifies the ungodly and if he didn't do that, if he didn't give a righteousness on credit, we would have no hope of ever being godly.

Saul of Tarsus was not a godly man: he went out killing Christians. But the time came when he could say, 'You know what manner of men we were among you for your sake.' And 'Ye are witnesses, and God also, how holily and justly and unblameably we behaved ourselves among you that believe' (1 Thes. 1:5; 2 Thes. 2:10).

James readers thought that imputed righteousness was the only thing that mattered, but James said, 'Be ye doers of the word, and not hearers only, deceiving your own selves.' Our righteousness is given first on credit, but our faith that brought about that imputed righteousness is fulfilled to the extent that we are obedient to what God gives to us to do. James shows that this righteousness not only determines our witness but God himself affirms it and, if we do well, we can be called the friends of God.

Rahab the Heroine

James is not finished. 'Likewise also was not Rahab the harlot justified by works, when she had received the messengers, and had sent them out another way?' Remember how Rahab the harlot hid the Israelite spies in Jericho? She said to them, 'I know who you are and I know that your God is the true God and he has delivered this land into your hands. Just remember me and my family.' Then she let them down by a scarlet cord which also served as a sign to protect her in the ensuing slaughter.

James says, 'Likewise also was not Rahab the harlot justified by works?' The Greek word for 'likewise' is *homoios*. It means 'after the same manner', 'in the same way'. He is obviously inviting a comparison with Abraham, about whom he has just talked. Since Abraham was given righteousness on credit, it follows that Rahab too was given an imputed righteousness.

Was Rahab imputed righteousness when she left the scarlet cord hanging out the window? Or was it when she 'perished not', as the writer to the Hebrews puts it (Heb. 11:31)? No, she clearly had faith before then – not a saving faith but an experimental faith. Was it when she received the messengers and sent them out? James calls that 'justification by works'. The answer is, she was given an imputed righteousness the moment she first believed. Joshua tells us that she hid the spies straightaway. But Joshua 2:9 reveals to us what lay behind her doing so. As soon as she saw them it was revealed to her that they represented the one true God and she called him by name: 'Yahweh. Jehovah. The true God.' Here was a pagan woman, a harlot, believing right on the spot and receiving an imputed righteousness.

James is showing not only how Rahab was imputed righteousness but how she, by experimental faith, did extraordinary things as Abraham had done. There are three comparisons between Rahab and Abraham. First, what Rahab did was as unprecedented as Abraham's offering of Isaac was. Second, what Rahab did was without anybody else's support or affirmation. Similarly, Abraham couldn't talk to Sarah, his servants or Isaac. It was between him and God. Rahab didn't have time to get anybody's advice. God wanted her to lean on him only. Third, both of their experiences involved a detachment from all that they held dear at a natural level. Abraham had to give up his only son, Rahab stood against her home town, culture, nationality and king.

But there were obviously differences between Rahab and Abraham and this is why James brings in Rahab. Alone, Abraham as illustration left things unsaid. Abraham offered Isaac thirty years after he was given an imputed righteousness. Rahab did what she did almost simultaneously with believing. Abraham had grown in grace over thirty years. But Rahab did something extraordinary the day she believed. Abraham was told by God what to do. Rahab did what she did spontaneously. Abraham was affirmed by God himself. Rahab was affirmed by the spies, and eventually Joshua.

Why Choose Rahab as an Illustration?

I think there are five reasons why James chose Rahab the harlot as an illustration for 'justification by works'.

- So that these Christian Jews would not be demoralized by thinking Abraham's awesome example was the only kind of righteousness by works.
- To show that great growth and a certain amount of time is not required in order to be righteous by deeds.
- To show that works do something for the kingdom of God that faith alone cannot do. Rahab illustrates all James has said in this chapter even more than Abraham does. James is concerned about his readers' witness in the community. Through Rahab, he is showing that works do something that faith cannot do. Rahab's faith was real and wonderful, yet it wouldn't have done a thing for those spies. It might have impressed them had she said, 'I know who you are. You serve the true God. God is with you. It's great to meet you', and let them go, but it would not have saved them. They needed to be hidden, advised when it was safe to leave, and shown the safest way out of town. What advances the kingdom of God is not faith only but works. What we believe isn't sufficient. It is what we do.

- To show what these works did for Rahab. The witness of what we do does something for other people, but it also does something for us. Rahab was spared. She risked her life and all that she had, but she got it back. Jesus said, 'Whosoever will save his life shall lose it: and whosoever will lose his life ... shall find it' (Mt. 16:25). Rahab found hers. Not only that. She prayed that they might remember her family too. Jesus said, 'And everyone that hath forsaken houses, or brethren, or sisters, or father, or mother, or wife, or children, or lands, for my name's sake, shall receive an hundredfold, and shall inherit everlasting life' (Mt. 19:29). Rahab got her family back.

  James' point then is that God will bless you by what you do. 'God is not unrighteous to forget your work and labour of love, which ye have shewed toward his name, in that ye have ministered to the saints, and do minister' (Heb. 6:10). These works will have an effect upon you in this way, said Peter, 'If these things be in you' – such as virtue, knowledge, temperance, patience, godliness – 'and abound, they make you that ye shall neither be barren nor unfruitful in the knowledge of our Lord Jesus Christ' (2 Pet. 1:8). You might stand alone in what you see, but it will be so clear that nothing can persuade you to the contrary.

- The ultimate reason that James selected Rahab the harlot was to show that works do not presuppose perfection. Both Rahab and Abraham did extraordinary things, but don't think that means they were perfect. Notice that Rahab was said to have been justified by works when she didn't even have a chance for growth, much less perfection. That James calls her 'Rahab the harlot' just emphasizes the point. God was not pleased with her prostitution, but despite it what she did was right, useful and productive. It saved the spies and made Joshua's entry into Canaan possible.

We all have our weaknesses, we stumble in many ways. God does not require an absolute perfection to use us. Mind you, the righteousness of Abraham and Rahab took some doing. It meant diligence, self-denial, detachment. And so must we resist the world, the flesh, the devil. But sanctification – good works – doesn't mean absolute perfection.

We learn from the stories of Abraham and Rahab together that what we do matters to God. Rahab wasn't told what to do, she acted spontaneously. It shows that we as Christians have a freedom to do what we can see needs to be done. You don't have to look for a precedent or wait for a divine command like Abraham received. Rahab knew what she had to do. She didn't have time to get support, advice or confirmation, and she makes the hall of fame in Hebrews 11. James says, 'She was justified by what she did.'

Faith Without Works Is a Possibility

James closes this section by saying virtually the same thing for the third time. 'For as the body without the spirit is dead, so faith without works is dead also.' He thinks that every time he says it, it should be clearer than the last time. Faith was never intended to exist without works but demands to be fulfilled by works. This is the subtle point that I think has kept many people from understanding James. He never says that faith without works is not a possibility. He's been showing clearly that it is possible, but that the consequences are damaging. Faith was never intended to be that way.

Some simply believe that James is showing that true faith always has works. But why, then, does James need to make this exhortation? Why is he labouring to get them to have works? If works flow automatically why does Paul have to say, 'What shall we say then? Shall we continue in sin, that grace may abound?' (Rom. 6:1)? James and Paul say this for the simple reason that all of us need to have things spelled out. We need to be exhorted. It's not enough just to say we shouldn't sin, ought to love God or if we are really Christians we'll be all right. We must do things. It's because faith without works is a possibility that James has to exhort like this. How many of us would have gone on and on and on in sin if God's minister hadn't stopped us? Through the preaching of the word we were warned. Many would be living a very shallow existence right now if God's word had not penetrated.

Temporary Faith

Note also that James is not talking about temporary faith, a false profession. You can find it in the parable of the sower, but it's not in James. John Cotton points out that the false profession is often the one that shows the flourishing of good works, and sometimes the true Christian will be one who for a while gives no indication at all of their salvation. Works by themselves do not prove that a person has faith. Neither does it follow that if people have faith they will automatically have works. 'A body without the spirit is dead, so faith without works is dead also.'

A body without the spirit is called a dead body. James' point is that it's useless. As Jesus put it in the Sermon on the Mount, 'Ye are the salt of the earth: but if the salt have lost its savour, wherewith shall it be salted? it is thenceforth good for nothing but to be cast out, and to be trodden under foot of men' (Mt. 5:13). There's only one thing to do with a dead body and that's to bury it. When somebody in the body of Christ is not obedient, there's only one thing to do and that's to get it out (1 Cor. 5:5). For faith without works is useless to God and to others. Others won't even know you are a Christian. If they do find out, the way you live will make them think so little of Christianity that they will blaspheme the name of Jesus. If you are a man or woman of faith but are not obedient it will backfire. You become useless to yourself. You have a divided mind.

Faith was designed not only for our salvation, but also for our godliness and our obedience. If faith is deprived of good works everybody suffers. But if faith is allowed to become all that it was designed, for not only do we leave the world without excuse, but it has a most wonderful effect upon ourselves. Peter called it 'joy unspeakable and full of glory' (1 Pet. 1:8). Paul said, 'The kingdom of God is not meat and drink; but righteousness, and peace, and joy in the Holy Ghost' (Rom. 14:17).

Our lesson from James 2 is that when we see the word 'justification' or 'righteousness' we must not see only one thing. There is a righteousness that is imputed and that's how we get to heaven. James calls it the 'law of liberty'. But there is also a righteousness that is produced when faith joins together with works and is made complete.

I leave you with this from Richard Sibbes: 'Esteem the doctrine of sanctification or justification by works as much as you do the doctrine of salvation or justification by faith only.' And if you do that the book of James will have served its purpose.

30

So You Want to be a Minister?

James 3:1–2

When James comes to a new section he usually uses the expression 'my brethren'. For example in 1:2, 1:16, 2:1, 2:14, 3:1, 5:7 and 5:12 he says, 'my brethren', and although each brings in a slightly new discussion, he almost always picks up a point he's previously made.

Works: The Second of the Epistle's Twin Themes

The theme in chapters 3–5 is the mastery of the tongue, the grace to control what you say. As he puts it in 3:2: 'If any man offend not in word, the same is a perfect man, and able also to bridle the whole body.'

When James mentions this matter of the tongue it is a point he has made twice already. In chapter 1 verse 19: 'Wherefore, my beloved brethren, let every man be swift to hear, slow to speak, slow to wrath.' Chapter 1 verse 26: 'If any man among you seem to be religious, and bridleth not his tongue, but deceiveth his own heart, this man's religion is vain.' The matter of the tongue focuses on the second of a twin theme throughout the epistle: word and works.

While chapter 2 was chiefly about works, James brought in this matter of the word first. In chapter 1 verse 18: 'Of his own will begat he us with the word of truth, that we should be a kind of firstfruits of his creatures.' It was repeated in verse 21: 'Wherefore lay apart all filthiness and superfluity of naughtiness, and receive with meekness the engrafted word.' And then he continues, 'Be ye doers of the word.' Verse 23: 'If any man be a hearer of the word, and not a doer, he is like a man beholding his natural face in a glass.'

At the end of chapter 1 he summarizes these two things. Verse 26 refers to the tongue: 'If any man among you seem to be religious, and bridleth not his tongue, but deceiveth his own heart, this man's religion is vain.' And then in verse 27, work: 'Pure religion and undefiled before God and the Father is this, To visit the fatherless and widows in their affliction.'

Much of the rest of the epistle is a return to this theme of the word and indeed is an elaboration of what he's already referred to as controlling your tongue. By 'the tongue' what James really means is that the tongue is an indicator of the heart, of what you really are.

Jesus said all this first. James, who was the half-brother to Jesus and who heard Jesus preach many, many times, quotes Jesus again and again in this epistle. For example, in Matthew 12:34: 'Out of the abundance of the heart, the mouth speaketh.' Verses 36–37: 'Every idle word that men shall speak, they shall give account thereof in the day of judgment. For by thy words thou shalt be justified, and by thy words thou shalt be condemned.' Chapter 2 emphasized justification by works. Now James will show a righteousness that is manifested by what you say. This same word for 'righteousness' or 'justification' that was used in chapter 2 is used to conclude the third chapter: 'The fruit of righteousness is sown in peace of them that make peace' (v. 18).

The Calling to Teach

James Warns Not to Seek Prestige

Again James is not telling us how to be saved or how we know we are saved. He's simply showing us how the Christian life is to be lived. He introduces this section in a rather odd way. The Authorised Version translation just says, 'Be not many masters', but it means rather: 'Let not many become teachers.'

Why do you suppose James introduces this subject of controlling the tongue with the subject of teachers? I suspect he wanted to kill two birds with one stone. I think that he wanted first of all to speak directly to an actual situation. It is obvious that some kind of a situation has developed in this community that he is addressing, namely an increasing number of people aspiring to be teachers.

The Greek word is *didaskaloi*. It is a word that is used interchangeably with 'rabbi'. It was used this way in John 1:38 and Matthew 23:8. It is translated 'doctors' in Luke 2:46. And when Jesus spoke to Nicodemus he said, 'Art thou a master of Israel?' (Jn. 3:10). And so it's translated 'masters' here in the Authorised Version.

It simply shows that among these Christian Jews there was a growing number who aspired to be a teacher or doctor or master, to be in a seat of some kind of power, to wield influence over the church. We already know they were class-conscious, social climbers, that they were very particular about who should come into their church.

So it follows that people like this would aspire to the position of teacher because it had already become a prestigious position in the church. The position of teacher at this time was often the function of an especially gifted person but not a standing office as such. Anybody who felt himself competent or learned would just step forward and offer himself for this position. James is putting an obstacle in their way. He suggests they'd better watch out what they're asking for.

The Need for Piety

The other bird that James wanted to kill with this one stone is that he wanted to establish a general principle for the church, that what is to be connected with the position of teacher in the Christian church is not prestige but piety. We all know that with other situations of teaching that may not be the case at all – with being a rabbi in ancient Judaism or a professor in a university who teaches. If you are erudite and you know what you are talking about, and you can say it well, it's quite all right. Whether it be history or physics or medicine or architecture or language, teachers must simply know what they are talking about.

But when it comes to being a teacher of Christian doctrine, a different kind of knowledge is at stake. It is knowledge that resides not in the head but in the heart. It is a knowledge of the Spirit, not of certain facts. It is exemplary knowledge, not descriptive knowledge, where the person himself is the embodiment of all that he teaches. He doesn't say, 'Do as I say,' but 'Be like me'.

In many disciplines one can be a teacher and not be an expert. For example, a piano teacher may himself not be a good pianist. The tennis pro is not the one you see playing at Wimbledon. He just knows how to tell you what to do and what not to do. This is what led George Bernard Shaw to say, 'Those that can, do; those that can't, teach.' Of course somebody added, 'Those that can't teach, teach teachers!'

The True Nature of Teacher and Teaching

Know this: that those who teach will receive the greater condemnation. 'Knowing', *eidotes*, is the knowledge of a well-known fact. When it comes to teaching Christian doctrine, suggests James, the man is responsible to God. And so it is not enough to be accurate or to be able to answer the question. One must answer to God not only for what he teaches but for the way he lives, his personal conduct and character, his own conversation. With any other subject, the teacher can actually be detached from his subject. He can teach all day from eight to five and go home and it doesn't matter what he does, how he lives, whether he gets drunk, whether he's faithful to his wife, what people say. As long as when he's teaching the subject he does his job well, he can keep from getting fired and so forth.

But when it comes to the teaching of Christian doctrine, how a man lives is as important as what he teaches, not only because he's answerable to God but so that he will have something worthwhile to teach. We're dealing with a kind of knowledge now that is not in empirical facts. It is revealed knowledge. Jesus said, 'If any man will do his will' – the will of God – 'he shall know of the doctrine' (Jn. 7:17). Peter said, 'If these things be in you, and abound' – such as virtue, knowledge, temperance, patience, godliness – 'they guarantee that you will 'neither be barren, nor unfruitful in the knowledge of our Lord Jesus Christ' (2 Pet. 1:8). The teacher of Christian doctrine can't rely on textbooks. He must have the Spirit show him things. And the Spirit will not show him things if he himself has not been obedient to God.

James says to these aspiring people who wanted to have the office of teacher to watch it. Many should not be teachers, because they 'shall receive the greater condemnation'. This is something that needs to be brought out at the present time as never before. For the modern church now is filled with academics, with theologians, with ministers who just think that if you know a little bit and you can dish out a good lecture or a good sermon you've done your job well.

I remember some years ago I had the aspiration of going to Germany rather than to England to do research, and the thing that ultimately turned me off of going to Germany was when I began to see certain things that the professors in Germany – not that this is the only country that this is true of, but it's well known there – that to get a teaching position in theology the professors in Germany have to have a new idea that will sell books and get a name for that professor. He gets where he is not because he's become a master of the truth, much less mastered by the truth, but simply because he's come up with something clever or brilliant. And if you look at the theologians that have come out of Germany in the twentieth century you see they're all innovative, saying something slightly different, and they sell books and they make their splash. But within a few years there's another idea that comes along. This is also true of the ministry.

Knowing the Terror of God in our Ministry

So much preaching today simply seeks approval. Jesus said, 'How can ye believe, which receive honour one of another, and seek not the honour that cometh from God only?' (Jn. 5:44). Paul said, 'If I yet pleased men, I should not be the servant of Christ' (Gal. 1:10). It doesn't mean simply being sharp mentally and reading up in contemporary literature and knowing that you're able to answer what's going on. 'I keep under my body, and bring it into subjection: lest that by any means, when I have preached to others, I myself should be a castaway' (1 Cor. 9:27). And so Paul could say, 'Knowing therefore the terror of the Lord, we persuade men' (2 Cor. 5:11). It is the motivating force in Paul's ministry. He had just said, 'We must all appear before the judgment seat of Christ.'

Although all men must stand before the judgement seat of Christ, teachers will be judged more strictly. We don't know much about James but here for the first time he puts himself in the picture. He says, 'we'. He therefore acknowledges that he himself is such a teacher. And he reveals that he feels what Paul felt. 'Knowing the terror of the Lord, we persuade men.' This is what motivated Paul, it is what motivated James.

The missing note in modern preaching is this matter of urgency. For the ministry has become professional. One doesn't get the impression from many ministers today that that minister has just come from the presence of God and when he leaves the pulpit he's going back into the presence of God. And so James, who has been pointing the finger up till now, turns the finger upon himself.

He deliberately wants to discourage men from entering the ministry because he knows what is motivating so many. Spurgeon used to say to young men, 'If you can do anything else, do it.' If you can do anything else you're not called. The very fact that you're able to do something else – you can be successful at it, you're happy at it, it's working – well, be glad. Don't worry about the ministry. Don't have any pseudo-guilt.

But Spurgeon also said these words because the ministry is no place for the man who is not called. For the sorrow that accompanies the ministry can often seem too great for the man who is called. Above all else, know what you're in for. James said the same thing 1800 years before Spurgeon. Not that he wouldn't rejoice over good men going into the ministry. It's in a sense an enviable thing that James was having to discourage people, because today the better men are going into other fields. It's a great tragedy indeed that so many lacklustre, colourless and unable men are those, on the whole, going into the ministry. There are exceptions, but we ought to encourage the better men to do it. Yet here's where we walk the tightrope: that he is called of God. James could see that here were those who were falsely motivated.

Apostles, Prophets and Teachers

Does James mean preaching as well as teaching? The answer is yes. What James meant by this Greek word *didaskaloi* is essentially what the ministry was becoming even then. In 1 Corinthians 12:28 the apostle Paul said, 'God hath set some in the church, first apostles, secondarily prophets, thirdly teachers.' In Ephesians 4:11 there were inserted also 'evangelists' and 'pastors'. Yet it really comes down to these three: apostles, prophets, teachers. Apostles were the original founders of Christian doctrine. When they died they were not replaced. Even James doesn't call himself an apostle but 'a servant of God'.

What about the prophet? Well, in this particular age when the canon of Scripture was being drawn up – in apostolic times – the prophets were not necessarily learned men. They only had something to say when the Spirit came on them, and then they were mightily used. There were a lot of prophets going around and James, Paul and John knew about this.

John said, 'There are many false prophets out in the world. There's a way to know a true from a false prophet and that's when the Spirit will confess that Jesus Christ is God' (1 Jn. 4:2). And Paul said, 'If any man is going to prophesy let him do it according to the proportion of the faith' (Rom. 12:6). The prophet must be sure that when he does have some kind of an utterance it is according to the prevailing understanding of faith that was accepted by the church.

In the days of Whitfield and Wesley, there were many lay preachers because the Spirit came on them and they were mightily used, as well as in the Welsh Revival. But when the revival subsided these same men didn't have the gift to carry on. The point is that it was the office of the teacher that was emerging as the apostles were dying off. As the revival atmosphere was subsiding there were fewer prophets. But the teacher remained and he became what we now regard as the minister. Preaching should be essentially teaching.

It is obvious that the teacher was to be a learned man. He didn't depend upon the prophetic utterance. Preaching should be teaching with, hopefully, the prophetic element, the evangelistic, even the pastoral, thrown in. Preaching is not merely exhortation. Preaching should be learned. And in non-revival times the Christian ministry is essentially a teaching-preaching phenomenon.

In James' time, the revival atmosphere was beginning to subside and this position of teacher was emerging and many were saying, 'Well, I'll be that.' So James is dealing with this situation. That then which refines and motivates the God-called teacher-preacher is this: his judgement will be stricter. The Greek word is *krima*. The Authorised 'He shall receive the greater condemnation' is not the only translation. The word *krima* means simply 'judgement' or 'sentence'. It can mean 'award'.

The word was used in Matthew 7:2 when Jesus said, 'For with what judgment ye judge, ye shall be judged.' We know that when Paul said, 'We shall all stand before the judgment seat of Christ' (Rom. 14:10), it was the *bema* seat. That was the place where not only were sentences for punishment handed down, but also rewards. So it's not necessarily condemnation that will come to the teacher, it's simply that he will be judged more strictly. As the RSV puts it: 'judged with greater strictness'.

Ministers Are Judged With Greater Strictness

Anybody going into the ministry should know ahead of time that you will be 'judged with greater strictness'. Many men in the pulpit today don't like that. But James is saying that if you can't accept that, stay out of the ministry, for you will have a severer judgment.

Is it fair that a teacher, a preacher, should be judged more strictly? He will be judged with greater strictness for three reasons. The first is because he knows more and that means much more will be required. Jesus said in Luke 12:47–48: 'And that servant, which knew his lord's will, and prepared not himself, neither did according to his will, shall be beaten with many stripes. But he that knew not, and did commit things worthy of stripes, shall be beaten with few stripes. For unto whomsoever much is given, of him shall be much required: and to whom men have committed much, of him they will ask the more.' The teacher has been given vast insights, and having full knowledge of his duty he's more bound to obey it.

The second reason he will be judged with greater strictness is that his position carries vast influence. For people will listen to him when they won't listen to anybody else. For this man becomes an authority figure and people will take seriously everything he says. He must watch what he is saying wherever he is. I find people quoting me back to myself and I don't even remember saying it. But they heard it. It's a very scary thing when one realizes that people are taking us seriously, every single word.

There's a third reason. That is: his own conduct, his own character, largely determines his credibility. A thousand times more weighty than learning or cleverness or the degrees after one's name is one's personal life. When Paul addressed the church at Thessalonica, he said, 'Our gospel came not unto you in word only, but also in power, and in the Holy Ghost, and in much assurance; as ye know what manner of men we were among you' (1 Thess. 1:5). He said in verse 10 of chapter 2, 'Ye are witnesses, and God also, how holily and justly and unblameably we behaved ourselves among you.' One's manner of life is what makes the minister credible. I can recall how I looked up to preachers as I was growing up. I can remember actually combing my hair like my pastor did! It's an awesome responsibility.

Stricter Judgment May Mean Greater Reward

But what James wants to convey here is that although the minister's judgment will be stricter, the reward can be greater. For it need not follow that his judgment issues in condemnation. Listen to what Paul says when he shows what is motivating him. He says, 'To the weak became I as weak, that I might gain the weak: I am made all things to all men, that I might by all means save some. And this I do for the gospel's sake ... Know ye not that they which run in a race run all, but one receiveth the prize? So run, that ye may obtain ... I therefore so run, not as uncertainly; so fight I, not as one that beateth the air: But I keep under my body ... lest ... when I have preached to others, I myself should be a castaway' (1 Cor. 9:22, 23, 24, 26, 27). For what motivates Paul, what motivates James, what must motivate the God-called man, is what God thinks.

It was my high privilege to meet Josef Ton, a man from Romania. I wouldn't take a thousand pounds for those two hours. Josef told me a chorus they sing in Romania. It was what kept him going when he was being interrogated by the authorities day after day after day. The chorus goes: 'I will look up to my God and say, "Father, are you pleased with me?" He'll look down and say to me, "Son, you've got the victory".' And Josef would say, 'Day after day, after the interrogation was over I would just say, "God, are you pleased?" A voice would come back, "Son, you've got the victory".'

But listen now as James follows his autobiographical comment with this heart-warming candour. He said, 'In many things we offend all.' This is better translated: 'In many ways we all stumble.' It's the Greek word *ptaiomen* that is used in 2 Peter 1:10: 'Give diligence to make your calling and election sure: for if ye do these things, ye shall never fall.' It's not talking about falling away from your salvation or a sin that brings you into ruin. It means 'to stumble'. It's used in Romans 11:11: 'Have they stumbled that they should fall?'

There's this contrast here. There is a possibility of stumbling or of falling and so it is a sin, but not of ruin. James says that we all stumble in many ways. As the RSV puts it, 'We all make many mistakes.' When a man like James can say this, that encourages me. After all, he had just used Abraham and Isaac as an illustration and he followed up with Rahab the harlot that we might not be demoralized. We can see that God can use us with our imperfections.

Faith may be made perfect, and that doesn't mean sinless perfection. The greatest saint always sees himself as the greatest sinner. Is it because he's just humble? No, it's because he's honest. The closer you get to anybody the more you'll see their blemishes. We all stumble in many ways. James is simply showing that this fact should make you think twice if you're going to become a minister.

Great Grief Is Caused When a Teacher Stumbles

James is putting this obstacle in the way of falsely motivated teachers or preachers because this stumbling causes great grief. The layman so-called can do the same thing and get away with it. The minister can't. We all stumble. But the teacher, if he stumbles, suffers because people want to think he's not human. James knows that he has suffered. He says not to think for a moment that becoming a minister is going to make you perfect. We all do stumble. But if you do become a teacher the same stumbling becomes more serious if only because the people will judge more harshly. But the main thing is that God will take it seriously as well. Spare yourself sorrow, James warns, and stay out of the ministry.

It is God's judgment that matters in the end. For there's something more painful than the criticism of people, no matter who they are. It's the terror of the Lord. God can hide his face and there is nothing more painful than that. And if he can hide his face now, God only knows what it will be like at the judgment seat of Christ.

The Honouring of God or the Honour of God?

Yet it is equally true that there's something more wonderful than the praise of people. It's the joy of the Lord. Nehemiah 8:10 says, 'The joy of the Lord is your strength.' I will look up to my God and say, 'Father, are you pleased with me?' I believe he'll look down and say to me, 'Son, you've got the victory.' That's enough. The honour of God.

31

So You Want to be Perfect?

James 3:1–2

James moves into the subject of tongue control by saying that we all offend in many ways. And he says that if anybody doesn't offend in word 'the same is a perfect man'. James takes up a theme that he really brought forward in the first chapter so that we might see how serious this matter is. I think all of us would have to admit that we need to hear this.

Tongue Control

This epistle is so practical that it is most painful. Nothing is more painful to us than to hear the subject of tongue control. Who is there among us who does not feel a deep sense of shame over what we've said to another person? Many of us have impaired relationships, almost destroyed them, so that there's nothing that can ever be done to bring them back. 'All the king's horses and all the king's men could not put Humpty together again.' All because of what we said. We may apologize a thousand times and do a thousand good things to offset what we've said, but we would wish more than anything that we hadn't said it.

James says that we all offend. And teachers are going to be judged more harshly than anybody else. So when he says, 'We offend all', he apparently means, in part at least, through the tongue. We know that James himself was slow to learn the vast implications of justification by faith. James himself was the one who was really dragging his feet in the earliest church. Perhaps he's thinking of this. I don't know. But it is not unlikely that he is aware of some scar where a person is repeating what he heard James say before James had a change of mind. There are very few of us who don't shift our position at some time across the years and know the horror of somebody quoting what we said years before. Take, for example, John Cotton, my favourite of the Puritans. In his early days he repeated what all of them were saying but he had a change of mind. And a lot of people didn't know about his change of mind after he got to England. Many of his followers had his old sermons reprinted even after Cotton died. Cotton Mather, his grandson, said that he knew his grandfather was grieved at this very thing going on.

You may say, 'This is discouraging to me. I want to be able to believe the minister.' But ultimately you must think for yourself. This is the glory of the priesthood of the believer. You should not accept any minister uncritically. The only exception is the canon of Scripture itself, for God in his sovereign providence let be included in the canon of scripture only that which is infallible. By the time James wrote this epistle he had it all together and said it perfectly.

This man James was not only the slowest and the one who was dragging his feet in the earliest church but it is likely that James had the most enormous stature in the earliest church. James knew of the influence he had and now he's saying that we have all offended. All of us have said things directly, indirectly, publicly, privately, a personal word, perhaps spoken impatiently, imprudently, and we've left scars on people.

Christian Perfection

Usually in the Scriptures we go from the general to the particular, but here James goes from the particular to the general. He's going to include everybody now. When James says that in many things we all stumble, and then he says, 'If any man offend not in word, the same is a perfect man', the impression would be that when it comes to the perfect man there's no such thing. If you are the type that can only think syllogistically you would say that there's no such thing as a perfect person because he says that we all offend. Your major premise would be that all of us stumble. The minor premise: whoever doesn't is perfect. The conclusion is that nobody's perfect.

But James goes on to a very difficult thing and yet a simple thing. The question is, does this word 'perfect' militate against everything the Bible teaches concerning Christian perfection? The Greek word is *teleos*. It means 'mature', 'full-grown'. It means 'perfect' in this sense, but there can be no doubt that the goal is a full growth that it can be labelled with the word *teleos* – perfect.

James says that we all offend so why does he go on to say what we shouldn't do? Take for example our Lord's word: 'Be ye therefore perfect, even as your Father which is in heaven is perfect' (Mt. 5:48). Why did Paul say to the Corinthians, 'We speak wisdom among them that are perfect' (1 Cor. 2:6)? Or in 1 Corinthians 14:20 he talks about being perfect in understanding. In 2 Corinthians 13:11 he actually closes his epistle by saying, 'Be perfect.' In Ephesians 4:13 Paul says, 'Till we all come in the unity of the faith, and of the knowledge of the Son of God, unto a perfect man, unto the measure of the stature of the fullness of Christ.' Listen to him in Colossians 1:27–28: 'Christ in you, the hope of glory: Whom we preach, warning every man, and teaching every man in all wisdom; that we may present every man perfect in Christ Jesus.' And Paul to Timothy: 'All scripture is given by inspiration of God, and is profitable for doctrine, for reproof, for correction, for instruction in righteousness: That the man of God may be perfect, thoroughly furnished unto all good works' (2 Tim. 3:16–17).

The Sublime Paradox of 'Perfection'

Is James saying that perfection isn't possible? Surely he's not saying quite that because he said in chapter 1, 'The trying of your faith worketh patience. But let patience have her perfect work, that ye may be perfect and entire, wanting nothing' (vv. 3–4). And he could say in chapter 2 verse 22, 'Seest thou how faith wrought with his works, and by works was faith made perfect?' Is it perfect or is it not? The problem is that we want to think so logically. But this is what I would call the sublime paradox – a statement that is apparently absurd or self-contradictory but true. The sublime paradox is that perfection is possible and impossible. Many of us will not have anything to do with that.

We jump to a conclusion partly because we don't really want to get at the fact or the truth. It's so easy to say, 'Come out with it. What do you mean?' You've heard the story about the man who goes up to another and says, 'What's new? Anything good?' The man says, 'Yes, somebody gave me a cheque for a thousand pounds.' The other says, 'That's good.' 'Well, no,' he says, 'the cheque bounced.' The man says, 'Well, then that's bad.' 'No, the man is bringing the money over today.' 'Well, then that's good.' 'Well, no. His car broke down on the way and he needed the money for that.' 'Well, then, that's bad.' 'Well, no. The insurance will pay for the car.' And you can go on and on. This is the way it is when it comes to the doctrine of perfection in Scripture. Because of this we tend to dismiss it categorically, but here we have all these references.

We need to see that there is a way of living that most of us don't even bother to investigate because we either say, 'Well, there's nothing to it', or we say, 'We all offend', then that dismisses perfection. Yet James says, 'If any man offend not ...'; he's showing there that there is something to be sought after.

As you read this epistle it is obvious that James is pushing for perfection without being self-righteous about it. And that was the spirit of Paul when he wrote to the Philippians, 'As many as be perfect, be thus minded', and yet he had just said, 'Not as though I had already attained, either were already perfect' (Phil. 3:12, 15). Here's the sublime paradox. What we have here is James bringing these in balance. His doctrine – what he calls the 'perfect law of liberty' (his nickname for justification by faith) – is vulnerable to antinomianism (rejection of the law). And his doctrine of justification by works (his nickname for the doctrine of sanctification) is vulnerable to self-righteousness.

What Really Matters in Seeking Perfection

We need to see that there is a balance, the sublime paradox which avoids the ugliness of the polarization that the Christian church has witnessed over the centuries. Many of us laugh at the story about Augustus Toplady getting off his death bed to fight a rumour that he and John Wesley had come to terms. But it's really not funny. It's sad. Let us not be afraid to break out of the mould. It doesn't matter what people say about us. They say, 'Are you Reformed? Are you Arminian? What are you?' What matters is that we follow this book and want to live it and be the manner of person that the world has not seen when it looks at Christianity. That is what we must strive for.

Our Lord Jesus suggests two ways by which one can come to perfection. How did Jesus put it? 'The young man saith unto him, All these things have I kept from my youth up: what lack I yet? Jesus said unto him, If thou wilt be perfect, go and sell that thou hast, and give to the poor, and thou shalt have treasure in heaven: and come and follow me' (Mt. 19:20–21). That was to be perfect in terms of worldly detachment.

Another way to be perfect that Jesus said is: 'I say unto you, Love your enemies, bless them that curse you, do good to them that hate you, and pray for them which despitefully use you, and persecute you ... Be ye therefore perfect, even as your Father which is in heaven is perfect' (Mt. 5:44,48). This was perfection in terms of forgiving others.

What James is talking about is perfection in terms of the whole man. Some have a perfectionist complex by nature. They've just been that way all their lives so when they come to Christianity they want to be perfect in that. That is a carnal motivation. Others simply have a self-righteous desire to negotiate with God without a mediator. We want to be so good that we don't need to plead the merit and blood of Jesus. That, too, is a carnal motivation.

James can say, 'In many things we all offend' because he has this doctrine of liberty, a doctrine of justification by faith. He knows that if we sin we don't need to panic. John said exactly the same thing: 'These things write I unto you, that ye sin not. And if any man sin, we have an advocate with the Father' (1 Jn. 2:1). If we sin we should be aware that it's a common occurrence and yet at the same time we should recognize the way the Christian life is meant to be lived.

What it Means Not to Offend

What does James mean then by not offending in word? It is not merely a perfection in doctrine. Especially in a day of evangelical decline, a feeling that you're perfect in doctrine can bring a person to a place of feeling very self-righteous to the extent that it makes it absolutely impossible to make any spiritual progress. People like this think that because they have arrived doctrinally that this is what matters. Nobody is perfect in doctrine.

Let me quote the great Calvin from Book 3 of *The Institutes*. He said, 'We certainly admit that so long as we dwell as strangers in the world there is such a thing as implicit faith.' By 'implicit faith' he means true faith but an inarticulate faith. Not only because many things are as yet hidden from us, says Calvin, but because surrounded by many clouds of errors we do not comprehend everything. The height of wisdom for the most perfect, according to Calvin, is to go forward and quietly and humbly to strive still further. If, when I come to the end of my ministry, there is a widespread consensus that the clearest and deepest truth has been taught, I predict that he who follows me will do even better.

James doesn't merely mean here a perfection of doctrine. He doesn't merely mean perfection in social graces. I admire people who never say anything wrong in public – like the Queen. I've never been like that. If I was ever invited to dine at Buckingham Palace I can predict that before the evening was over if I didn't first spill the coffee or, while trying to eat like an Englishman with two hands, flick a pea like a Polaris Missile across the room, before the evening was over I would reveal that I was from the hills of Kentucky and not educated in an English public school. Neither does James simply mean not losing your temper. Some have a temperament by nature that means they always seem to be in control, and this is an attractive thing. And yet James means all of these things. He is concerned about doctrine, about how you speak and act, having social graces and not losing your temper, but that still would be to miss his point. For James is continuing what he meant by patience having her perfect work (Js. 1:4). It was repeated in verse 19: 'Wherefore, my beloved brethren, let every man be swift to hear, slow to speak, and slow to wrath.' He's talking now about what patience can do in contrast to what temptation can do. As sin has its 'perfect' work that began with temptation, so does patience have its perfect work. We know that sin begins with temptation. 'Every man is tempted, when he is drawn away of his own lust, and enticed. Then when lust hath conceived, it bringeth forth sin: and sin, when it is finished' – the same Greek word *teleo*, 'finished', 'perfected' – 'bringeth forth death' (vv. 14–15). James wants to show that there is also a grace that comes in the Christian faith whereby it can have a perfection. Sin has its perfection. It's death. So faith can be perfected when one offends not *in word*.

Our Reaction to Temptation

Why, then, would James say that this lack of offence is with reference to the tongue? And why would controlling the tongue enable you to bridle the whole body? Remember that the first impulse when you're tempted would be to say, 'I'm being tempted of God.' That's the most natural thing in the world to feel, especially if that day you prayed, 'Lead us not into temptation,' or, 'Lord, guide me today. Just overrule in my life.' And then before the day is over you are tempted. You say to yourself, 'I prayed this morning that I wouldn't be led into temptation, and look what's happened here.' James said, 'Be slow to speak.' He doesn't want you to react that way.

As long as there is the remotest thought that God can be tempting you, then you're going to give in to it. But once you deal with this and know once and for all that God doesn't tempt, it will affect the way you live. You will recognize that it's your own responsibility.

Two Kinds of Temptation

The next impulse when temptation comes is to speak so as to yield. James has referred broadly to two kinds of temptation in verse 21 of chapter 1: sexual temptation and temptation that affects your self-esteem. How many young people have said, 'Well, I've only got two problems: lust and losing my temper'? This is why James said, 'If any man offend not in word he's bridled the whole body.' Because everything else comes easily if you deal with those two.

Do you know that sexual temptation can be aborted by refusing to say what you think? You may say, 'Look, there's also non-verbal communication, you know.' I know. For James knows – and hear me well – if you resist bringing out into the open what you feel, you will save yourself much grief and much sorrow. Sexual lust can be stopped if you don't say anything.

What about losing your temper? It, too, can be stopped in time. You may be steaming inside. Your face may be getting red. But if you will resist bringing it out into the open and avoid the confrontation verbal-wise, you will save yourself much sorrow. What James means, then, is that it is not perfection *not* to have the thought. Perfection is to *have* the thought but to cast it down. 2 Corinthians 10:5 says: 'Casting down imaginations … and bringing into captivity every thought to the obedience of Christ'. Strength of character is refusing to say what you feel when you know that saying it will make things worse.

The Tongue Shows What Is in Our Hearts

The tongue, then, is the indicator of the heart. Jesus said, 'Out of the abundance of the heart the mouth speaketh' (Mt. 12:34). You might want to say then, 'If it's in the heart you might as well say it. The tongue just says automatically what's in the heart.' But how we control what we think determines really where the heart is. Where a man's treasure is there will his heart be also (Mt. 6:21).

Jesus said that if you lust after a woman you commit adultery in your heart, or if you hate you commit murder in your heart. There are those silly people who say, 'Well, you might as well do it.' But wait a minute. No. The tongue will indicate where the heart really is by your refusing to say (and do) what you feel when you know that saying (and doing) it will make it worse. The tongue is an indicator of whether you do lust and hate in your heart. There's a difference between temptation and sin. The tongue will indicate whether temptation is aborted before it grows into sin.

This is why James continues: 'If any man offend not in word, the same is a perfect man, and able also to bridle the whole body.' The tongue proves in the end whether you are in control of your total being. When he says 'the body' that means the total man, the total person. Never forget that Christianity deals with the total man – the soul and the body. The soul is what is saved through the death of Jesus Christ and it will live on throughout eternity. Living the Christian life is not saving the soul. That has already been done by the engrafted Word (Jas. 1:21).

But the Christian life that we're talking about and the living of the Christian life has to do with your total person, not only your soul but your body. After all, your body is the temple of the Holy Spirit. Paul could say in the light of the fact that your soul is saved, 'I beseech you therefore, brethren, by the mercies of God, that ye present your bodies ...' (Rom. 12:1).

Your body can only be in one place at a time. Therefore watch how you spend your time and where you go. It's your body that people see, which is the temple of the Holy Spirit. You're aware that you're not your own, that you're bought with a price (1 Cor. 6:20). And thus the perfect man is not the one who doesn't have the thought or the feeling. But he is the one who refuses to say what he feels when he knows it will make things worse.

Bridling the Tongue

This word 'bridle' is used in connection with the body in this verse. Earlier James talked about bridling the tongue because the tongue is really a negative thing left to itself. The tongue is never to be seen as a positive thing unless God overrules, because the tongue has no ability to come up with the right thing. It has no gift automatically to produce the fruit of the Spirit. Its function in the Christian life is to abort temptation by refusing to speak. James will come to the positive later on in this chapter, but at this point in time he's simply saying that when it comes to your tongue, say nothing. Be slow to speak. It is his conviction that if we take care of the negative by what we don't say, God will enable us to produce the fruit of the Spirit and the wisdom that comes from above. The wonderful thing is that, by controlling the tongue with reference to sexual temptation and self-esteem, you are then able to bridle the whole body.

We Should Strive for Perfection

Our job, then, is to watch what we say. Yet this is no easy thing. The problem with some who teach a doctrine of perfection is that they want to make it easy. They believe that you just consecrate your life and let God do the rest and then you go out in the world and see whether it works. You'll find out that it doesn't. It's not that simple. It is a matter of discipline, control.

Perfection in the end, then, is to accept our imperfection but strive no less for perfection. That's the sublime paradox, and if you can live with that then God will use you in ways that he hasn't been able to use you up to now because you've said, 'Well, it's black or white.' Do you want to be perfect? Well, you should. Because then you will strive for this and begin to see that there is the possibility to gain self-control. Maybe you'll have the blemish now and then that will keep you humble, but still you can say as John Newton put it: 'By the grace of God I am what I am. I'm not what I ought to be. I'm not what I want to be. I'm not what I hope to be. But thank God I'm not what I used to be.' Paul summed it all up: 'Do all things without murmurings and disputings: that ye may be blameless and harmless, the sons of God, without rebuke, in the midst of a crooked and perverse nation, among whom ye shine as lights in the world' (Phil. 2:14–15).

32

The Tongue and Self-Control (1)

James 3:1–8

Now James wants to go into some detail with regard to the tongue. When you first look at this passage you wonder what his point is. He's simply stating facts here. There's not really a contribution with regard to Christian doctrine. He's simply putting a series of illustrations that make this Christian perfection seem more remote than ever.

Man Cannot Control Himself

The first thing he does is to show how man easily controls an animate object: 'We put bits in the horses' mouths, that they may obey us; and we turn about their whole body.' Then he shows how man easily controls an inanimate object: 'Behold also the ships, which though they be so great, and are driven of fierce winds, yet are they turned about with a very small helm, withersoever the governor listeth.' Man controls animals, things, unfallen nature, unfallen creation. He can control his own inventions – the ship (v. 7). But he cannot control himself. James says, 'The tongue can no man tame; it is an unruly evil, full of deadly poison' (v. 8).

I want to know why it is that man cannot control his tongue. But what I want to know even more than that is what James' purpose is in telling us this about the horse and the ship. It doesn't give me a lot of encouragement to know that you can control a horse, you can control a ship, but not the tongue. Obviously James is not revealing any new doctrine. He's not telling us anything that is controversial. Obviously this is true about a horse. This is true about a ship. Why does he say this?

The first reason is this: that perfection via tongue control cannot be attained by excelling in any particular gift we may have, even by getting involved in Christian service. If God has given you a gift, use it and be thankful for it, but be careful concerning your own motivation. If there is carnal ambition then it's a false motivation. But it is equally false to answer the call to Christian service if there is really at the bottom of your willingness to do so this latent desire to compensate for some fault that you have. This is an old habit of people in the church. If they can't deal with a particular weakness they get involved in the Lord's work and they feel slightly better about it. It compensates for some guilt.

Some go into various kinds of Christian service not because they're truly called but because they think it will help deal with a certain problem they have. This is true outside the church. Take, for example, a medical doctor who decides to go into psychiatry. Now what I am about to say is not always true – but it's often true that the reason one does this is to help oneself. What motivates many doctors to go into psychiatry is that they hope along the way that they'll know something about themselves. It's true then in the church with regard to Christian service. Some will have a problem that seems never to go away. They say, 'What I need to do is to get more involved.'

Throughout the history of the Christian church this has been done in almost bizarre ways. This is why some women become nuns. Sometimes a prostitute who becomes a Christian just feels so bad she goes into a nunnery. Or sometimes a girl who has lost her boyfriend cannot reckon with it so she becomes a nun. It's true of some men going into the monastery. Actually this was a bit true with Saint Augustine. He had followed a profligate lifestyle and when he became a Christian he became completely different, even refused to get married, and it set some kind of example for the Middle Ages. But it is really wrong to think that by taking a certain line it's going to solve a particular problem.

Somebody might take a Sunday school class or try to do something religious or just be around at church more. They think that's going to cause a particular problem to go away. And especially this matter of the tongue. You can become more dedicated and get more involved in doing this or that, you could even be useful – but you will find out some months later that the problem of the tongue is still there and you are no closer to tongue control than before you started.

God's Gifts and Calling Won't Control our Tongues

Now there is a difference between a gift and grace. Paul said, 'For the gifts and calling of God are without repentance' (Rom. 11:29). That verse has been interpreted two ways. I think both interpretations are right on target. One interpretation is that God doesn't give a gift according to one's repentance. And the other way of looking at it is that God doesn't take it back once he has given it. In either case what we have here is that a gift may come to a person who may be unworthy of it in so far as the way he lives his life, and that gift may still be used with great effectiveness. The use of the gift doesn't presuppose spiritual acceleration. It doesn't help him to be what he ought to be spiritually.

There was a particular minister some years ago whom I admired very much. He was holding a two-week revival meeting in Iowa. They were into the Wednesday of the second week when the pastor of the church who was hosting the revival meeting was told that this particular minister had been living in adultery for two years and that there was a woman following him wherever he went. She was in the town even at that moment. This pastor had to make a decision whether to confront the minister there and spoil the whole meeting or to let him go on. The pastor, who was the only one who knew of it, had to hear the minister preach for the next several nights. The odd thing was that on the Sunday night there were forty conversions. Then after it was over he was confronted and he was put out of the ministry. (I think he's been restored since then.) But this just shows that you can have a gift and it can be effective although repentance has not even come in.

James' point here is that you don't get over the problem of the tongue by becoming a teacher or by using a particular gift. More involvement in Christian service will not bring one closer to godliness or tongue control.

Neither is there anything we can do pragmatically to bring about this perfection via tongue control. Now again this might seem demoralizing. You may think, 'What on earth can we do?' This obviously puts the attainment of the kind of perfection James is talking about beyond the remotest possibility. 'The tongue can no man tame.' Jesus put it like this, 'If thy hand or thy foot offend thee, cut them off, and cast them from thee: it is better for thee to enter into life halt or maimed, rather than having two hands or two feet to be cast into everlasting fire' (Mt. 18:8). He says the same thing about the eye. In any case, if you cut a hand or a foot off you've still got one left. What about the tongue? Are you supposed to cut it off?

There have always been those in the history of the Christian church who have tried various things to attain to a certain kind of perfection. Even those who went the route of emasculation were no closer to this perfection. The fact is, short of actually cutting your tongue off, nothing will work whether it be New Year's resolutions made every night 365 days a year or entering into full-time Christian service or going into a monastery or sleeping in the church (not during the services!). These things just haven't worked.

God Won't Control our Tongues for us

Nor is there anything that God will do in connection with tongue control. Here's where the rub comes in because we all thought, 'No man can tame the tongue but God can.' That's the point many make about this text. But James' chief point is: don't expect God to do it. God can do anything. He could institute the second coming of Jesus right now and deal with the problem of sin and evil before sundown. God can stop earthquakes, volcanoes from erupting, famine, war, crime. Boys and girls, God can do your homework for you – but he never did for me!

There are many things God can do, yes, but James' point is that he won't do this. You may say, 'I'll pray more,' or, 'I'll just consecrate myself to God all the more.' Consecration and prayer are the biggest cop-outs in the world on this matter. I have sometimes refused to use the hymn 'Take my life and let it be …' because we sing that song and we say, 'Well, I mean it.' But then we wake up the next day and find we still have the tongue problem. All of us want God to do it for us.

Uncle Buddy Robinson who a colourful, unlearned preacher – but a man with great common sense – in my old denomination. And he was mightily used of God. I'm told that up to a quarter of a million people were converted under his ministry. They would have at the front of the church what they called an altar, a wooden rail about twenty-five to thirty feet long where people could come to the front and kneel. They would often use the expression, 'Lay your all on the altar.' You know: 'God can have my hands, my feet, my job, my family …' After one of the services one lady was praying and sobbing. Uncle Buddy knelt down in front of her and said, 'Sister, what's the problem?' She said, 'I can't get my tongue on the altar.' Uncle Buddy said, 'Stick your tongue out.' So she did. He said, 'Looks like it's three inches long. Let's measure this altar here. Twenty-five or thirty feet long. I don't see what the problem is. Surely you can get your tongue on the altar.' We all want to do it that way.

The fact is, no amount of prayer or consecration has ever dealt with it yet. We can pray, 'O God, help me not to do it', but it happens. And as for the 'speaking in tongues movement', what this means is that you let God have your tongue and you will speak in tongues. That's wonderful. You can speak in tongues for an hour, but you've got twenty-three more hours of that same day. What happens then? The problem doesn't go away with the Pentecostals either.

James' purpose in these lines is to bring us to the place that we realize there is no hope of bridling the tongue until we accept the fact that God is not going to do it. If we think there's one chance in a thousand God will do it, every one of us will wait for God to do it and the problem will never go away.

The key to this passage is what James has already said with regard to lust. It's the same principle inverted. 'Let no man say when he is tempted, I am tempted of God.' You will never do anything about lust until you recognize that God has nothing to do with it and that it's up to you. It is not until then that you'll begin really to say, 'This is my problem.' When you really believe that God isn't behind the temptation and that it's in your hands it has an effect on the way you live. This is precisely James' point now.

Live in the Real World!

When James talks about the horses and the ships he's not telling us anything we couldn't learn in the almanack. He's making these Christians realize that they live in the real world. This is often the problem. When a person first becomes a Christian he has a great sense of the power of God and the whole world looks different. Now it didn't change, you did.

I had a friend who was converted in Alabama and on the night of his conversion he was so thrilled he drove in his car from Sylacauga to Birmingham and as he was driving he began to sing the chorus: 'God can do anything, anything, anything. God can do anything but fail. He's the Alpha and Omega, the Beginning and the End, the fairest of ten thousand to my soul.' He just faintly began to hear a siren behind him and he looked at his speedometer – he was going at a hundred miles per hour. He looked in his rear-view mirror and there was a blue light going off and on. It didn't bother him one bit. He pulled over and said, 'Hallo, Officer, praise God.' And the officer said, 'You were going at a hundred miles per hour.' He said, 'I'm not under law, I'm under grace.' I know you're not going to believe this, but the policeman didn't like that! He gave him a hundred-dollar fine. That's what grace did for him – it cost him a hundred dollars and he realized that he was still in the real world!

There comes a time when the Christian needs not new doctrine or new teaching about justification, sanctification, redemption. He simply needs to know certain facts of life: that he's still in the world. You cannot change what is true even though you're a Christian. You can't change the past or what is. The Christian has a tendency to live in a dream world. He says, 'My God can do anything.' He can, but when it comes to the tongue he's not going to do anything about it. That's scary, isn't it? You ought to be scared.

In the real world there are certain facts of life. They're true of a non-Christian. They're true of you. What you say will bring much sorrow. God does not work with us apart from the real world. Oswald Chambers used to say, 'Some people are so heavenly minded that they are of no earthly use.' We're all guilty of behaving along these lines.

Although you are a Christian you still have to eat to live. You have to get your sleep and you must obey natural laws. If you're due to catch a train and you get there late you'll miss the train. If you were a diabetic before you were a Christian you still need to take insulin after you're a Christian. If you violate your body you will suffer. Young ladies, if you live promiscuously you might get pregnant. Young men, live promiscuously and you might catch a disease. If you want to smoke you may get lung cancer. If you start drinking it will have an effect upon you and it could be disastrous. These are facts.

What we Say Causes us Sorrow

The tongue is a small member. Non-Christians know this, but as a Christian you need to be told that you will suffer untold harm and sorrow by what you say.

This is true at three levels. First, what it will do to yourself. When James brings up this matter of being slow to speak it is in connection with temptation and the wrath that will follow. James now calls it a tongue of fire (v. 6). When you lose control because of what you have just said then it is worse than ever because now you have no control at all. Once you say it something happens and things are never the same again. When it comes to sexual temptation you may have thought it but until you say something the problem can be contained.

This is also true with regard to your self-esteem. Your words will grieve the Holy Spirit and you are then further impoverished. In these two areas, sexual temptation and your self-esteem, if you speak so that either you make temptation become sin or by being defensive you justify yourself, you are impoverished and the result is double mindedness. When you speak without thinking you lose control, nothing is right and you live in confusion. The only hope is that God will bring you to repentance.

But you still have to live with what you did not only to yourself but to the other person – this is the second level of suffering. If you make a sexual reference to someone, look what you've done to that person. You've opened up a new world. Never again will things be the same between you and that person. Or in protecting your self-esteem – putting the other person down or in his place – the worst thing is that the relationship that you have is never quite the same again. The interesting thing is that the unguarded comment is often forgiven because you can say you really didn't mean what you said. But what's bad is when you really did mean it and it was obvious you thought it.

Finally the third level. We call it gossip. 'How great a matter a little fire kindleth!' You see the effect it has on the person you say it to. You do that person no favour to make another person look bad. I can remember hearing something about a particular minister. I wish I'd never heard this. I checked it out and everybody said it was not true. But I heard it and I can't forget it. I still think, 'It might be.' When you say this kind of thing to another person you hurt that person.

Look at the effect it has on the person about whom you've said it. They're defenceless. We're told that it is like defiling the whole body, setting on fire the course of nature. Before you know it it's a forest fire started by a little spark.

Then there's the effect it has on you after you've done it. You're so sorry you said it and you think, 'Why was I so little as to make that statement?' You're impoverished when the third party is hurt.

The saddest thing of all is that you can't really take it back. It's fire. It burns and once it's burnt it's never the same again. You can say, 'I'm sorry. Please forget I said it.' In America many times a witness will say something and one attorney will say, 'Objection', and the judge will say, 'Sustained', and the judge turns to the jury and says, 'You are to disregard this comment.' But it was said. They can't disregard it. They can't bring it into evidence but it still colours things.

When God Overrules

You may go to God and say, 'O Lord, I'm sorry I said it. I wish I hadn't,' but you can't erase the past. You've got to live in the real world. You may say, 'Can't God overrule? Can't he stop me?' There's only one promise that I know of in the Bible concerning anything like this. It's in Matthew 10:16. It says, 'Behold, I send you forth as sheep in the midst of wolves: be ye therefore wise as serpents, and harmless as doves.' That's tongue self-control right there. But he also says, 'Beware of men: for they will deliver you up to the councils, and they will scourge you in their synagogues; And ye shall be brought before governors and kings for my sake, for a testimony against them and the Gentiles. But when they deliver you up, take no thought how or what ye shall speak: for it shall be given you in that same hour what ye shall speak. For it is not ye that speak, but the Spirit of your Father which speaketh in you' (vv. 17–20). That's the only place I know of that talks about God overruling but that is an emergency, life or death situation.

The whole message of James is that the Christian life is mostly to be lived under non-emergency conditions. It will have an effect upon our tongue when we see that it is up to us. Once we're confronted by the fact that God isn't the author of temptation but it's us, it has an effect on the way we live from then on.

So with the tongue, it's up to you to live in the real world.

By the way, you will begin to see great progress here. That's what James is after. Nor will you be able to gloat or feel that you've done something great, because tongue control is its own reward. You're the winner. In Luke 17, Jesus said, 'Likewise ye, when ye shall have done all those things which are commanded you, say, We are unprofitable servants: we have done that which was our duty to do' (v. 10).

33

The Tongue and Self-Control (2)

James 3:1–10

Who among us feels good when we read this passage about the tongue? But James defuses the situation and right at the beginning puts himself at the front of the queue. He says, 'We all offend in many ways' (v. 2). Sometimes I get as much help and strength from seeing the weakness of the great saint as I do from seeing his strength. James' task to speak to us in such a manner that we will not be demoralized and yet to sober us and still encourage us. To be able to do that is the mark of a great teacher.

Temptation is Our Problem

Here's what happens to every Christian: Satan slips in right after every conversion to draw away that new convert from a sense of responsibility. He says that since God saved us, surely God is able to work these things out for us? Satan appeals to our desire to be spiritual. We are told, 'Just tell the Lord that you want to do his will and turn it over to him.' We take this to be the sign of great spirituality. But which pleases God more: your being willing to please him or actually doing what he says? In the words of that hymn by Frances Havergal: 'Thou hast made us willing and thou hast made us free.' As long as we entertain the remotest hope that God will do it all we're not going to do anything ourselves.

As you read the history of the Christian church, God has always used those who had an extreme view of the sovereignty of God and an extreme view of the responsibility of man. God uses self-starters. Men like Luther and Calvin and Zwingli, with their robust views of predestination, have always baffled the historians. The historians, the secular minds say, 'I can't understand these men. They claim to believe in the sovereignty of God but look at the way they do things.' James will not let us just turn it over to the Holy Spirit. His whole approach is to box us in and not let us escape our responsibility even by our most spiritual motives.

Mourning for Sin

James has another motive at work here: what we have in the third chapter of James is a true demonstration of mourning for sin, the heartfelt lament that we are God's special creation, and yet we lag behind beasts and birds and reptiles. 'For every kind of beasts, and of birds, and of serpents, and of things in the sea, is tamed, and hath been tamed of mankind: but the tongue can no man tame; it is an unruly evil, full of deadly poison.' James is showing that this is a very melancholy thing and we should be grieved. There is no greater evidence of true spirituality than mourning for sin.

True mourning for sin is something that the devil cannot counterfeit. Wherever you find superficiality in the church you will find an absence of mourning for sin. The great lack of the modern church is real conviction of sin. We can talk about where we are but we don't really grieve about it. James is grieving.

What makes James' profession remarkable is that it is not merely a personal sense of shame. Isaiah experienced that when he said, 'Woe is me! for I am undone' (Isa. 6:5). But James is bewailing for humanity generally, identifying himself with the totality of God's fallen creation. He has elevated himself from the preoccupation with personal matters and personal conviction of sin.

It is much like with Moses who reached the place in his life when his concern shifted from the personal concerns of his own life and family to the greater concern of the kingdom of God. The early Moses was worried about himself and his own security – how God was going to take care of his life. But the mature Moses was concerned about the greater kingdom of God. There's that moving account where he goes before God and intercedes for the people. God is getting ready to destroy the whole lot. And Moses stands there and says, 'No, don't' (Exod. 32).

This is what we find in the account of Ezra when he said, 'I fell upon my knees, and spread out my hands unto the LORD my God, and said, O my God, I am ashamed and blush to lift up my face to thee, my God: for our iniquities are increased over our head, and our trespass is grown up unto the heavens' (Ezr. 9:5–6). It is the sign of true godliness when there is a lamenting for sin generally, when it becomes a national mourning and an identification with all of humanity.

This is how Isaiah put it: 'We hid as it were our faces from him' (Isa. 53:3). Many of the great saints have experienced this. You find it in Newton's hymn when he said, 'I saw my sins his blood had spilt and helped to nail him there.' Or Wesley put it like this: 'Died he for me, who caused his pain?' Or as Isaac Watts put it: 'Was it for crimes that I had done?' This is a love for God and a sense of the glory of God that Satan cannot counterfeit. James is mourning, 'Out of the same mouth proceedeth blessing and cursing. My brethren, these things ought not so to be' (v. 10).

James proceeds then to show what it is about the tongue that should be the ground of mourning. He says that 'the tongue is a little member, and boasteth great things.' At this stage James gives us four comparisons. The first comparison is that of the tongue to a spark in a dry forest: 'Behold, how great a matter a little fire kindleth!' The NIV puts it: 'Consider what a great forest is set on fire by a small spark.' Why would James compare the tongue to a spark in a dry forest? Why couldn't he compare the tongue to the salt that's in the earth, or to the light that's in the world? Primarily it's because he's describing unfallen nature first and then he turns to fallen nature.

The Tongue Represents our Fallen Nature and Influences the Whole Body

James talks about the bits in horses' mouths. The horse is part of unfallen creation. Ships are created by man. But James says that the tongue does not represent God's unfallen creation, but rather fallen creation, and has no positive good of its own. In fact, Eve's first mistake was talking back to the devil. Would to God that Eve had never opened her mouth!

It has been man's tongue ever since that has kept him in this awful state. This is why Paul put it like this, 'They are all gone out of the way, they are together become unprofitable; there is none that doeth good, no, not one. Their throat is an open sepulchre; with their tongues they have used deceit; the poison of asps is under their lips: whose mouth is full of cursing and bitterness' (Rom. 3:12–14).

James gives the reason he must compare the tongue to a spark rather than to light or to something positive. It is because the tongue is a fire, he says. By 'fire' he's not referring to the positive advantages of fire such as heat or warmth. He's referring to the negative things because he goes on to say that the tongue is 'a world of iniquity'. Indeed the tongue has a monopoly on God's fallen creation. It controls mankind and ensures the continuity of chaos and injustice.

A second comparison is this: he is mourning for sin because the tongue is compared to a member that defiles the whole body. It is not the arm, it is not the leg that defiles the body, it's what goes out of man, says Jesus. He said, 'Out of the abundance of the heart the mouth speaketh' (Mt. 12:34). And therefore by your words you shall be justified or condemned. When you see what Jesus says about the heart and what James says about the tongue you begin to see that they're talking about the same thing. The tongue is an indicator of the heart.

Yet James says that it is the tongue that defiles the whole body. 'If any man offend not in word, the same is a perfect man and able also to bridle the whole body.' By 'whole body' he means the whole man. When we think of the whole man what do we mean? We can say four things:

- his motivation,
- his personality,
- his mind,
- his own physical body.

James is saying that the tongue actually lies behind man's two most basic urges. James said it 1900 years before Freud and Jung and the whole psychoanalytic movement did. They have been saying now for a hundred years that sex and self-esteem are the two basic urges and this is what James has been saying throughout the epistle; it is the tongue that sets these two on fire.

The Way to Avoid Sin

You don't pray about it, you do it. This is why Jesus said, 'Watch and pray' – in that order. The way to avoid sin is to avoid the temptation and the way to avoid the temptation is to have a prior commitment: tongue control. There are those who are what they are right now because of the years of ability or inability to control the tongue. What makes a person like they are? It's the years of tongue control. What makes a person balanced or odd? It goes back to the ability to control words. What makes a person popular or unpopular is that people will recall what they said. The months and years of tongue control shape your personality. Once you speak without thinking you lose control.

I mean not only motivation and personality but also mind. I'm referring to man basically at a natural level, not to his spiritual side. We're talking about the person that we know and what people see in us. It is the tongue that largely determines our whole emotional stability. Proverbs puts it like this: 'He that is slow to anger is better than the mighty; and he that ruleth his spirit than he that taketh a city' (Prov. 16:32). James' term for emotional instability is double mindedness.

Gaining Emotional Stability

Have you ever wondered why there are so many Christian neurotics? There is an explanation for it. The natural man won't accept this and I'm not justifying it, but I am explaining it. The Christian has the devil as an enemy and the non-Christian doesn't. Our ineffectiveness in resisting the devil can lead to our emotional instability.

The Christian often falls into the trap of a false kind of dependence upon God. The devil makes you think it's a sign of spirituality. But James is trying to help us, for Christianity ought to produce the finest kind of person. Would you want your own child to be pathologically dependent upon you? Surely you want your own child to grow up and develop into autonomy and independence. 'A wise son maketh a glad father' (Prov. 10:1). It's when that son has ability of his own and creativity, and industry, and by perspiration and inspiration becomes the type of person that makes the father glad that there's real autonomy. If that pleases us as parents, how much more does it please God when we develop into those kind of people because we want to please him by what we do? The apostle Paul recognized this when he said to the Galatians, 'Let every man prove his own work, and then shall he have rejoicing in himself alone, and not in another' (Gal. 6:4).

The mind, then, partly means emotional stability. But it also means clear thinking. If we control our tongue it enables us to think clearly. Many times we defend a position that we no longer believe but, because we've said it, we've got to keep showing we still believe it. If only we had learned tongue control we wouldn't be in that predicament. 'It's a small member that controls the whole man.' It will affect our decision-making process. It is what will give us an assessment of the times, a world-view. The Christian ought to be the finest citizen, the best businessman, the best worker, the best secretary, the best lorry driver. But we've got to do it, James tells us.

Gaining Bodily Control

Another thing with regard to the whole man is not only motivation, personality, mind, but the body itself. When sexual lust gets out of control it can lead to unwanted pregnancy, to disease of the body. Self-esteem if it gets out of control can lead to ulcers and high blood pressure and migraine headaches. We become threatened. We internalize and it breaks out upon us physically.

I've heard Dr Lloyd-Jones say more than once that one of the principal reasons he left medicine is because the illnesses that he was confronting were so often spiritually derived. You may think that I'm telling you to develop autonomy and independence while Christianity teaches that we should be dependent upon God. It should not be a pathological dependence. So much Christianity today is not robust and strong. We turn it over to God and we cease to be real people.

James Makes us Face the Real World

The devil slips in and robs us of being the kind of persons we ought to be because Christianity alone can produce the best kind of person. Psychology, Islam, Marxism, raising socio-economic standards will not do it. James is making us face the real world. Will we listen to him?

Yet he's not finished. There's a further comparison. The first: the spark to the forest. The second: the small member to the body. The tongue not only defiles the whole man but it even sets the 'course of nature' on fire (v. 6). The Greek word means 'wheel of nature'. Not only is the tongue man's worst enemy, but the tongue is the greatest enemy of all of God's unfallen creation. Look what man has done with reference to ecology. Unclean air, unclean water, endangered species. Nuclear war threatens to annihilate man and all life of any kind. It is traceable to the tongue. Only the Bible can give us that kind of world-view and understanding of what is happening. We as Christians ought to be the first to see this and ought to be taking the lead. But we've been lagging behind.

The Reality of Hell

James' ultimate statement in his fourth and final comparison is this: that it is the tongue that is 'set on fire of hell'. The word 'hell' is the Greek *gehenna*. It's a difficult translation here. The Authorised Version says that it is 'set on fire of hell'. The Greek literally means – and most versions get it right – that it is the tongue that is inflamed by hell. The word for 'hell' here is the same word that Jesus used to denote the place of actual punishment. There are three Greek words in the New Testament translated 'hell' in the Authorised Version. One is *tartarus*, used only once: 'If God spared not the angels that sinned, but cast them down to hell ...' (2 Pet. 2:4). The other is *hades* which means 'death'. 'The gates of hell shall not prevail against the church' (Mt. 16:18). 'And have the keys of hell and of death' (Rev. 1:18).

But there's a third Greek word translated 'hell', and that's *gehenna*. Without exception it means a place of eternal damnation. It is used synonymously with, everlasting fire, weeping, wailing, gnashing of teeth. The question is, how then can the tongue be inflamed by hell because we're not there yet? If you're not a Christian thank God it is future, because it's coming and yet it's having its effect now. How can this be? It's very simple. Hell was created for the devil and his angels, as Jesus said in Matthew 25:41.

I don't know whether you believe in hell but the devil certainly does, and he knows all about hell. Listen to what the demons said when Jesus was casting them out: 'Behold, they cried out, saying, What have we to do with thee, Jesus, thou Son of God? Art thou come hither to torment us before the time?' (Mt. 8:29). And we're told in the book of Revelation chapter 12: 'Woe to the inhabiters of the earth and the sea! for the devil is come down unto you, having great wrath, because he knoweth that he hath but a short time' (v. 12).

There is one consensus in the satanic world: that there is a hell. The demons are going to be plunged into hell. They know the time is coming and they know the time is short. And so, according to James, it is the fire of *gehenna* that motivates the devil to work so violently. It is the devil that is wanting to see that there's continuity of chaos, of injustice even, in your own life. It's the devil who wants to paralyse Christians, to achieve a passivity in Christians. This also shows us just how much James believes in this matter of hell. It's said, 'Jesus said a lot about hell, why is it the New Testament writers don't say much about it?' It was an assumption. Jesus said it all. And it's something we must never apologize for. We may not naturally like the doctrine of eternal punishment. I don't know that anybody does, but it is to be held to.

The Route to Self-Control

This fourth comparison: James says it is hell that sets the tongue on fire. It is the devil who is at work to get you to say things that you ought not to say.

What does James hope to accomplish by saying all this to us?

- First, so that the true Christian will have a mourning for sin so that we won't justify it.

- Second, so that the true Christian will be motivated to take hold of himself, to be different from the rest of mankind and refuse to be upstaged by beasts and reptiles and birds.

We all know we can do far more than we do. Do you wonder sometimes why the non-Christian can be so productive? It's because he doesn't know anything of this pathological dependence that sets in with so many Christians. It's a painful truth that many Christians were more productive before they became Christians. Why? The devil started to work. This is one reason why Jesus said that the children of the world are wiser than the children of light (Lk. 16:8). But if we become convinced that God isn't going to control our tongues for us, we will begin to control them for ourselves.

34

The Tongue and Self-Control (3)

James 3:6–10

We continue in this third chapter of James dealing with his discussion of this most painful matter of the tongue. (If a minister waits until he himself is free from anything he's going to have to deal with, he will never preach at all.) But however painful it may be we are going to look at it carefully.

It makes me think of a time some years ago when my wife and I were listening to a series on the radio in Florida. A good man, a rather superficial preacher but what he was saying was good, was preaching through Romans. He took several weeks on chapter 4, several weeks on chapters 5, 6, 7, weeks on end. It wasn't too deep, but I was really looking forward to chapters 9, 10 and 11. He got to the eighth chapter and for some reason we missed a Sunday. Two weeks later we tuned in and he was on chapter 12! I was quite tempted to do James just like that.

The Tongue Is Fire and Poison

James has told us that the tongue is two things: fire and poison. The tongue is inflamed by the fire of *gehenna*, hell itself. If you knew that you were going to hell it would have an effect upon you. You would cry out to God for mercy. The devil knows he is going to hell, but the effect it has on him is that he wants to do as much damage as he can along the way.

And it is the tongue, in fact, that is the devil's best weapon. He can use the tongue of man to conserve the damage he's already done, to do his own dirty work of spreading evil throughout the world. The tongue is not a neutral thing to start with. It is by nature already leaning toward hell's pull. For the tongue is the official spokesman of fallen nature. There's nothing sinful about nature generally, but the tongue represents fallen nature.

So Keep Your Mouth Shut!

The tongue is the indicator of man's evil heart, perhaps best described as being like a pilot light in a gas oven. It is ready to set something ablaze. It is the immediate indicator of man's own motivation. And it is the easiest thing in the world to give in to what is in the heart. Keep your mouth shut and you can save yourself a lot of trouble.

It is because the tongue is the indicator of man's fallen heart that this fire is so easily inflamed by hell itself. You can see why it is called 'fire'. Like fire, it so easily gets out of control. Like fire, whatever it burns is destroyed and is brought to complete disuse. It is called fire because we ourselves get burnt when we speak without thinking, not to mention what we do to others. This is why James goes on to say that 'the tongue can no man tame'. He compares the tongue to that of fallen nature. He says that 'every kind of beasts, and of birds, and of serpents, and of things in the sea, is tamed, and have been tamed of mankind' (vv. 7, 8). Man can tame anything else. By the ordinance of creation we can tame the beast. We can kill for food. We can put animals into a zoo.

We Remind the Devil of Jesus

The chief reason that the devil attacks man is that man is created in God's image. 'Similitude' is the word used in the Authorised Version. Jesus Christ was the image, the perfect image, of the invisible God as Paul said in Colossians 1:15. The writer to the Hebrews says that Jesus Christ is 'the brightness of God's glory, and the express image of his person' (1:3). Jesus Christ reflected the image of God perfectly. We do it imperfectly because we're fallen. Yet we all have the image of God stamped upon us, and because we remind the devil of what he hates, he attacks us.

Satan's arch enemy is Jesus Christ. We remind him of Jesus. Jesus is the invisible God made visible. He was God made flesh and we have the image of God upon us. The devil is attacking us because he's attacking Jesus.

Why the Devil Attacks us

Satan is jealous of us and so he attacks us. If a person is jealous of you, you can't ever do anything right, no matter how hard you try. You might try to call a truce, but they'll still be jealous of you. Those who have worshipped the devil are the biggest fools of all because Satan possesses and destroys them. There's no way we can please the devil.

Satan attacks us best through the tongue. It makes us realize how thankful we ought to be that we have the high privilege as men and women of being made in God's image and not to be a fly or a dog or a cat or a mule. It's almost too good to be true that we would be called the sons of God not just by creation but by redemption.

Defeating the Devil

We then, by being Christians, are called to participate in this cosmic war between God and Satan. To the extent that we learn to control our tongues, to the extent to which we practise being swift to hear and slow to speak, it is to that extent that we honour Jesus Christ, the arch-enemy of the devil. To the extent we resemble Jesus Christ who defeated the devil, we then will also defeat the devil.

There are no exceptions. 'The tongue can no man tame.' It's a way of saying that no man can save himself. James has earlier said that 'if any man offend not in word, the same is a perfect man, and able also to bridle the whole body' (3:2). He's saying that no man can cleanse himself because the tongue is poison. And no man can be sure what the devil is up to and what he's going to do next. James says that the tongue is 'an unruly evil', 'untamable'.

If the tongue were controlled not only would the man who controlled his tongue be a perfect man, but if everybody did it there would be no evil in the world. There are two ways of doing away with evil. One is, if God just stepped in and instituted the second coming of Jesus and the final consummation of things; evil would be done away with. The other is, if all men controlled their tongues, you'd have the problem licked. But you see the tongue is not tamable right now.

James' Total Solution

You say, 'Doesn't James have a solution then?' He does. We come to it in the latter verses of this same chapter. But it will do us no good to jump to the solution until we are absolutely convinced of all that he's saying right here. It's like trying to lead a person to Christ. Unless they see they've got a need, you can never do anything for them.

We must admit that we have failed, that nothing has worked. Even though we have said God can do it and we've put our tongue on the altar, as it were, we still have the problem.

But that's not all. Poison is a substance that either kills or makes a person deathly ill. 'So the tongue,' says James, 'is poison.'

When you speak without thinking, something actually clicks inside or snaps and you don't have control from that moment on. You grieve the Holy Spirit and you're not aware, it's a painless thing. But then you suddenly realize that nothing's right. You become divided within. Speaking without thinking is tantamount to swallowing poison. But the uncontrolled tongue also has a poisonous effect upon others.

Speaking Without Thinking

I want to talk about two categories. First, what you say to another person directly – when you speak to another person without thinking. When you speak to another person, never assume that he will react indifferently. We may think that when we're speaking to another person they're not listening, that what we're saying will have no effect upon them, but such is never true.

Here's another principle. Never impute to another person as having grace that keeps him from being affected by what you say. Never say, 'I can say this to that person because he's so mature. It wouldn't bother him one bit.' But it does. You do that person great harm. It's the worst assumption you can make. There's the child in all of us. We tend to treat others as parents sometimes and we say things to them as though that wouldn't bother them. But what our children say to us bothers us. What we say to our children bothers them. They hear us when we speak.

This reminds me of a lady I knew. I had to deal with her daughter in counselling some years ago. The mother would say to the little girl as she grew up, 'Well, you're just going to grow up not having any morals. When you come of age you'll just become immoral.' Do you know, she did. She believed her mother. The fact is, there is nobody who is unaffected. Even Jesus Christ our Lord was affected by what was said to him. He was without sin but he was tempted, and once he had to say to Peter, 'Get thee behind me, Satan.' When he was told that John the Baptist had had his head cut off it had an effect on him. We're told he went to a solitary place. We sometimes think that Jesus, because he was God in the flesh, didn't learn anything new. Oh, no. He was man.

When you speak without thinking you not only put temptation in another person's way, but you may lead them to sin. Jesus was tempted without sin but we're not like that. This is why the tongue is poison.

I think of that awful verse in the Old Testament: 'Jeroboam who made Israel to sin' (1 Kgs. 14:16). This is the responsibility we have.

The second category is what you say about another person indirectly. Again, never assume that the person you tell it to will react indifferently. What you say will not be forgotten. You are helping shape another person's opinion of somebody, and that person can never feel exactly the same way again about the other person. If what you say is damaging to that person, it is tantamount to homicide.

Always assume that what you say to another person will be quoted. If you don't want it repeated, shut your mouth. I don't care how close you are to that person. We all say, 'I can keep a secret.' We all impute that ability to ourselves. The person who really can is an exceedingly rare person. But just because he can keep a secret doesn't mean he can really handle it. It may be a great thing for him to have to bear in holding that secret within. So remember, what you say will probably be quoted or implied. And when it's quoted it will continue to have its poisonous effect, like poison that spreads throughout the whole body. And then, of course, there's always the possibility that what you say about that person will get back to him or to her and they'll be crushed and may never recover.

Three Reasons to Control our Tongues

We must see that God isn't going to control our tongues for us so we will assume that the tongue is like the evil that is in the world that's going to remain until the final consummation. We live in the real world even though we're Christians. But further, James wants us to mourn for our sin and cry out as James did, 'Brethren, these things ought not so to be.' And finally, he wants us to see the damaging effects that we have on ourselves and others.

The Tongue Has Opposite Functions

At this stage, James brings out this unthinkable, embarrassing – you could call it scandalous – incongruity of the same tongue having opposite functions. He says, that it's with the tongue that we bless God, that we praise him and pray to him and tell him how much we love him. But with the same tongue we curse men. It is with the tongue that we actually worship God, in public worship and in private devotional life. 'Therewith bless we God, even the Father' (v. 9).

Why did he throw in that? He's showing that the same tongue talks about the God and Father of our Lord Jesus Christ.

Talking to the Father

One of the major contributions of Jesus Christ was to tell his followers to call God 'Father'. They were thrilled that they could do that. Now James is saying that we bless 'God, even the Father'. It's about as sound doctrine and orthodoxy as you can possibly get, that there is an intimate relationship with the Father. We cry, 'Abba Father' because the Spirit of adoption is with us (Rom. 8:15). He's not talking about a superficial worship.

False Ideas of Piety

His purpose is to counter the objection that people who lack tongue control simply aren't praying enough, that your problem is that you just aren't reading your Bible as much as you ought to, or you're not going to church as much as you should, or your theology isn't sound enough. This is the way all of us want to deal with the tongue. Just an extra ten minutes a day in prayer or an extra thirty minutes or an extra two hours, or we'll go to Bible study. James is trying to show you that if you lack tongue control you should not think that it's because you're not praying to God enough or because you don't have a good view of God.

Note that James says, 'We bless God'. He's including himself again. And if this absolute perfection of tongue control were attainable, surely James would have had it. Wouldn't you think that this man James would have it. What James is saying here is that it's a lovely thing to have an intimate relationship with God and know your doctrine. As far as it goes that's wonderful. He said, 'Here's the problem. We curse men with the same tongue.' Is it not true that some of the most pious people, some that are most doctrinally sound, are the greatest gossips? But the sad thing – the most shocking thing – is that it doesn't seem to bother us.

Popular Piety is not Sufficient

Here's the big mistake we make – that popular piety will be sufficient. We don't smoke. We don't drink. We don't go out into the world. We don't fall into gross sin. Therefore a little thing like gossiping just doesn't bother us. We think it's not really that bad. We tend not to take seriously this matter of gossiping.

Now he adds, with regard to the men we curse, 'who are made after the similitude of God' – created in the image of God (v. 9). We're defiling men who are created in God's image. We don't curse the rest of God's creation, only God's image. The same principle was at work when John said, 'If a man say, I love God, and hateth his brother, he is a liar: for he that loveth not his brother whom he hath seen, how can he love God whom he hath not seen?' (1 Jn. 4:20). James' point is that we nullify our worship when we turn on those who are created in God's image. When we do that we don't always feel bad at the time. 'Samson wist not that the Lord was departed from him' (Jdg. 16:20).

Avoiding Gossip and the Need for Repentance

Grieving the Holy Spirit is almost always done unconsciously. It's sometimes hours later, sometimes years later, we realize that what we did was wrong. True spirituality seeks to close the gap between the moment we did what we did and the time when we feel bad about it. And if we close the gap we will stop. We'll be swift to hear, slow to speak. Gossip is nothing but a defence mechanism to preserve our self-esteem. It arises out of an inferiority complex. We build up ourselves by tearing another down. It is a violation of the principle of John 5:44: 'How can ye believe, which receive honour one of another, and seek not the honour that cometh from God only?'

Men made in the 'similitude of God' means that God loves every other man as much as he loves you. Who said that you could talk about another person the way you do? Do you think God loves you more? You want God to be indignant when somebody says something about you, don't you?

I want us to ask ourselves why we aren't as spiritual as we ought to be. If we have said anything about another person that makes that person appear less than perfect, we have grieved the Holy Spirit then and there. But if James can lead us to a true mourning for sin, then the time we've spent on this will be worth it.

35

The Tongue and Self-Control (4)

James 3:6–18

We can summarize what James has said, regarding tongue control, that God isn't going to do it for us. And James wants us to mourn genuinely for sin and to see the damaging effects that follow from the uncontrolled tongue.

Gossip Is a Defence Mechanism and a Curse

Gossip is a carnal defence mechanism, the most perverted way to preserve our self-esteem. At the spiritual level it arises from a dearth of our own grace. At the emotional level it shows our insecurity. In any case, it betrays that we want our approval from men and not from God.

It is a poisonous habit that is very difficult to break. If you don't think so, start trying to break it and you'll be shocked at how many times in a given day you've been doing it. It's so hard to break that we tend to sweep it under the carpet. Misery loves company, and it is our inferiority complex that makes us gossip. Its perversion is this: we build ourselves up by tearing down another. That is exactly what motivates a person to gossip. James calls it 'cursing men'.

If gossiping ever makes you feel better, then it shows how unspiritual you really are. Doing it and hearing it is an exercise in rejoicing in iniquity, not rejoicing in the truth. 'Ah,' you'll say, 'but what if it's true?' In the words of William Perkins, 'Don't believe the devil even if he tells the truth.' The devil quoted Scripture to Jesus and Jesus rejected it. And gossiping has the very breath of Satan behind it. It is not to be listened to. It is to be rejected utterly. Gossiping has the most under-estimated potential to grieve the Spirit of any sin in our theological vocabulary. It is the easiest thing in the world to excuse, and if we knew how much it grieved the Holy Spirit I'm certain it would make a difference in our lives.

Grieving the Spirit and Accepting Responsibility

The thing about grieving the Spirit is that it is almost always done unconsciously. I want now to give you a definition of gossiping: it is any effort to make another person appear less than perfect. James laments that the true worship of God and the putting down of people proceed from the same tongue (v. 10). 'These things ought not so to be.' If we can indeed be convicted of gossiping as much as we are convicted of the grossest immorality, it will make a noticeable difference in the way our lives go. There is a wonderful world out there waiting to be explored if you become convicted of sin at this level – you'll even feel better. Don't insult God and say, 'Lord, help me.' Recognize that you are sinning.

We can think of the grosser forms of immorality and there's not much argument. Why do you suppose James said earlier on, 'He that said, Do not commit adultery, said also, Do not kill' (2:11)? These Christian Jews, who outwardly were moral, were respecting persons. And so he said, 'Whosoever shall keep the whole law, and yet offend in one point, he is guilty of all' (2:10).

The Need for a Prior Commitment

That's exactly what James is saying – a full and predetermined commitment. Jesus said in the Garden of Gethsemane, 'Watch and pray, that ye enter not into temptation' (Mt. 26:41). If we have to watch, that puts the onus on us. Because the only way you can avoid temptation is by having a prior commitment not to listen to it.

For example, if you had to meet a train in Victoria Station in ten minutes and you estimate that it's a six-minute walk, you're going to get there. Many may come up and say, 'Could I have a word with you?' 'I'm sorry I've got to meet a train.' 'I won't take a minute.' But you've got to go and you go, don't you? When you look at temptation that way it will make a difference in the way you live your life. That is the way it must be with regard to gossiping. The temptation will come, and the only way to deal with it is to be really convicted and to have a prior commitment not to do it.

Gossiping is not Excusable

Our problem is that we have looked on gossiping as an excusable evil. It makes me think of a friend of mine from this country who had been preaching in America with a Christian group of people who are well known for their very strict way of living. He said, 'I've really enjoyed myself. But there's this odd thing about this group.' He said, 'They're all fat. I never saw such fat people. Come to think of it, I've gained ten pounds myself since I've been over there. What's the explanation?' I said, 'There's no difficulty about that. These people that you're with, they don't smoke, they don't drink, they don't go to cinemas, they don't play cards, they just don't do anything. But when it comes to eating they do that very well!' Why? They regard it as an excusable evil.

We have looked at gossiping as an excusable evil. Outwardly we're moral. We may have holy affections. We come and sing the hymns and we're moved. The minister speaks and we say, 'God spoke today and we just felt the presence of God.' Until you fear gossiping as much as you do a venomous snake you will make no progress.

At this point James counters a series of objections. The objections are these: that one who truly worships God, who is sound in his theology, who has an intimate relationship with God, is always pleasing God. We tend to think this. We've got an appetite for spiritual things. We want to come to the Bible study and pay tithes and support everything. We say, 'Well, surely the Lord is pleased with me.'

To put it in a slightly different way, James is countering the idea that if one's devotional life, one's worship and orthodoxy are all in order, it follows that the tongue will be in control. James is saying, 'That just isn't so.' For with the tongue we bless God and with the same tongue we curse men.

Be Swift to Hear, Slow to Speak

It's interesting that this was true in James' day. It shows that man has always been the same, that the same gospel is still vulnerable to all sorts of slurs. Many who spot the popular piety and see its superficiality want to blame it on the gospel. The fact that they can see so many Christians who are gossips makes them say, 'What do you expect?' But it's not the gospel, it is we who develop a comfortable provincial piety.

The easiest thing in the world is to take a certain witness of the Spirit, such as joy or peace, and take that to mean a categorical approval from the Lord of our total lifestyle. If we've had an answer to prayer we say, 'The Lord is smiling upon me.' Or we feel his presence in a church service. Or just sometimes the Lord will come down and bless us and we wonder why he's doing it. Don't take it as a sign that you're categorically all right.

Here's the principle: a little bit of grace often leads to a false conclusion which a whole lot of grace would prevent. Yet the fault is with us, not with a little bit of grace. For a little bit of grace will open our eyes, but then we tend to jump to a conclusion.

The fact is, there is a lot more grace and a lot more knowledge out there waiting for us. And it will come in proportion to your being swift to hear, slow to speak. James is saying that our experience with God is good as far as it goes. 'The problem,' says James, 'is that with the same tongue we expose a serious defect in our total personality. We curse men.' How? By making them appear less than perfect. We all like to look for the chink in someone's armour and then talk about it. The same tongue shows how deficient our worship really is, for if we were content with the honour that comes from God only, there would be no need to speak evil of anybody.

There is only one single reason under the sun why we make others appear less than perfect and that is because nature is in command rather than grace. 'The worst thing of all,' says James, 'is that if you knew whom you were cursing you wouldn't do it. You are cursing God's creation, made in the likeness of men.'

We Are not Qualified to Judge Others

What are the implications of this? The first is: when we speak evil of another person we're taking upon ourselves the prerogatives of God, presuming ourselves in a position to judge. But God alone is qualified to judge another person. And God doesn't want anybody trying to rival him in what is his prerogative.

The second thing is: when we speak against those who are made in God's image, it is an implicit assumption on our part that we are somehow special. It's all right for us to do it. You smile – but we all somehow want to think we're the exception.

Driven by Self-Pity

We don't want others to say anything about us that makes us appear anything less than perfect. In fact, if others say anything about us that doesn't make us look really good we want God to deal with them. We tend to think that our doing it is the excusable evil. That shows the blinding power of self-love.

Some are so deceived on this point that they don't know the difference between self-love and the witness of the Spirit. There are some who actually feel led to say these things. The image of God means that all men have the same Creator. We can all of us say with the Psalmist, 'I am fearfully and wonderfully made' (Ps. 139:14). We all want to think ourselves the exception. If you gossip God will deal with you, and if another gossips and God doesn't deal with them, they are to be most pitied.

I read yesterday in Psalm 147: 'Who can stand before his cold?' (v. 17). If you get away with the things I'm talking about you're to be pitied. It means you're standing before God's cold. He's giving you the cold shoulder. He's not even chastening you or dealing with you. Perhaps the chief lesson from Jonah is that Jonah couldn't get away with what he did. Are you getting away with it? You think you're clever. You think you're the exception. I'm very sorry for you.

Foolishly Playing God

James says that an attack upon another human being is an attack upon God. You may think that you're trying to do to another person what God ought to do. But gossiping is just your way to upstage God.

James moves on now to describe what I would call the typically immature Christian piety. Having described it, he abominates it. 'Out of the same mouth proceedeth blessing and cursing. My brethren, these things ought not so to be.' The word 'proceedeth' is the Greek word which means 'to emit', 'to send forth'. His point is this: blessing God, praising the Lord, doesn't really originate with the tongue. The heart that wants to praise God is prompted with the Holy Spirit that comes from without. The worship of God is not an enterprise at the level of nature. Cursing men is. It comes from the tongue. And yet the same tongue now is doing both.

A Ray of Hope

When James tells us that 'these things ought not so to be', he for the first time gives us a ray of hope. Up to now the tongue has been referred to as 'an unruly evil'; it's not going to go away. The tongue is something we can't control. We think we can't ask God to do it and expect it to happen automatically. Our temptation is to jump to the conclusion. We're swift to speak. We say, 'Wait a minute, we can't do it. God's not going to do it. It can't be done.' James has a solution here and we ought to have seen it by now.

James is trying to convict us, and our hope is that we are convicted. If we are convicted, something might happen. If we justify gossiping as an excusable evil then we haven't heard James yet. And unless we are convicted of all gossiping, there's no hope. There's no use looking for the solution when we haven't seen the problem. If you are really sorry and if you're really convicted but, best of all, if you've been granted an unfeigned repentance, then you're ready to move on.

Spirituality Is no Excuse for Slander

James makes the case that spirituality can never be responsible for our slandering others. This is nothing new. We have seen already in the first chapter: 'Let no man say when he is tempted, I am tempted of God' (v. 13). As long as somehow there's the remote thought that God has been responsible for your own peculiar temptation it's not going to affect the way you live one bit. This is his way of looking at the tongue.

Temptation comes from below. 'Every good gift and every perfect gift is from above' (v. 17). He's now saying the same thing about the tongue. With this matter of gossiping, even if you have prayed a lot and maybe you've made great spiritual progress and you've got holy affection, gossiping can seem right at times, especially if it's true. But if you think that godliness can lead to gossiping you are as guilty of error as the one who says, 'God is the architect of temptation.'

This is James' whole point. 'Doth a fountain send forth at the same place sweet water and bitter? Can the fig tree … bear olive berries? either a vine, figs?' (vv. 11, 12). Simple question. He's showing there is that which comes from below and that which comes from above.

James says you can't have it both ways. He uses this analogy from nature, a metaphor. A fountain doesn't emit sweet water and bitter water from the same place. The fig tree doesn't produce olives. A vine produces grapes. It is James' conviction that the spirituality of which God is the author is of one kind and one kind only. And if you wonder what it is you find it in verse 17: 'The wisdom that is from above is first pure, then peaceable, gentle, and easy to be intreated, full of mercy and good fruits, without partiality, and without hypocrisy.'

A Little Bit of Grace is not Enough

If there is the slightest taint of bitterness or envy in us when we're talking about somebody, know that God isn't in it, no matter how spiritual you may think you are, no matter how much you prayed the same day, no matter how much money you gave to the Lord, no matter how much you've been witnessing. It's impossible. It came from below. You may have had a little bit of grace but you jumped to a false conclusion that a lot more grace would have prevented. The biggest mistake we make is that we confuse our spirituality with our personal grudges. We say God is always on our side – my side. James laments that this could be the case and so he says, 'So no fountain can yield both salt water and fresh.'

James has taught us two things here. The first is that there's no hope for us unless we are convicted of gossiping. There's no hope unless we see that God is never behind our efforts to make another person look less than perfect. Until we see that it is the flesh only that provides the impetus to speak to anybody or about anybody we just go right on saying, 'Lord do it for me.' Let us pray that we're convicted.

If you take this seriously you're going to be surprised, you're going to feel better in every way. This could be the turning point in your life. You've been looking for some kind of breakthrough, a blessing, here it is. It's right at your fingertips. Stop gossiping. The world will look different. You'll feel clean. More grace will come. Knowledge and joy. That's a promise.

36

Wisdom in Action

James 3:13–18

When James raises the question: 'Who is a wise man and endued with knowledge among you?' he is restating the thesis that we have seen throughout this epistle, namely the living of the Christian life, the essence of which is Christlikeness. Having said what he has said about bridling the tongue, he is putting it in a more positive way when he talks about showing 'out of a good conversation our works with meekness of wisdom'.

Wisdom for Christian Living

James is bringing us back to the central thesis: 'Who is a wise man among you?' We have the twin subsidiary themes under the general theme of the wisdom that he envisions for Christian living, the emphasis upon works and the emphasis upon the word. In chapter 2 we have the emphasis upon the works, in chapter 3 the word and how we bridle our tongues and how we must do so.

Divine Wisdom Is Different from Earthly Wisdom

James now continues to elaborate beyond the word by talking about the wisdom that comes from below and the wisdom that comes from above. What comes from below is temptation, as well as a wisdom that is bitterness, envying, strife. There is a wisdom that comes from above. But at this point he simply wants to bring together all that he's said concerning non-verbal sanctification, namely works and verbal sanctification, that is, how we control our speech by thinking before we speak. Therefore James is ready to apply the question, Have you got the message? 'Who among you then is wise and endued with knowledge? If so, prove it by showing out of a good conversation your works with meekness and wisdom.'

The emphasis is on the word, that is, what we say. He's going to show what Paul calls 'the fruit of the Spirit'. James calls it 'wisdom that is from above'. The first thing he focuses on as he brings in this new section is what we would call wisdom personified. This Greek word *sophia*, translated 'wisdom', is a quality, never an activity. Having dealt with wisdom in abstraction, now he wants to raise the question, 'Who among you is wise?'

This word *sophos* or *sophia* implies in ancient Greek literature the highest kind of wisdom and knowledge and ability. Many of the ancient pagan Greeks regarded this *sophia* as something that pertained to the gods alone. People just didn't naturally have this self-knowledge, critical objective knowledge about oneself.

This is the sort of thing that doesn't come to us easily because we all look in the mirror and see what we want to see. We reflect upon our past and recall how we were and we pick out the good. We really fear looking at ourselves with objectivity. These ancient Greeks made a distinction between *sofia* and *philosophia*, which was an ability to dispute in rhetoric, in argument – hence the word 'philosophy'. *Sophia* was knowing you didn't have wisdom. *Philosophia* was knowing you had a certain ability to argue or to dispute.

This wisdom, then, that James is talking about is a wisdom that had to be learned by the fear of the Lord. In fact, it's the word that was used in the Septuagint when Proverbs was translated. 'The fear of the Lord is the beginning of wisdom' (Prov. 9:10). This wisdom is not the ability to dispute, or having a craft or skill or natural cleverness.

James wants us to see that there is a difference between wisdom in abstraction and wisdom that is personified.

I'm hoping that by this time we are beginning to think like James. Now it's time to take the examination, 'Who among you is wise?' He says, 'If you do claim to have this, show it by a good conversation matched with your own good works with meekness of wisdom.'

James introduced this chapter with a warning to those who might aspire to the ministry. He is pointing out here that this wisdom that must characterize the ministry is more than having an art or a craft, than having the ability to speak in public, than a technical ability or having cleverness or being able to dispute.

Wisdom personified, then, is something that applies to all and invites an unusual competition among men. We all know about sibling rivalry and competition, and all of us grow up with the thought of what we are going to do in life and how we are going to get ahead. We know there'll be examinations we have to take and we want the best score. But here James dangles before our eyes a goal as he says, 'Who among you has this?'

We're now talking about a quality of life that is exceedingly rare. And yet the extraordinary thing is that it's open to everybody. The fact is, having the ability to dispute in logic or rhetoric or having a clever mind or having a particular gift or art or craft really is not an advantage in this. We're all at the same level.

The Greatest Challenge Ever – Demonstrating Your Gifts

Are you by nature an ambitious person? You're a highly motivated person. You like a challenge. Here is the greatest challenge you'll ever get and that is to become a truly wise man or woman. Actualize that ambition by this kind of wisdom. You may have been frustrated by everything you've ever done in your life. What James is talking about throws out to you a challenge that all things have not been mastered because they cannot be mastered by education or money or any natural ability. But here is an opportunity to be somebody that really matters.

Or perhaps you are the one who has always managed to get ahead, to achieve. You like a new challenge. But what about this other wisdom? Here's the challenge for you. Here's what separates the men from the boys. Who is a wise man among you? 'Let him shew out of a good conversation his works with meekness of wisdom.'

What we're coming to, then, is actualized wisdom and understanding. 'Who is a wise man and endued with knowledge among you?' Here's a new word for this epistle, *epistemon*. We get the word 'epistemology' from this word. It means 'to be versed in', 'to be master of'. It's a general term that supercedes all of the other Greek words for knowledge.

Students in philosophy know that epistemology is a branch of philosophy that deals with knowing, the way we know. James is anticipating the genius who says, 'I've got all of those skills, abilities and knowledge.' Some of us don't have any of these things, but there are those who are clever, who have intuitive knowledge and a high IQ. They've got it all. James says to them, 'This will include you.' Here is the greatest challenge in the history of man. In other words, if you're so sure you've got everything, James says, 'Who among you is wise and endued with knowledge? Show by a good conversation your works with meekness of wisdom.' Keep in mind that James is also thinking about those who aspire to the ministry.

Making Good Use of Wisdom, Words and Works

James was always looking out for future ministers, as was Paul. He said to Titus, 'Ordain elders in every city' (Titus 1:5). It's part of the task of the minister to have his eye out for the one that God may call. There's nothing more thrilling than to have somebody called to the ministry right under one's own ministry. For this is the way we think of the future of the Church.

But James, whereas he wants the gifted man, is walking on the knife edge. It's not enough to have the gift. Who is wise? Who has knowledge? Who is a master of things? Let him show it by the good conversation, his works. Because there's nothing worse than having the gift and then being a failure because one does not have the godly walk and the kind of works that honour that very calling. Wisdom is to be actualised. This genius is to be demonstrated. James says, 'Demonstrate your wisdom. Show that you've really got these things by the kind of life you live.' It's really the greatest challenge in the history of man.

Maybe you feel that you have something to offer and you've just never been recognized. If you will actualize what James is talking about here you will have people banging on your door for advice, for help. You'll be in demand on your street, in your neighbourhood, in your community. For this wisdom that manifests itself by the good conversation, the works with meekness of wisdom, is rarer than gold and diamonds. Proverbs puts it like this: 'he that ruleth his spirit [is greater] than he that taketh a city' (Prov. 16:32).

Demonstrating Wisdom

Here's where the rub comes in. You may say, 'I believe that I have got this.' And you're not meaning to be proud about it. James says, 'Show it.' It's the same word that Paul used to the Colossians when he referred to Jesus: 'Having spoiled principalities and powers, he made a show of them openly, triumphing over them in it' (Col. 2:15). What Jesus did is no secret. It's open for anybody to see what has been done by the death of Jesus on the cross. This wisdom, then, is something that is to be shown and to be demonstrated.

As James put it in chapter 2 verse 18 when he chastised them, 'Shew me thy faith without thy works.' It can't be done. Now he's saying, 'You also show your wisdom by your works.' How? Three ways.

Blameless Lifestyle

First, 'out of a good conversation'. This is a quaint seventeenth-century expression that really means 'behaviour'. In Hebrews 13:7 the writer says, 'Remember them which have the rule over you, who have spoken unto you the word of God: whose faith follow, considering the end of their conversation.' James is warning us now that this good conversation means not only your non-verbal, but also your verbal, witness. It denotes a total lifestyle so that your life, that anybody can see, is what is going to speak first. In America they say, 'Get to the bottom line.' In other words, get to the point. The bottom line here is that James is saying, 'Beware of the one who says, "I don't hear what you say because I can see what you are".'

Our works mean nothing if not put in the context of this good conversation, this total lifestyle. James says, 'Show it by a good conversation.' Only then does he come to works. This is so important, because all of us are living in a generation where many churches and ministers are talking about the social gospel, even though it empties churches. You would think that by now these apostate liberals would have learned their lesson. They say, 'We've got to end poverty, war and all this.' But the things they get very uneasy about are their own lives, their own morals, their own faithfulness to the Lord Jesus. They're quick to quote 'Pure religion and undefiled is ... to visit the fatherless and widows', but they don't like the last part: 'to keep himself unspotted from the world'.

It is our responsibility as Christians to know that the good works must be preceded by a lifestyle that is blameless. For our works will mean nothing if not backed up by godly living. You might spend more time witnessing or praying so that you will not have to deal with certain areas of your life where you know the Spirit has convicted you. The fact is, our conduct, our verbal and non-verbal lifestyle must be there first. The good conversation, the behaviour will present your good works on a silver platter to those who know you.

This word 'good conversation' means two things: one, simple morality; two, bridling your tongue. You may say, 'You may not believe this, but God has helped me and I feel that I've come a long way.' But wait a minute. James gives a second thing now. The proof of this wisdom.

Good Works

This makes a lot of us uneasy because we feel that if we have, under the grace of God, progressed to the stage that we have this total lifestyle, we think surely that's enough. That is not enough. 'Show out of the good conversation your works.' Not God's works, your works. What you are. It's what you do that they see. This, then, is our responsibility.

You cannot stop at having disciplined your life, controlled your spirit and temper, subdued your lusts. This is progress, but you must show good works out of that. Do you take the time to do for others what you know they would like you to do for them? Remember that word 'visit' back in chapter 1 verse 27 about visiting the fatherless and the widows. It means to get to the bottom of the matter, to find out where people are hurting. When it comes to not being a respecter of persons as James put it in chapter 2, do you prove your works by an indiscriminate witnessing to all men? Or do you just witness at a certain time?

A lot of people, a lot of ministers are like this. They can be bold in church or in the pulpit, but they don't want to say anything to anybody anywhere else. Many of you may pass out tracts. It's one thing to do it where nobody knows you, but what about those all around you? The good conversation is not enough. Your works must be there. Churches must grow on the basis of conversations and conversions.

The thing that struck me so deeply when I visited certain churches in America, although the theology that lay behind the preaching wasn't always as sound as many of us might demand, was that I saw lives being changed. I stood on the platform with the minister of the First Baptist Church in Fort Lauderdale. There were a thousand people and he bent over and said that half those out there had been converted in the last eighteen months. Incidentally, that's how long he'd been the minister there. I felt convicted.

When we took the local minister of the church in Islamorada down in the Keys out on the boat fishing, the captain who had never met him said, 'So you're the pastor of this church. What is it about your church? Three of my friends in the last few years have started going to your church and their lives have changed. Their marriages have gotten together. They've quit their use of dope and alcohol. They're even happy.' It's the gospel. His people were witnessing. It is not enough to have the good conversation and the lifestyle that is blameless. Many of us have this and thank God for that. But there's more. It's doing something for people and going to them.

Meekness

You may say, 'If we start doing that, that's going to breed self-righteousness.' James thought of that, and that's the third thing. He said, 'Let him show out of a good conversation his works with meekness of wisdom.' The ultimate proof of this wisdom is the meekness that characterizes it. The happy disappointment that follows the one who has this wisdom is that he can't talk about it because true wisdom is always self-effacing.

Paul put it like this: 'I say, through the grace given unto me, to every man that is among you, not to think of himself more highly than he ought to think; but to think soberly, according as God hath dealt to every man the measure of faith' (Rom. 12:3). He went on in the same chapter to say, 'Be not wise in your own conceits' (v. 16).

A disputer in rhetoric or logic wants to be noticed. The artist, the craftsman, always loves the compliment. People with the greatest intellects are the most insecure people in the world. They need to be reminded that they are clever. But true wisdom never calls attention to itself. True spirituality is never self-conscious. It is like Moses who did not know that his face was glowing. This is James' plea. When will we take him seriously? It's not enough to be godly. There must be the works that show you care about people.

Wisdom in Action

I wonder how many of you have won a soul to the Lord or at least brought somebody to church who was unconverted. We may not like this. It is much easier to be a sermon taster and come and say, 'Wasn't that good? It was worth coming for.' That is not going to be the wave of the future.

This is the message of James. He says: 'Show me your faith without your works.' You can't do it. May God help us to see it. He says. 'Demonstrate you works. Do you have a good conversation? Good. What about your works? Maybe you are a doer and an activist. What about your good conversation?' For what James challenges us with, what we must produce, is this high wisdom in action. Then the world will take notice and we'll begin to see blessing. And that's a promise.

37

Counterfeit Wisdom

James 3:13–18

One of the questions I get asked most often in the vestry is simply, 'How can I know God's will?' or 'How can I test a particular feeling or leading so that I can be sure that I'm in the Spirit and that God is saying to do this or that?' It is a very important question and yet one not always easy to answer. But it is dealt with in a direct way in our text today: 'But if ye have bitter envying and strife in your hearts, glory not, and lie not against the truth. This wisdom descendeth not from above, but is earthly, sensual, devilish.'

This matter of what comes from below and what comes from above is a recurring theme in this whole epistle of James. Temptation comes from below. When it came to the discussion on the tongue we saw how easy it is to feel that what you're saying is really given to you from the Lord. But James raises the question, 'Doth a fountain send forth at the same place sweet water and bitter?' Obviously that can't be. So he talks about what comes from below and what comes from above.

The Possibility of Being Godly but Wrong

The most godly person can sometimes have an unbridled tongue. It's scary when you think of the possibility of being godly and still being grossly in the wrong. It's humbling. James makes us face this. The following discussion can be most helpful in knowing whether our leadings are from below or from above.

In introducing the subject James brings up again this theme of wisdom. He refers to the possibility of having bitter envying and strife in our hearts and he calls that 'wisdom'. But he says, 'This wisdom descendeth not from above, but is earthly, sensual, devilish.' He begins with this contrast. We need to understand early on in the Christian life that every authentic grace has its counterfeit, though of diametrically opposite origin. It's possible that true grace can be counterfeited so that we are deceived ourselves, thinking the whole time we're being led of the Spirit, only to realize later – and sometimes so late that it's too embarrassing to admit – that we weren't led of the Spirit after all.

So the first thing we must examine today is this sobering possibility. 'If ye have bitter envying and strife in your hearts …' James is not talking to the unregenerate. He's talking to Christians. We need to recognize that being envious and being bitter and having a contentious disposition is a possibility.

It's possible simply because the most godly are not exempt from making a mistake. It's the wise man who agrees with Jeremiah: 'The heart is deceitful above all things, and desperately wicked: who can know it?' (17:9). The devil is still around. If he doesn't stir you up, he'll stir up somebody around you who will play into your weakness so that you will be stirred up after all! This is the way the devil works, and he is always around doing this.

Yet we need to remember that there are many things that at first glance may seem to provide just cause for bitterness. Sometimes the more persuaded you are of something, the more vulnerable you are to bitterness. You say, 'Why doesn't somebody else see this?' And you begin to get bitter inside and say, 'I'm sure I'm right.' Sometimes you become enraged with the conviction. James is going to talk about this.

Surprised by our own Ungodliness

If we are not aware of this sobering possibility of bitter envying then we're going to give Satan an even greater opportunity to have a victory with us and we have a naive, non-biblical view of man and sin. It's often the case that a Christian who has been obedient to the Lord thinks that at last he's solved a particular problem. You say, 'I had this problem for a long time but I don't have it anymore', and then unexpectedly you find yourself acting the same way you did before. And you are mortified. This is because we tend to think that when we've solved a problem we've put aside this sobering possibility.

All of us like to think that we can outgrow preaching, we can outgrow Bible study and we can outgrow this sobering possibility. In fact, you get so holy and godly that you can just say, 'I don't need James. Let's see if I can find a book that I can use.' It's ridiculous. But we all unconsciously slip into this. We must never let ourselves feel exempt from the possibility that we can behave in a most embarrassing and ungodly manner.

A Likely Temptation

James progresses from this sobering possibility to what he puts as a likely temptation. 'If ye have bitter envying and strife in your hearts, glory not.' It means, 'Do not assume superiority.' The most natural thing in the world is to think that your own reaction as a Christian is surely of divine origin. If you're a new Christian and you can count the days that you've been a Christian, there may be a feeling that because God is with you and he's for you and you're doing something right for a change then everything you're going to say is going to be right. And then you find yourself saying something that is wrong and somebody rebukes you for it. You're embarrassed and the devil will say, 'You're not even a Christian or you wouldn't talk like that.'

Sometimes a particular Christian has reconsecrated himself. It has happened to many of us that God deals with us and we come back to God in a fresh and sincere and mournful manner and say, 'Lord, I wandered but now you can have me.' We begin to set our alarm clocks to get up a little earlier to pray more and to read the Bible more and we begin to think that we're being led of the Spirit. Often the person like that is a sitting duck for the devil's onslaught. It's like the person who begins to tithe and that week his car breaks down and costs him a hundred pounds. The devil says, 'That's the Lord saying you shouldn't do it.' It's often true that the person who begins to pray more and wants to be led of the Spirit will say something he ought not to say and somebody will say, 'The trouble with you is you're just trying to get too religious. Back off a bit.'

The True Nature of Righteous Indignation

When you have bitter envying, James says, 'Don't feel superior about it. Just because now you're more spiritual and you are praying more than you have been and you're getting more involved in things at the church and then you find yourself able to be bitter, don't assume that that bitterness is a sign that you're more spiritual.' 'Glory not.' It is a supreme test of spirituality to be able to judge yourself and realize that your natural reaction may be quite wrong. If a feeling of envy creeps in or there's a threat to your self-esteem, these are natural feelings. When we feel God is on our side we begin to think that God thinks as we do. Jealousy and bitterness have a camouflaging effect upon our own emotions. We sometimes call it 'righteous indignation'. Very few people ever truly experience that, by the way. All of us like to feel that when we get angry it's righteous indignation. Would to God more of us really knew what that was. But what happens when bitterness creeps in or a feeling of envy or a threat to your self-esteem? Instantly it turns objectivity into subjectivity and it inserts the jaundiced eye before we know what has happened. All looks yellow to the jaundiced eye. We speak before we think and wrath sets in and we think, 'I've done it again.' James said, 'Be swift to hear, slow to speak.' Before you know it, wrath is there and you think, 'God, why did I do that? Help me not to do it again.' You are ashamed.

It often happens in the heat of the moment because you think you're right, perhaps because you've been more spiritual. And we become entrenched in a position. We say something and we feel we've got to keep saying it. When the heart is affected like this the Spirit is grieved.

Why? The heart is the seat of faith. Paul said, 'With the heart man believeth unto righteousness' (Rom. 10:10). God has given you the heart for the capacity to believe. Augustine said, 'Thou hast made us for thyself. Our souls are restless until they find their rest in thee.' Our hearts are for faith. Nothing else has any right to be there.

A Second Probable Temptation

But if you have bitter envying in your heart it's as though you have a foreign body as a Christian, for your heart should be occupied by faith. Faith is pushed aside for envy to be there. That ought not to be. 'Do not,' James says, 'glory or assume superiority.' And he gives us a second probable temptation while he's at it, 'Do not lie against the truth.' 'Surely not,' you will say. 'Who as a Christian would lie?' James had to talk like this. Maybe you feel you don't need this, you're so honest and you never say anything wrong, never have an evil thought. It shows how profound the recesses of the human heart are. Deep within us is this inability really to know our motives.

How, then, does the Christian lie against the truth? By insisting he is right when in fact he is wrong, by not facing the bitter envying that is there. If bitter envying is ever in your heart, mark it down that you are wrong at that moment even if you are right on the whole. To the extent that you have bitterness you then and there surrender true righteousness. You lie against the truth by trying to vindicate yourself. Vindication is God's privilege.

Vindication Comes Later – God's Way

Do you know what it's like to want to be vindicated? When everybody thought you were a fool or everybody said, 'You were wrong.' Or you've taken a stand on a matter and you just know you're right but nobody else thinks so, and it's painful. 'Vengeance is mine ... saith the Lord' (Rom. 12:19). You will be vindicated when it won't matter to you. While it is the thing that preoccupies your mind it will elude you.

I can recall over twenty years ago when I wanted vindication with regard to a particular matter more than anything. I remember coming in one day and my wife said to me, 'I've got good news for you.' Immediately I thought, 'It's come.' It was something else. In the last five years not only was I vindicated, but I've actually had someone apologize to me and ask for forgiveness. I can truthfully say that I was annoyed that they would ask me for forgiveness, that I didn't even care. Twenty years ago that would have meant more to me than anything in the world. But not now.

Jesus said, 'Whosoever will save his life shall lose it: and whosoever will lose his life ... shall find it' (Mt. 16:25). You'll be vindicated when it doesn't matter. In the meantime, just let God do it. 'Let God be true, but every man a liar' (Rom. 3:4). 'Vengeance is mine.'

A Contradiction in Terms

Let's look at this contradiction in terms. James calls this bitter envying 'wisdom'. We've seen that it's the Greek word *sophia*, the highest kind of knowledge, objective self-understanding. Why call it 'this wisdom'? Because your first impression, in the heat of the moment when you have the flash of insight or opinion or inclination, would be to call the way you feel 'wisdom' – this bitterness you have. But James says, 'This wisdom is not from above.' The conclusion is that there is such a thing as counterfeit wisdom.

Counterfeit 'Wisdom'

James is showing how the child of God, even the most godly, can be sidetracked while thinking the whole time that he's the mouthpiece of

God, as it were. Such a thing is counterfeit wisdom, an apprehension that presents itself to the believer as being wholly valid, as being the only way to look at a matter, when in fact it's wrong. How can you know whether you are carried along by counterfeit wisdom? James says, 'If any of these three are there, remember to disassociate yourself from this': that is envy, bitterness and strife.

Notice this distinction. It doesn't mean that what you see you don't see correctly. It doesn't mean that you are wrong in the way you think about a matter. But what James is saying is that if you are unable to talk about it without bringing in what you know is a threat to your self-esteem – envy, bitterness, contention – then that's your clue that this wisdom doesn't come from God.

Recognizing Bitterness

How do you detect bitterness? First of all ask yourself this: when you're talking about a particular matter, do you have a personal interest in the outcome which concerns you? If so, and you cannot speak about it without your self-esteem being right there at the bottom of it all, James would say, 'Don't say anything.' The moment you know that what is really motivating you to speak is your concern about what another thinks of you, refuse to talk about it.

Perhaps your own reputation is at stake and you know that others are aware of your stand. It can happen in politics. Some people attach themselves to a particular politician, and if he makes a big mistake they'll begin to defend him. They're not able to detach themselves. This is the way we all are.

It can be a petty problem in the household, and we take a stand. We just don't like to admit that we might have been wrong. It can happen in theology. It can happen when deciding on what you ought to do, what your job should be, what your career should be. You say what you want to say and people hear you, and now you have to defend it. How much better it is to stay detached where you're not so personally involved. What may have begun as a valid issue, if it becomes your issue, ceases to be the objective truth that you're seeking and you disqualify yourself from speaking about it. If what you're after is really right, let God vindicate you.

The question is, how to know whether your leading is of God. If you are motivated by self-esteem, this wisdom descends not from above. You may not like that, but that's James' answer. Let God vindicate you. If he doesn't, it just might be that you should consider the possibility that you weren't right after all.

Is there bitterness there? What is bitterness? When you so hurt within that you can't speak about it unemotionally. When your words are calculated to get even. And, however right you may have been, the bitterness disqualifies you from speaking of it.

Recognizing Contention

What about strife? That could be translated as 'evil spirit', 'evil disposition', 'contentious spirit'. It's when you've really lost your temper. Anybody can see this, though you might not be able to. When that happens, the Spirit of God has departed a long time ago.

The problem is that when we lose our temper we don't see it for a good while. But no matter how right you are, you're wrong when you lose your temper. You may be of the opinion that you're right in what you're wanting to get over. You may be absolutely sure you've got a case, but what has really happened is that the devil has moved in and stolen the issue from you, and now you just have to be quiet about it.

Earthly, Sensual and Devilish 'Wisdom'

James goes on to give us three words regarding this counterfeit wisdom: 'This wisdom descendeth not from above but is earthly, sensual, devilish.'

Earthly

'Earthly' – that's the Greek word *epigeios*. This word is used in John 3:12. Jesus is talking to Nicodemus: 'If I have told you earthly things, and ye believe not, how shall ye believe, if I tell ye heavenly things?' Paul used it in 1 Corinthians 15:40: 'There are also celestial bodies and bodies terrestrial' – 'earthly'. And in 2 Corinthians 5:1 he said, 'We know that if our earthly house of this tabernacle were dissolved ...'

This is a word consistent with creation, what is commensurate with common grace. In other words, no special grace is required to produce this wisdom. Any non-Christian would do the same thing, would have the same reaction as you. We may feel something and we may think that we've got the flash of insight, but James punctures our balloon – 'earthly'.

Sensual

The second word is 'sensual'. This is sometimes translated 'natural'. It's the Greek word *psuchike*. It's used in 1 Corinthians 2:14: 'The natural man receiveth not the things of the Spirit of God.' Jude used it in verse 19: 'These be they who separate themselves, sensual, having not the Spirit.' Paul used the word to describe the unregenerate. Jude used the word to describe the hypocrites who had wormed their way in and turned the word of God into lasciviousness. The question is, does it follow that only the unregenerate and the hypocrites act like this? No. It's equally true that a true Christian can act like a non-Christian for a while.

James shows that not everything a Christian does or says has a divine origin. As he put it in chapter 3 verse 10: 'Out of the same mouth proceedeth blessing and cursing.' So that which may characterize the hypocrite and the unregenerate, may also characterize the Christian. It's humbling to think that, but if you've got bitterness you must not glory. You ought to know that this wisdom is earthly, sensual and natural.

Devilish

Then James uses a third word, 'devilish'. *Daimoniode* – 'demonic'. Sometimes the devil himself gets in, and for a time the true Christian will be the very instrument of the devil. For the whole time, mind you, you think that you are right, you become blind to objectivity. You're preoccupied with how you feel. You want to get your point of view across and you don't know that really the devil has captured you. He couldn't get his point of view over any better if he'd picked the most wicked man in the world. You're doing the job perfectly well.

This is what had happened to these Christian Jews in the early church. By the way they behaved they caused the world to have the feeling that it would be all right to blaspheme. They were doing the very job the devil wanted done.

I hate to think of the possibility of being an instrument of the devil, but it can happen. After the devil has done his dirty work through us we later see how foolish we were. Most of us are too proud to admit this, resulting in months and sometimes years of retarded growth. Retarded development takes place simply because you let a personal issue ruin, destroy and cripple you emotionally in your personality. Even though you're a Christian, you're bitter. That wisdom 'is earthly, sensual, devilish'.

Closing the Gap Between Sin and Repentance

True spirituality seeks to close the gap in time between sin and repentance so that you eventually reach the place when, just before you're ready to do what you're about to do, you can see it coming and you stop and no sin is committed at all.

Have you done something last week or last year or ten years ago that you now see is wrong? Here's a chance to get some great peace and get it quickly. Just say, 'I'm so sorry, but I was wrong.' Make restitution. By the way, that takes special grace. Nothing earthly, nothing sensual, nothing devilish about saying, 'I was wrong.'

Finally, James adds a PS, a descriptive statement that seems almost redundant. 'For where envying and strife is, there is confusion and every evil work.' Confusion means the opposite of clear thinking. Evil work means that once you let self-esteem take over and you lose control, you are vulnerable to committing any sin in the book. 'Every evil work.' You now become the target of the devil. Whereas at one time he had to throw a dart at you to get you, now he can just blow you over because you've become so weak.

Would you like to have some real peace and joy? Say, 'I was wrong. I really was wrong. I'm sorry.' The person you say it to may not even forgive you and you may think, 'I'm sorry I said it.' It's all right. You have cleared yourself and the joy and peace will come back. Believe me there's nothing more wonderful than that.

38

Godly Wisdom

James 3:13–18

We are now coming to the conclusion of the third chapter of this General Epistle of James. We need to remind ourselves once in a while of what James is after and what his concern is. His concern is the future of Christianity generally but the witness of his readers particularly. This epistle is written so that they might see how the Christian life is to be lived and how their witness itself must be rebuilt.

Wisdom from Above

The genius of Christianity is its wisdom, that is, its source of wisdom. Now we look at what is to be described as godly wisdom. 'Wisdom that is from above is first pure, then peaceable, gentle and easy to be intreated, full of mercy and good fruits, without partiality, and without hypocrisy.' If this godly wisdom is manifested in us, it ensures that our witness in the world will be all that God meant it to be.

We ought not to forget what James said earlier in the epistle, before he brought in wisdom: 'Count it all joy when ye fall into divers temptations' (1:2). The Christian faith and the Christian character that must be built do not come apart from suffering. Even our Lord Jesus Christ who was without sin learned obedience by the things he suffered. How much more then do we need God's chastening?

Hebrews says: 'No chastening for the present seemeth to be joyous, but grievous: nevertheless afterward it yieldeth the peaceable fruit of righteousness unto them which are exercised thereby' (12:11). It is the same word that James uses. 'The wisdom that is from above is first pure, then peaceable,' and he goes on to say, 'The fruit of righteousness is

sown in peace of them that make peace.' As chastening produces the
change in us that really has an effective witness, so suffering will bring
about this wisdom. If in fact you're not going to grow without
suffering, and suffering does come, it should thrill you to know that
God is tapping you as one he wants to make into the kind of Christian
that the Bible was written for. Be thankful for it.

Wisdom – Gift or Grace?

Now as we look at this matter of godly wisdom we need to see a very
important distinction, between wisdom as a gift and wisdom as grace. The
charismatic movement often mentions gifts. In 1 Corinthians 12 the
various gifts of the Spirit are listed. The Greek word is *charismata*, and
indeed it is a most excellent gift of wisdom that is named there. But the
godly wisdom that James is talking about is separate and distinct from that
charismata, or gift of wisdom.

It is quite likely that the gift of wisdom is present where there's already
an abundance of common grace, where the person already has a high level
of intelligence. The gifts often come from the Spirit, sovereignly of God,
to the person who has the embryonic form already by nature, because
God by common grace gave it.

When Paul spoke of the *charismata* to the Romans in Romans 11:29 he
said, 'The gifts (*charismata*) and calling of God are without repentance.'
This is another thing to remember when you think of the various gifts of
the Spirit. Spirituality is not required. Repentance doesn't bring it about,
and if it does come, the absence of repentance doesn't mean that you lose
it. God doesn't repent himself that he gave it because it is sovereignly
given.

I don't mean to be unkind and critical, but it ought to be said. Where
you see so many who are involved in the charismatic movement, have
you ever wondered why there is often a flippancy about them, a lack of
real spirituality, a lack of godliness and, most important of all, a lack of
understanding of spiritual truth, and yet they have these gifts? Because
repentance isn't involved in wisdom as a gift.

We're talking now about godly wisdom that is distinct from the gift of
the Spirit – wisdom as a grace.

Wisdom – Grace and Unction

This godly wisdom is unction. It is described by John in 1 John 2:20:
'Ye have an unction from the Holy One, and ye know all things.' It's

interesting that the Greek word for unction is *chrisma*, not *charisma*. Not 'charisma', which is used to describe the person who has a certain kind of personality, just *chrisma*. It is a similar but different word. This unction is not something you have by nature. It is special anointing from the Holy One. And *this* is *not* given apart from repentance. This is why when John said, 'But ye have an unction from the Holy One', he was showing the contrast with those who 'went out from us' because 'they were not of us' (v. 19). Indeed John had just said, 'Love not the world, neither the things that are in the world. If any man love the world, the love of the Father is not in him' (v.15).

We're talking now about something that comes from God that *does* affect our lives, our attitude, our love for him and our willingness to obey him in any detail involved. So that if there is a love for the world – as John put it, 'the lust of the flesh, and the lust of the eyes, and the pride of life' (v. 16) – this godly wisdom need not be expected. It is exceedingly rare today. This wisdom that comes from above is not intelligence, a natural gift, or common grace. It is a special thing, an anointing. It is the consequence of God's own dealing with us. This is so encouraging because all of us can have this. You may not feel that you're very learned or bright or clever. But we're talking now about something that bypasses nature.

Wisdom from Above

The first thing that we see is its origin, 'from above'. The contrast here is not that of common grace which, as James 1:17 puts it, is also from above so that the person who has certain gifts ought to know that he got them from God. But the contrast here of being 'from above' is the contrast with counterfeit wisdom, which is 'earthly, sensual, devilish'.

What, then, does James mean by 'above'? It means that we're talking now about that which is not to be found in the created order. This wisdom that comes from above – this unction – is not given to one naturally. It is specially given. It is not inherited. It is not acquired by education. And it is most certainly utterly unlike devilish wisdom, which is fostered by your own projection rather than the truth.

By 'above' James means that here is a wisdom utterly unlike what we are by nature and what we would naturally project. Thus this wisdom that comes from above is always surprising. It is always refreshing. And it always brings great relief. When it's there you think, 'I just hadn't thought of it being like that.' It is utterly unlike you. You almost become a spectator and you're amazed at yourself.

It's what Paul means by 'the fruit of the Spirit' (Gal. 5:22). It's not your fruit. It's the Spirit's fruit just flowing through you. This is what is meant by being 'from above'. Devilish wisdom is when your projection is seized upon by the devil and keeps you awake at night. But this wisdom lets you sleep like a baby.

How to Recognize Godly Wisdom

Purity and Peace

James says it is 'first pure, then peaceable'. This Greek word 'pure' – *agne* – means 'chaste' or 'blameless'. It is void of any mixture of ambivalence, of personal feeling, of a private vendetta that you may have. You might say that this wisdom is always neutral so that you know that it's not your personal feeling. It's void of even cultural or provincial colouration. It's pure. It's unconditioned. It's void of any dependence or obligation to anybody. You recognize it because it is so different from what you have imagined as pure. Our projections are always filled with anxiety or envy or strife, but godly wisdom is what we by nature would never have come up with.

James then shows the confirmation that it is godly wisdom. It is 'first pure, then peaceable.' The purity of it is confirmed by the peace of it. The purity of it is almost always self-authenticating. When God's wisdom is present you just know that it is right. When a minister preaches with unction there is just a consensus among the people of God that this is right. We may not like it, but we know it's right. It cuts deep, 'piercing even to the dividing asunder of soul and spirit', says the writer to the Hebrews (4:12). It's when God deals with you and convicts you that you're guilty.

Do you know what it is to have God deal with you in a direct way and convict you of your duty? You may try to shake it off, but then when you do it you find that it brings peace. This is why James said, 'It is first pure, then peaceable.' For when the godly wisdom is there and you know what he's saying, then the breakthrough comes. If God puts his finger on something, you know in your heart of hearts that it's right and no peace will ever come until you do it. Doing it gives you peace and begets peace.

Gentleness and Openness

The next thing James does is to elaborate in detail how you can further but unmistakably detect this godly wisdom. It's gentle. *Epiekes* means 'moderate, orderly, reasonable'. There's nothing extreme, nothing rough, nothing off-putting about it. God will not lead you to do something that is ridiculous or extreme as when the devil said to Jesus, 'If thou be the Son of God, cast thyself down from hence' (Lk. 4:9). God doesn't do that. His wisdom always reaches us where we are. If God wants us to make changes he doesn't lead us from A to Z, he leads us from A to B and from B to C. When I think of the patience that God has had with me, to bring me to a certain place, and how kind he was in doing it, I couldn't have known all that he was trying to get me to see eventually from the way he began. He led me from A to B. I think now I'm at J or K or L. And I think, 'If God had tried to get me from A to L, I would have collapsed.'

God's wisdom is 'pure, then peaceable, gentle' and it doesn't try to show another up or make another feel put down. If you ever put another person down because you say something that makes him feel rather stupid, that is not godly wisdom. That is sensual and devilish. If a person leaves your presence feeling oppressed and wishing that they hadn't heard you say that, you have been a victim of devilish wisdom and you've foisted it onto another person. For this wisdom makes you feel good. It's the way Jesus wants you to feel. If you show this wisdom you will make other people feel good.

'Easy to be intreated' is the next expression: *eupeithes*. It's the only time this word used in the Bible. It simply means 'pliant'. It comes from a Greek word that means 'to be easily persuaded'. The person who is governed by this wisdom is non-defensive. He's willing to be wrong about something he may have said. The person who has this kind of wisdom makes you feel it's okay to bring anything up. Why? This person is being like Jesus who is not 'an high priest which cannot be touched with the feeling of our infirmities' (Heb. 4:15). This wisdom enables one to sympathize.

All of us have our weak spots. All of us know what it is to bristle when a certain subject or a certain person is brought up. But when we're governed by this godly wisdom we don't bristle. It's like Stephen praying, 'Lord, lay not this sin to their charge' (Acts 7:60). How could he pray a prayer like that? It's not natural. For here's the person who has mistreated us and we can just love him. It's the fruit of the Spirit, godly wisdom.

Mercy and Good Fruits

James goes on: 'full of mercy and good fruits'. Mercy is given without any commensurate exchange. It's the way we are before God. We have no bargaining power. Mercy is that which can be given or withheld and justice be done in either case.

God deals with us that way. God doesn't get even with us. He got even on the cross when he punished his Son. He's 'rich in mercy' (Eph. 2:4). If we have been the object of such mercy then we can take seriously Jesus' words: 'Love your enemies, bless them that curse you, do good to them that hate you, and pray for them which despitefully use you, and persecute you' (Mt. 5:44). That is godly wisdom. If vengeance is handed to you on a silver platter, you walk away from it. You refuse to say, 'I told you so.' Rather you say, 'Let's see what we can do.' 'Gentle, easy to be intreated, full of mercy and good fruits.'

Why did he add: 'and good fruits'? Because mercy must be visibly demonstrated. It's putting your money where your mouth is. You don't just say, 'Go in peace. Be warmed.' The person who receives this mercy truly enjoys it. The good fruits keep the person from feeling patronized. If you show me that mercy which is 'full of mercy and good fruits' I won't get the feeling that you're enjoying heaping coals of fire on my head. I'll feel you are being like Jesus. That is mercy that is God-like and divine.

Even-Handed Sincerity

Next expression: 'without partiality'. James is still thinking about the fact that these Jewish Christians had been respecters of persons. But this wisdom is not controlled by any subjective bias. This is what was meant originally by this word 'pure' or 'blameless'. There is no ambivalence. If you are showing this wisdom there will be no vendetta involved. Sometimes we can't be used of the Lord simply because we're too emotionally involved in a matter. If somebody says something to you about your parents or your children or a brother or a sister or a close friend which is negative, and you get involved, it's hard to be objective.

We're all this way, and yet this wisdom is without partiality. Godly wisdom completely transcends personal feeling. You may not like it if a person isn't partial to you. But real love is to be objective. A person does you the greatest favour when he is impartial, for God is no respecter of persons. Sometimes you must say something to another person that is hard for them to take. You know it's going to hurt them, but it's really love even if you hurt them at first. This is what is meant by 'without partiality'. That is true love in action.

Then James adds finally: 'without hypocrisy'. My first reaction when I came to 'without hypocrisy' was that that surely goes without saying. But why did James say it? Because it's possible up to this point to put on an act. It's not very likely you can do it successfully, but it can be done, so that the whole time you're just acting nice, but it's not godly wisdom.

This wisdom means that you have got personally involved in the right way. You are not emotionally involved but at the same time you're not able to react with another person in a detached manner completely. You're not able to put on an act and just be nice. This word really means 'sincere', so that in the end you're not able to show this wisdom unless you care about that person and show that you really care. It's the same thing with this unction. It is always impartial but compassionate and involved. It's not like a professional man who just makes a judgment, but it's like Jesus who is 'touched with the feeling of our infirmities'.

The Harvest of Wisdom

'And the fruit of righteousness is sown in peace of them that make peace.' Why does James add this PS? For two reasons. One, it contains a promise and two, it is yet another confirmation of this godly wisdom. What's the promise? If you sow peace you have the promise of personal peace. 'Blessed are the peacemakers' (Mt. 5:9). There's no greater reward than this: the peace that comes. The Bible talks about 'the God of peace' and that describes God. The Bible talks about 'peace with God'. That describes justification. But then the Bible talks about 'the peace of God'. 'Peace like a river', as it has been put by the hymn writer. This peace is so wonderful that if you have it you would not want to be anywhere else or to have anything else in its place. That peace is beyond description. It passes understanding and will keep you (Phil. 4:7). James says that if we show this kind of wisdom where we are sowing righteousness, then the harvest is peace. In other words, the fruit of this godly wisdom is first that you show righteousness and true justice, and that helps everybody. But the actual carrying out of this wisdom is called a fruit or a harvest where you yourself have this great peace.

What's the confirmation? Simply, the joy of seeing godly wisdom actually working and knowing that you are a participant. It's a wonderful thing to be involved in this way, to be a peacemaker. Do you know of anybody you don't have peace with right now? Is there something you can do about it? Begin there. It can be that you are being a peacemaker by helping others to be reconciled. It can be among believers or among relatives. But James' point is that you get your cake and eat it too. You see justice carried out and you yourself are given great peace.

When you participate in this godly wisdom you really do manifest the kind of Christianity that James is after. He's thinking of the future of the church, but also of the actual witness of these people. He saw it passing behind a cloud in his day. And we must admit we are talking about something that is exceedingly rare at the present time – the self-effacing, impartial, non-defensive, merciful and caring Christian. Are we that?

Scripture Index